Between
ME
and the
RIVER

Between
ME
and the
RIVER

A MEMOIR OF WISDOM, HOPE AND HEALING

CARRIE HOST

BETWEEN ME AND THE RIVER

First published as hardcover in 2009 by Harlequin Enterprises Limited.
Copyright © 2009 by Carrie Host
This trade paperback edition published May 2011.

Library of Congress Cataloging-in-Publication Data
Host, Carrie.
Between me and the river : living beyond cancer : a memoir /
Carrie Host. -- 1st ed.
p. cm.
ISBN 978-0-373-89214-3 (hardcover)
ISBN 978-0-373-89246-4 (trade paperback)
1. Host, Carrie. 2. Cancer--Patients--United States--Biography.
3. Carcinoid--Patients--United States--Biography. I. Title.
RC265.6.H67A3 2009
362.196'9940092—dc22
[B]
2009010729

www.Harlequin.com

Printed in U.S.A.

To Amory, Chanel, Marco, and William—for loving me back to life

"Do what you can, with what you have, where you are."
—Theodore Roosevelt

"All changed, changed utterly: A terrible beauty is born."
—W. B. Yeats, Easter, 1916

Contents

Prologue

April 13, 2004

I hate having to stand by like a stranger in my own life.

I have to watch as the babysitter does what I want to be doing. I'm jealous of her physical strength and of her health. I can't believe I'm actually feeling this as I lie on the couch in my room. My emotions swing wildly from extreme gratitude, to resentment, to complete apathy. Sinking deeper into these dense thoughts, I tell myself that I'm just not interested anymore in taking care of my family.

My two older children, Marco and Chanel, are at school and my fifteen-month-old baby, William, is napping, but when he wakes up I won't be the one to lift him from his crib. I can't. It would take the house being on fire to get me off this couch.

I'm angry but too weak to show it, so I decide not to care anymore. I try to find things that are safe to think about. For a long time, nothing comes to mind. Then, two distinct moments emerge from my memory. The first is from my childhood.

One frozen February evening in 1972, my family of eight is eating dinner. We're all sitting around the long dining room table. We never eat in the kitchen because we don't fit. My parents are involved in a stiff conversation with my two older brothers, Jack and Steve, at their end of the table. They're on a subject called "war." War is really hard for me to picture.

"What's a war, Dad?" I interrupt them.

"Honey, it's something I'd rather not tell you about."

"Were *you* in a war?"

"Yes, in Korea."

"But where's *this* war?"

"Vietnam," he says. I don't like the sound the word makes coming from my father's mouth.

"Now don't worry about that. Just eat your dinner," my mother directs, her beautiful brown eyes softening her words.

"If they draft me, I'm not going," my brother Jack says, looking straight at my dad through his John Lennon spectacles.

"Me, either, man," Steve sides in, tipping his chair back.

"Those turkeys can't take you. You're sixteen. You won't be drafted yet," Jack consoles him.

"Far out," he replies, tossing his shoulder-length hair back with a flick of his neck.

"Take him where?" *I'm only eight.* "When can the turkeys take me?" I ask, convinced that each of us six kids will be taken away by turkeys to a drafty place called Vietnam.

"They don't take girls, Carrie, just boys," Jack answers while Steve starts to snicker.

"But I don't want them to take you." I start to cry, picturing my big brother being taken away.

"Me, either," Marisa chimes in, not looking up from the Hot Wheels car that she's pushing in circles around her dinner plate, the racetrack.

My two older sisters, Wendy and June, are quiet in the middle of the table and in the middle of the family. Quiet is not for me.

"Now I told you boys not to talk about this in front of the girls," my mother admonishes them, too late.

"But *how* do they take you?" I press on for an answer.

"*They* don't take you, Uncle Spam takes you...*Lu-Lu Bell,*" my brother Steve chides, using the name he made up for me that he knows will make me mad. Then, using his pointer and middle fingers to pull his lower eyelids down as far as possible while using his thumb to push his nose up, he makes himself look like a red-eyed pig.

"Who's that?" I wonder, innocently afraid of some uncle I've never heard of.

"Uncle *Sam*," my sister June says to correct him more than to inform me, jumping at any chance to have a fight involving intelligence. This is where she shines.

"The president of the United States," my father says with finality, trying to end the discussion and appease my mother before her dinner is ruined.

"President Nixon?" I ask.

"That's right, yes."

"Well, *I'm* writing him a letter! I'm telling him that he can't come here and take my brother away."

"You can't write to the president, *Lu-Lu Bell*," Steve taunts.

"Duuuh – George!" June agrees with him, only as an opportunity to use the refrain that she knows will infuriate him. And that's it; they're in a fight.

"Yes she can! She's smarter than *you two!*" Wendy shouts over them, always coming to my defense.

"Yeah!" Marisa snarls with a six-year-old-face, not knowing anything more than that Wendy and I are forever loyal to her, our baby sister. Therefore, she should take *our side* in all family arguments.

I cry. Storming from the table to my room, I rifle through my little desk drawer for paper. Big Chief is too babyish. I want something more grown-up, so I take a circus-animal valentine from the box of twenty-four that I'll be filling out for my friends next week. I write on the back of it politely, and neatly, so that it all fits into the tight space of the heart shape.

Dear President Nixon,

Would you please stop the war in Vietnam.
My brother doesn't want to go there.
I won't let you take him even if you
come to our house to get him.
Happy Valentine's Day
anyway.

Love,
Carrie Farland

I put it in the envelope along with a stick of Juicy Fruit, in case he likes gum, and properly address it, just like the nuns taught me to do in school. I first lightly draw three lines across the center of the envelope with a ruler, in pencil. Then I carefully write the address with my fountain pen, and erase the pencil lines once the ink is dry. Nuns don't like anything crooked.

I find my dad in the den, in the shifting blue light of *Gunsmoke,* the only television program I can ever remember him watching besides golf. I crawl up next to him on the couch.

"Dad, can you mail this to the White House for me?" I ask timidly in a whisper, hoping that my brothers won't hear and start making fun of me again.

"Why, sure, honey."

"Really?" I check, looking up at him.

"Of course. My friend Mr. Allen works in Washington. I'll see that he gets it to the president," he says.

"Thanks, Dad!" I say, thrilled that someone in my family takes me seriously.

Several weeks later, when I come in the door after school, my mother hands me an envelope. It says, THE WHITE HOUSE in the upper left-hand corner and is addressed to me, Miss Carrie Farland, 735 Williams Street, Denver, Colorado 80218, complete with an eleven-cent stamp on it. I am instantly satisfied. My eight-year-old brain gives no credit to the detail that my father's friend, having hand-delivered my card to President Nixon, had anything to do with the fact that I am now holding the president's reply, a typed letter. His signature is not typed, but signed in thick black ink, which impresses me.

> February 16, 1972
> Dear Carrie:
> During a busy day it is especially delightful to hear from my young friends, and I particularly appreciate your kind greeting on Valentine's Day.
>
> I am grateful for your thoughtfulness in thinking of me, and I am pleased to have this opportunity to return your best wishes,
>
> Sincerely,
> Richard Nixon

Now an adult, I have a slightly different take on this response from the president. He's nicely managed to completely avoid addressing any of my concerns. His letter is a politically perfect masterpiece. That fact aside, I recall the way that holding that letter in my hands made me feel. I got a response from the most important person in the world. If writing could do that, then I wanted to be a writer.

Aside from writing letters, essays, short stories and poetry, all of which were promptly deposited into an antique suitcase and snapped shut inside that compartment of my life, there were only a few times I really indulged my deep desire to write. The second memory was of one of those times, in 1996.

It's a particular day during the Summer Writing Program that I'm attending at Naropa University, in Boulder, Colorado. This is the home of the Jack Kerouac School of Disembodied Poetics, and I'm taking a four-week poetry-and-prose writing workshop. Various well-known poets and writers come and teach us style-specific courses. It's in the session that we have with Allen Ginsberg that I learn probably the best single thing that I can learn about writing and, as it's turning out, about life: choosing a place to start.

One morning, he has us working on an odd piece of prose. The subject is "5:30 a.m." and any dialogue within it should not name whatever is being talked about. So, anybody talking should not actually talk about what they're talking about, and all of this should have something to do with 5:30 a.m. We have to begin this piece on the spot. He sees that I am still struggling to get my piece going as the class ends and the room slowly empties. I sit there with my hand in a death grip on my pencil, taking stabs at slices of dialogue. He taps on my desk with a rather knurled old finger and says, "Just write the end."

"What?" I look up at him, puzzling. "How can I do that? I don't even have a beginning!"

"I know. Just write an ending and I'll look at it tomorrow before class," he instructs me. His tone holds a certain abrupt kindness, the type that poets like him bestow upon the rest of us who are new at trying to crawl out of our minds onto the blank pages that lie before us.

Back at home, long after the family is asleep, I stay up far too late and write an ending to beat all endings. The next morning, I spot Ginsberg just outside of the old one-room cabin which is our classroom. I'm looking forward to his personal attention, and because I'm an hour early, to a full critique of my masterful paragraph. Greeting him, I hand him my "ending."

He barely glances down at it or up at me. Instead, he hands it back without an apology and says only, "Oh. Good. So, now come up with all the ways you can get there, and you've got your beginning, or at least your middle." Then he walks away to say hello to some old friend waving in his direction. My ego crumples. Like a piece of paper towel, I try to sop up what the genius just said. I wanted him to say so much more. But I know that he's right. There isn't any more to say. All writers know this. That is why we don't talk, we write. This is how Mr. Ginsberg leaves me and my tremendous ending all alone in the middle of the courtyard.

Now, eight years later, sitting here about to become one with my couch, I embark on taking a peek at my life as if it were a writing assignment, and immediately feel at ease. I start to work out the way that something like a life might end, in this case my own. I begin to see that this whole horrible experience is really an opportunity to shape the chapters that are yet to be written. I do still *care* about something; something that cancer can't take from me, something that will give me inspiration and my life back in the process. It becomes quite clear to me that that something is writing.

In 1972, at eight years old, I felt that even the president valued my words. In 1996, at thirty-three, I was still chasing down post-college courses on the craft of writing. Here in 2004, at forty-one, and five months into dealing with carcinoid cancer, the knowledge that the end of my life may be much nearer than I had ever considered possible resurrects my long-buried desire to write. The threat of imminent death invites me to leave my dread of rejection behind. I used to fear the rejection my writing might meet with, but now I'm afraid of dying. What have I been waiting for? I feel the corners of my mouth press out into a huge, quiet smile. The things that used to *stop me,* now amuse me. I finally get it; I finally understand that endings are not only about the final page.

Comparing my situation to writing somehow gives me courage and comfort. In the written word I trust. I decide to find some type of deranged consolation in writing an ending. Rolling onto my side, I reach past a bowl of soup gone cold—the oyster crackers, now large pillows of mush. Picking out a pen from the mess on my coffee table, I tear off one of those instructional sheets stapled to my prescription bag, the one that lists exactly how bad the pills inside are for me. I've stopped reading those as I already know all of the side effects of my meds and which ones to take with what. I turn the warning side over and make the back of it into something useful. It is now the blank slate I need to write an ending that will stop my mind from wandering down dark, cancer-filled alleys.

When the end of my pen is chewed flat, I finally pull it out from between my teeth. I write an ending that sums up all the parts, a final paragraph I can live with and, conveniently, live for. When I'm finished I fold it up too many times, like a third-grade love note, and I fall asleep holding it tightly to my chest. I promise myself that someday when I have the strength I will write the rest.

Part I

The River

Miles and Miles

November 5, 2003

Hardly any other word leaves us as numb or as frozen in time as *cancer*. That six-letter word, paired with the phrase "you have" is like being emotionally trampled by elephants. It's been a year and a half since those words were directed to me. Also, it's been a lifetime.

So this is the beginning of my journey with cancer. That single word took a split second to change my life and a lot longer to write in that last sentence, the writer in me too afraid to put the word *cancer* on paper, for fear that seeing it in my own handwriting might make the humming in my head even more real.

Oncologist is a captivating word that tumbles carelessly out of our mouths until we are using it in regard to our own situation. Then we finally meet the oncologist whose job it is to deliver the most frightening news and who, in so doing, instantly becomes the grim reaper. This doctor is the first person on the scene who we know we don't want to see again but to whom we are going to become intimately tied. This is the person you run from in your nightmare, the one who keeps showing up at every turn with a disturbingly calm demeanor.

Tumor board? Who coined the term *tumor board,* I wonder? But what other title could be assigned to the group of oncologists and radiologists who meet to evaluate your medical case? They sort through all of your various scans, X-rays, blood work and tests, and then collectively decide the course of treatment that should be proposed to you, the patient.

They "stage" your cancer and then they write the script, the script in which you are billed as the main character. They hand it over to that guy you keep running from in the nightmare. He will show up at the head of the table in his conference room. This room has a ceiling that is too low and getting lower every minute. The thick medical reference books and journals are packed too tightly on the crammed bookshelves at one end. There are windows on both sides of the room, but they don't open. Half of them separate you from the hall of the clinic, and the other half allow you a treetop view. You notice all of this while you wait for him to say something. He taps the stack of paper like a deck of cards, making sure the edges are neat. This will be his only prop and will also serve as his silent defense against your certain denial.

He already knows how to deliver the lines. He's had a lot of practice. This makes you like him less. He's the kid in fifth grade who sits in front of you and has done all of his homework. Yet because he sits up so nice and straight, he protects you from the teacher's scanning eyes. Ironically, he will now protect you again.

He knows a lot more than you do about the condition of your body, and this is disturbing beyond words. Because he's spent so many years in medical school, and so many more actually being a doctor, he has learned to dish this up on one of those compartmentalized trays, keeping the parts separate while still putting it all on your plate.

He will begin to recite directly from your medical file. You will wish he would stop and say, "My mistake, this isn't you. You can go now," but he doesn't. He will turn a page and lift his chin slightly, slowly breathing in through his nose and looking up at you appraisingly. He is checking to see if your bags are packed for the trip he is about to send you on. You pretend to be looking in his eyes. Actually you are staring at the mountains in the distance, reflected in the excruciatingly clean lenses of his wire-rimmed glasses. Just like that, you have stepped onto the platform and are heading toward the train you are about to board. You will hear the ticking of your watch, even though it's digital.

A nurse wearing a happy-puppy shirt will walk by the other side of the glass window, her stethoscope draped around her neck, her clipboard in hand. She does not look your way, because she already knows what you are doing here. She's the person in that same nightmare to whom you keep shouting for help, but she can't hear you. She is on the other side of the glass, on her way to someone in more immediate need. She will see you later.

The oncologist continues to read the lines in front of him. "...the octreotide scans lit up in these areas...the bulk of the carcinoid is...there are metastases to the liver...tumor on the left lung...it has completely covered the omentum wall and the peritoneum..." Wait!...Stop!...I can't breathe.

I consider myself a word person and there are already three words that I don't understand. Each probably has a whole textbook to define it. I keep looking out the hallway window for the nurse in the puppy shirt to save me. He stops reading. He is finished describing you in the medical terms that the tumor board has agreed upon. You realize that a description this big and complex took a group of doctors to write. You want to hit delete and go back to the old description of yourself, the one without the medical terms mixed in. You can't. He is waiting for you to say something. You can tell this because he has set down his script in a neat stack and his back has now come in contact with the rest of his chair. He has far too much compassion in his eyes. He is not going away. He waits. You are speechless.

He asks my husband and me if we have any questions. We have, but we only ask those with answers we think we can swallow without choking. "Which surgeon do you recommend?...How did this start?...What is a low-fiber diet?" We leave.

Without exchanging a word, my husband and I take the elevator down three floors and walk out. I know that my legs are there, but I can't feel them. I move my body forward, down the eight steps to the sidewalk. My senses are smacked by the crisp November air. I want to take in a deep breath, but find I am only taking shallow sips. The familiar scent of the coming snow in the mountain air, full of pine, is suddenly too bold and full of life for me to bear.

My eyes well up at all the questions still running through my head that we didn't ask. "How long do I have?...Will I have Thanksgiving in my sister's cabin, or will I be too sick to make the four-hour drive?...Will I miss the baby's first birthday, December 17?...Will I make it home for Christmas with the kids?...Will I make it through the surgery?"

Having been told that I should have the surgery immediately is more than enough information on how fast this train is moving. We find we are holding hands, my mitten in the clasp of his glove, walking silently toward St. John's Church on Pine Street. For my problem, I figure that I probably need the big church but it's locked, so we naturally cross the courtyard to the chapel. I'm grateful to enter the dim light and for the wooden pew that holds the five tons of lead that have filled my body.

My gaze is resting on the stone floor, the colors from the stained-glass strewn unevenly across it. I let the tears come. I just sit there and cry. I'm crying in a way that I don't recognize. At forty, these are tears that are coming from somewhere I don't feel ready to know about. My husband cries right beside me. I've never heard such sadness emerge from him before. We hold on to each other as only two people who might be separated forever do.

You will hear the wind for the first time, as you never have before.

Hear it whipping around outside of the chapel. Hear its delicate whistle through the highest branches. You will hear those branches click and rattle softly. Through tear-rimmed eyes, you will notice its cold breath whispering in under the heavy wooden doors, stirring a dried and dead autumn leaf into a slow dance across the vestibule.

Time passes. How much, I'm not certain. I stand and walk to the candles in their rows. Some are lit—each, I imagine, with a whispered prayer. The wooden matches tremble in their box under my shaking hand. I take one out and light three candles, one for each of my children.

The sound of my own fear, a noise which I have never heard before, arises from deep within, shaking my body with all the possibilities of loss. The sound of a mother sobbing at the threat of being taken from her children, the most unbearable sound in the world, reduces me to stone.

Thank you for this chapel where I can fall apart. Help me find my way through this maze. Please don't take me from my children. They need me. I want to see my baby grow up. I'm not ready to let go of his little hand. Help me, please, I'm so afraid. I'm so heartbroken.

This might be the first time you find yourself praying. You may wonder to whom you are praying, or you might already know. Either way, you might become more familiar with this part of yourself as the train departs. You will mentally wave goodbye to loved ones as it slowly chugs out of the station. The people you love can't come with you. You will have to ride this train by yourself. You know this, and you are so scared that you can feel every nerve standing at attention. You are acutely aware that this is your train.

Then you turn to take your seat on that train and you are relieved to find that there are others, lots of others who are already here. Their knowing glances tell you that you'll have company for the ride. This may be the single most important thing to know during your journey. You may be scared, but you are not alone.

* * *

Cancer is like that. At first, you can't believe that you are in the waiting room of a cancer center. It's not like the waiting room anywhere else, because all of these people are in some way affected by cancer. You don't want to be one of these people. You don't want to believe this. It's the person next to you in that waiting room, looking like he is doing well, who helps you see the first piece of tangible evidence that there are people who survive this. One moment you are spiraling down, sure that you are utterly alone, and then circumstances reveal that you are not. This is where hope comes and puts an arm around you.

Still Searching

October 8, 2003

O nce on the train, you might reflect on how you first arrived at the station. Each of us approaches the station in a different way. This is how I showed up.

It is the quintessential October day in Boulder, Colorado: a dazzling blue sky, autumn at the peak of her glory, a nip in the air. Suddenly, during lunch with my friend Kirsten, the pain that had launched me into the emergency room in agony exactly one year before comes creeping back into my stomach. I'm setting my fork down after the first bite. I know this pain. I know right where it started and where it will end up.

My friend is multitasking. She is catching me up on her recent trip to New York to find a showroom for her jewelry line, filling me in on her latest love interest, and taking a few calls on her cell phone. She looks effervescent compared to me.

I observe her animated energy in amazement, thinking that I don't know how she keeps up with herself. I'm also thinking this used to be me before I was pregnant with my third child: glowing, energetic, in shape, and able to whip any situation under control with one hand tied behind my back.

"I feel sick to my stomach," I'm saying. I know something is wrong. As soon as the pain begins to radiate around to my back, I push my plate across the table to join her side salad, positive that I cannot eat. Too busy to answer me, she answers her cell phone and begins to sample the delicious dish in front of her. I place an ear on her phone call, as she is motioning me to do, between a sip of her wine and a bite of my entrée, a mischievous look in her eyes. I strain to focus on the distant voice coming over the line. Instead, I hear the loud one in my head, which is shouting, *"This isn't about your lunch, and you are in trouble."* She's finished the call and picking up where we left off.

"I wouldn't worry about it. We all hold our tension there." I hear her saying in the distance, her delayed reaction to the pain in my stomach. I want her to be right, but I know that this is different. With my seven-mile-stare straight over her shoulder, looking blankly at Walnut Street, I absently watch her take three more calls. I watch her gracefully polish off my asparagus omelet with hollandaise as she spins a business deal with the person on the line. Since *I* am mentally answering the pain that is besieging me, I am actually grateful for her distraction. I am no longer present. We wrap up and pay the tab.

Driving up Broadway, I head home, popping Tums, hoping the pain will go away as suddenly as it appeared.

October 9, 2003

Just about eighteen hours later, at 5:30 a.m., this mysterious pain does just that: it vanishes without a trace. My husband and I are both delighted and relieved that I am suddenly fine after a long night. He leaves at 6:30 a.m. for work and ten minutes later I drive the kids down the road to meet the school bus at 6:45 a.m. A surprise awaits me back at home. No sooner do I step into the front hall than the pain which had totally vanished hits my abdomen like a prize-fighter. It knocks me to my knees, my ten-month-old baby still in my arms. I gently lay him down on the rug beneath us, turning my face away so as not to scare him with my contorted expression. I try to breathe.

I hear the phone ring once and stop. It's my neighbor, Sara, giving me the "one ring" to let me know she will be leaving for a run in five minutes with her two dogs if I want to join her; it's our usual morning routine. I consider trying to crawl to the kitchen to return her call and ask her for a ride to the hospital. Instead, I am immobilized by pain that is off the charts. If I can manage for five more minutes, Soccoro, my housekeeper, will be arriving at 6:55 a.m. sharp. In the eight years that she has worked for me, she's never been late. A wonderful fact that, at the moment, I'm counting on. *Her brother will drop her off, and I will ask him to take me to the hospital on his way to work.* From my position in the hall, I can see the driveway, but instead of their car, a taxi rolls in.

I want that taxi to wait for me and I get lucky. Because she is just short of the fare, she heads inside to see if I can help her out. She comes in the side door as usual and hears me call out for her. She rushes through the kitchen and the dining room to find us in the hall. The baby's all bundled up and cooing and I'm still in my coat, crying as quietly as I can. She scoops up the baby and helps me to my feet. I try to explain, but abandon my attempt.

Grabbing my purse I head out the door, doubled over, to the waiting cabbie who is clearly confused when I get in and say, "The hospital, please." Holding up my cell phone, I look at Socorro standing in the doorway holding the baby. I mouth the words "I'll call you" through the closed window, pointing to my phone.

As the taxi cruises toward town I'm calling the gastroenterologist who saw me for this same pain when I was pregnant. He is out, but his "on call" will come to see me at the hospital. I am at the point where the pain is so severe that I can no longer complete my sentences. I call someone who can finish them for me: my mother. She already knows part of my story, since I called her before I went to bed last night asking her what she thought the pain might be. Together, we had talked it through.

"Do you think this could be the same pain that I had at the end of my pregnancy?" I'm asking her. "Don't you think that it's weird that the pain's never returned since I delivered the baby ten months ago?"

"That doesn't make sense." She's thinking out loud.

"Could one bite of hollandaise at lunch give me a stomach ache this severe?" I offered.

The minute she hears my panicked voice this morning she says, "I'm on my way to meet you at the hospital." I am relieved that she's coming and that she can fill them in for me. Next, I try my husband's office. "He is already on the way to a closing. Unfortunately, his cell phone is sitting right here on his desk. I'll get the message to him though, as soon as I can," his assistant tells me.

I'm hoping to see my neighbor Sara's husband, Laird Wolfe, a longtime doctor in the emergency room and family friend. Soon I find out that this is not his shift, but I am seen, and immediately I am given some type of shot for pain relief. It seems that none of the doctors is able to make immediate heads or tails of my excruciating pain, so I am admitted. The testing begins. Tests that will change everything. Tests I've never heard of are proposed and executed.

The blood draws and urine collections are just the beginning of the next twelve hours. I have a colonoscopy, an upper intestinal endoscopy, a CT scan of my pelvis and abdomen with oral and intravenous contrast, X-rays and last, and hardest of all because of the unexpected pain, a vaginal ultrasound. Along with all of the tests, my breasts are beginning to rebel for lack of my nursing baby to empty them.

The on-call doctor turns up on the scene. She remains, to this day, one of the best things that could have ever happened to me. Dr. Coco Dughi comes around the corner carrying her clipboard sideways under curled fingers, like a surfboard, and looks across the emergency room as if she's sizing up the swells. I find out later that my first impression of her is not far off. She hails from Hawaii and actually *is* a surfer. She's just recently moved her internal-medicine practice here from Mayo Clinic in Minnesota.

"So tell me what's happening to you here, friend," she says, in a "let's figure this out" kind of voice. She looks me directly in the eyes. She appears to actually absorb, process and analyze information as I am relating it, rather than simply listening. She keeps me informed. She is calm and positive. She gives me the feeling that I am worth listening to. She is not wishy-washy. She seems to know that I am not crazy when I insist that this is exactly the same pain of a year ago.

She puts a strong hand on my back when I begin to cry after being informed that I will have to stop nursing my baby immediately due to the drugs they are about to pump into me. I ask my mom to drive home and bring the baby to the hospital as soon as she can. I want to nurse him one last time. Dr. Dughi takes my request seriously, and decides to have the nurses hold off on the drip to my IV until I have nursed my baby. Then she sees that I am given some privacy to do so.

My mom and I decide with the exchange of a glance that we want to keep her. We want this smart, strong and endearing woman at my side. She is the first doctor on the scene that I feel is "dialed in." This doctor, I feel I can trust.

"It appears that you have Crohn's disease," the gastroenterologist tells me that evening. I lie awake in my hospital bed, seven tests and fifteen hours later, in total disbelief. I'm missing my kids and weeping over my baby, who is way too far from my arms.

"What's Crohn's?" I ask. I get a brief description, and the night nurse tries to explain it further for me at one o'clock in the morning. I try to think with this. I am not settled with this Crohn's disease diagnosis. It doesn't fit. I don't believe it; partly because I don't want to, and partly because it doesn't feel right. My husband takes a crash course on the definition and tries to help me approach it that way. When Dr. Dughi comes by my room in the morning clad in hiking gear, on her day off, I tell her, "When I get out of here, I'm finding a way to get off of this Prednisone drug for Crohn's. It is making me crazy. I can't sleep, my heart is racing, and I just know this isn't right...I just don't feel like I have Crohn's disease, but I can't explain it," I finish, starting to cry out of deep frustration.

Instead of trying to convince me that the gastroenterologist must be correct in his working diagnosis of Crohn's and that I am wrong, she hands me a Kleenex and surprises me with a question. "What do *you* think is going on?"

I tell her about the 3-cm ovarian cyst that everyone is ignoring, that has been there since my pregnancy began. She looks me straight in the eye and says, "Okay, when you get out of here, I want you to go straight to your gynecologist and get that checked out right away. It is possible that it ruptured, which could explain the pain." She releases me the next morning. I take her advice. I make the necessary appointment to be seen two days later.

October 17, 2003

My fifth day back at home, my mom and I are waiting for the nurse at the other end of the line to give me the results of the blood work that was sent to Mayo Clinic to verify the diagnosis. This is what I hear: "Your blood work did not test positive for Crohn's."

"I don't have Crohn's," I whisper excitedly, covering the phone while the nurse on the other end continues. My mom and I are all but jumping up and down, so relieved to be checking that off of my list.

Yet, I keep knocking on doors, looking for answers. I still want to find out what's been causing the intense pain which strikes so randomly. Pain that comes on like a sudden storm without warning then quickly builds to hurricane force and then vanishes just as suddenly without a trace. Pain that is so forceful it has me holding on to the furniture, panting and grunting like a woman in labor. Pain that leaves me worn out and beaten, sure that pain cannot possibly be worse. Pain that has most doctors looking at me as if I need to have my head examined.

I confirm upon one solid look in the mirror that I do not look well. My eyes are red and bloodshot and have been for months. I am having hot flashes that flush my face, neck and chest a disturbingly bright red as though I had been in the desert for a week without cover. I endure these flushing incidents anywhere from twelve to twenty times a day. This horrible flushing, bloodshot eyes, and unexplained abdominal pain have had me running for an answer to five different doctors, as well as a chiropractor, a nutrition specialist, an optometrist and a lactation consultant.

The answers I am given are varied. "Your pineal gland is not functioning properly. Take this supplement and expose your eyes to light without wearing your contacts one hour a day and you will be fine....You need to balance your chi with these herbs and supplements....Your eyes are fine, but you should change the brand of lens that you are wearing, and the solution you are cleaning them with is probably irritating your eyes. Try this ultrasonic machine to clean your lenses and your eyes should clear right up."

Finally, the lactation consultant informs me: "I have been around breastfeeding mothers for over twenty-seven years and I have never heard of any having hot flashes. I highly doubt that you are menopausal or even pre-menopausal, dear. After all, you've just had a baby. I'm so sorry, I'm truly baffled. Have you seen your doctor about this?" she asks.

"Yes, as a matter of fact, I have," I sadly reply, thinking about how I have gotten nowhere in the last nine months.

Fire and Ice

October 20, 2003

I see the gynecologist who delivered my baby and witnessed my pain firsthand during the final nine weeks of my pregnancy. After his examination, this is what he tells me: "I know that you say that this is the exact pain you were having from thirty weeks on in your pregnancy, but I have checked you over and I find nothing you should worry about. The small nodules that I feel are most likely hardened stool."

"I've just had a colonoscopy two days ago!" I object. My words fall on deaf ears and he continues, running over my words.

"The small ovarian cyst you had prior to your pregnancy would not cause this kind of pain, and I've never seen one rupture during pregnancy. I don't agree with the cyst theory, so I'd have to agree with your gastroenterologist on his diagnosis of Crohn's," he continues, *never once* looking at me.

"But I just told you that I've tested negative for Crohn's," I say, dismayed at his lack of ability to connect the dots. I hand him the case history that I have written myself, a simple and straightforward list of events and tests. There are also the results from Mayo Clinic stating that I *don't* have Crohn's disease. He does not even look at these. He tosses it onto the counter and shrugs, saying, "Well, I don't agree."

I sit in stunned silence on the examining table as the door shuts behind him. I get dressed and leave. I am outraged. As plain as that, I am dismissed along with my case and my apparently unimportant results from Mayo Clinic. Vowing never to see this doctor again, I storm across the parking lot to my car. I don't believe that he cares or that he's listening. This is the merry-medical-go-round and I have to find a way off it. This is the dream where you know someone is after you, so you dodge into the safest places that you can find. Still, it is to no avail. You can't get anyone to help you.

In tears, I drive up Mapleton Hill toward the Still Mountain Clinic, calling the one doctor besides Dr. Dughi who I know will, at least, *listen*. Since he has helped me in the past, I hope he will help to sort this out and give me some intelligent direction. His receptionist tells me that he is completely booked, but asks me to hold. When she returns, she tells me that he said to come right over and that he'll fit me in as soon as he can.

Dr. Gottlieb is trained in both Eastern and Western medicine, giving him a unique perspective when addressing a medical issue. I hand him my case summary, and I tell him, "These are the CliffsNotes that cover the past ten months but most of all, the past three weeks. If you would just review them, you'll be caught up on my current situation."

Instead of tossing this collection of information aside, the map which has led me to his office, he slowly reads my concise, yet clear notes as if they actually matter. Already I start to feel encouraged that help is on the way.

When he has finished reading, he says, "Yes, I agree with you and it would seem appropriate to accept the results from Mayo Clinic. You really don't profile as a Crohn's patient as the onset of the disease is generally seen at nineteen or twenty years old. I've had several Crohn's patients come to me for treatment of their symptoms, and from what I see physically, you simply do not present the signs and symptoms of it. I also agree that you should have this cyst checked out as Dr. Dughi suggested." Finally, he does some tests of his own and sends them to the lab for evaluation.

He tells me, "While I was in medical school, my father once said to measure twice and cut once." It's a good piece of advice and one which this doctor seems to emulate in everything he does. He is never in a hurry, and he considers the facts before speaking, which makes me trust his judgment. When I ask him whom he would have his wife see if this were *her* situation, he smiles and says, "Well, *me*, of course."

He cheers me up with this little quip and, in the same breath, chooses my next doctor, the doctor who will discover my cancer, Dr. David Thayer. "I've seen Dr. Thayer in surgery and I was impressed with his ability and his manner. He's both a gentleman and a tremendous doctor," he says without a trace of doubt in his voice. I am getting good at noticing if people are certain of what they are talking about.

"Let's call his office right now to ask if he can see you today. If not, then we'll try for tomorrow morning, all right?" he says, dialing the number himself.

October 24, 2003

Doctor number five—three hours and two radiologists later—offers a logical explanation for my unexplained "episodes," as we are now referring to the baffling mystery of my pain. We seem to finally have an answer!

They have discovered a 5-cm ovarian cyst in *addition* to the 3-cm one that appeared earlier! I hear Dr. Thayer say, "I suspect these cysts, along with possible endometriosis, could definitely cause this kind of severe pain, particularly during the last trimester of pregnancy."

He tells my husband and me that these cysts should be removed, and we schedule a laparoscopy for early December, his first available appointment. My only concern is our upcoming family vacation to the British Virgin Islands scheduled in four weeks, over Thanksgiving.

My husband Amory and I have planned a sailing trip with the kids. We have chartered the boat, and the necessary flights are booked and paid for. I am thinking, like any healthy person would, about my vacation and that if I have to *wait* until December for surgery I won't get clearance to travel. I tell his scheduler in earnest, "I want to fill the *first* cancellation that he has." I get my wish five days later.

October 29, 2003

The phone is ringing. Good . It's Dr. Thayer's office, they must have an opening.

"He has a cancellation on Friday morning, do you want to take it?" the scheduler asks.

"Definitely," I answer quickly, but the moment I do, I feel the back of my head tingle right behind my ears.

"Can you come in for the pre-op exam today then?"

"What, *today?*"

"We have to do your pre-op exam today, if your surgery is day after tomorrow."

"Oh, yes...I can...yes," I answer, much less assertively.

"Is everything all right?"

"No, yes...I'm okay. I'm just...really scared."

She asks the one question I don't want her to ask: "What are you scared about?" There's an ample pause. She's waiting for my answer...damn it. I'm afraid to give it to her, but then I do.

"I'm scared that I have cancer."

"Really? Why would you be thinking that?"

"That's what's scaring me, that I *am* thinking that."

"I don't think you should worry about that. Many of our patients have ovarian cysts removed, all the time. This is a very easy procedure, and finding cancer with this is so rare. Now if you want to talk more about your concerns with a nurse when you come in...I can make a note here...."

"No, don't. I mean, please don't make a note, I'm very superstitious...you know."

"Well, all right then, can you come in at two o'clock?"

"Yes, sure, that'll work, I think...yes, that's good. I'll see you then."

"Great. And really, don't worry. I just know you'll be okay, all right?"

I hang up, trying to believe her, staring blankly at the mountains in the distance.

When cancer happens, none of us is ever really ready. I'll be thinking that the tack I'm on is perfect, until a rogue gust forces me to point in a different direction altogether.

October 31, 2003

"Happy Halloween!" I call out to my kids from the stairway where I descend, carrying the baby in his puppy costume and putting him in his high chair. I squeeze fresh orange juice and cook up a full breakfast of eggs, toast and fruit salad because I know it is definitely the first and the last decent thing that they'll eat today.

My eighth-grade daughter, Chanel, adjusts her Disco Diva purple wig and tries to glue on her thick false eyelashes to match. She is in front of the mirror in the hall, yelling out to me between bites saying, "Mom, eggs are *so* stupid, I don't want to eat eggs!" Her sixth-grade, motocross-clad brother, Marco, finishes the food on his plate, knowing it's not worth the fight. He puts his helmet in the trunk with the backpacks.

My husband, on the other hand, is grateful for my breakfast and says, "This is delicious." Both kids look over their father at each other with that "he's trying to set a good example again" smile and say in unison, "You always say that, Dad."

We load up the car with the coats, treats and baby William. I'm thankful that Marco's motocross gear now doubles as his costume, as I recall how last year he went as a refrigerator when I was eight months pregnant. Suffice it to say that just getting all of us into the car was a feat.

So far, it is a typical Halloween morning, like so many happy ones in the past. The morning air is brisk and nine pumpkins of various sizes are carved and sitting on the brick steps of the front porch; one for each of our family of five, three for the cats, Coal, Minkie and Sailor, and a tiny one for Bob, the toad that lives under the porch but has retired for the winter.

Once at school, Chanel and Marco hop out and wave goodbye to the baby, who is smiling brightly from his car seat. "I'll see you after school. Don't forget you'll take the bus today. I'll be waiting for you at home," I call out as they rush toward their friends. I won't be there to help with the school party today as I normally would, because I am going to have an outpatient procedure to remove the offending suspects, two ovarian cysts. The baby and I return home. The sitter is there to meet us.

I remove all of my jewelry and shower. I do not apply makeup, lotion or perfume per the preoperative instruction sheet I was given the day before. I am practically running to get to the Stan Brenton Surgery Center downtown. I just know that once they remove the cysts by laparoscopy, I will feel great. This will be a minor procedure according to my friend who has had one herself. Compared to what I've hazarded lately, this will resemble a trip to the dentist. I'm driving myself there and Amory will walk over from his office and take me home.

I will recover easily. I will be completely healed and ready for adventure by the time I reach the azure waters of the Caribbean next month. All of my unexplained hormonal symptoms will stop, and I'll be back in the game, sailing in the lovely British Virgin Islands with my family. At this point, ignorance is bliss. Little do I know that my dream vacation will be replaced by a complete nightmare.

A Different Life

Being Halloween, it's not an ideal day for a full-time mother of three to have anything done, much less surgery, but I expect to be back at home by noon. By four o'clock in the afternoon when the kids get home, I figure that I will be snapping photos and getting them set to head out for a night of fun.

In our neck of the woods we only get about three or four kids knocking, so it won't be too much to stay home with the baby and answer the door for those few. Amory will run Chanel and Marco out to their usual trick-or-treating neighborhood. I have got it all figured out.

At the surgery center, I change into the uniform of late, the hospital gown. This time I don't mind, because I will not be wearing one of these after today for a long time. As I lie here waiting to go into pre-op, I see my orthopedic surgeon, Dr. Wieder, across the room. He comes over shaking his head. He wears a sly smile and says, "Geez, you just can't stay out of this place can you? Didn't I already fix your shoulder up this month? What are you doing back in here again?" So I tell him, adding sarcastically, "I thought that blood and stitches were just the thing for Halloween. Anyway, after today I plan to be done with all of you doctors, you included!" He agrees with a hearty laugh.

Dr. Thayer stops by to talk with me. I ask him a question strictly based on intuition, which is pretty much how I decide a lot of things in my life. Feeling shy and unsure, I ask, "Well, I've been thinking that since nothing was found during my colonoscopy, particularly in the ileum, where they had been taking a biopsy for Crohn's, could you...

well, can you look at my intestines from the outside? Is that possible since there were no problems seen on the inside?" Just hearing this string of questions I feel nauseated. I'm on to something.

While he accepts my question thoughtfully, he becomes interested that I had been thinking all of this through to this point. "I will already be in roughly the same quadrant, so I might be able to take a look." He was clear to point out, "This would not be considered routine." Like any smart doctor, he is careful not to promise me anything.

"Thank you for considering this. Whatever you can do in the way of looking around while you're in there would make me feel a lot better," I say. He smiles and says, "We'll sort this out. We will." I believe him. I had no way of knowing to what end his "sorting" would deliver me. Unfortunately, it would not be to The Bitter End Yacht Club, where I had been featuring myself, cocktail in hand, watching the sun set in this glorious destination on Virgin Gorda, well known to sailors of the British Virgin Islands. The nurse administers a dose of Versed, or "patient-be-gone" as I have fondly named the drug, and I float away.

As I wake up, I wearily begin to focus on the upper corners of the room. They are too close. In fact, the whole room has shrunk substantially. I don't remember anything about this room at all. Also, it is rocking slightly. It feels like I'm moving. I *am* moving. I close my eyes, I let the rocking soothe me and I imagine that I am in my berth on the sailboat, drifting off to sleep, soft waves sloshing rhythmically against the hull with the halyard clinking against the mast.

I open my eyes again. I am not on a sailboat. I'm in an ambulance. Unable to speak, I look at the paramedic at my side and ask with my eyes, "What am I doing here?" It is the silent question he has undoubtedly answered a hundred times. "My name is Mike. We're in an ambulance right now on our way over to the hospital, Mrs. Host."

"Why?" I whisper. Momentarily consulting his handy clipboard, he looks at me and says calmly, "Let's see...well, it looks like you've had your appendix removed and they usually keep patients overnight with that."

The already shrunken room just squeezed itself around my tiny bed frame. I gasp and try to object. I want to shout out and tell this obviously confused man that no, that isn't me, he has the wrong patient in his little ambulance. I had a cyst removed, not my appendix!

Though groggy, I quickly conclude that I am one of those medical mistakes we hear about on Oprah for whom we shake our heads in quiet disbelief, relieved that it is not us. They've mixed me up with someone who is probably now dead of a ruptured appendix! I am trying to speak; no words come out. My voice is stifled by the dry cotton that has apparently taken the place of my throat.

"Your husband is following us." He fills me in, answering my next silent question before my useless attempt to ask it.

I am drifting in and out, nauseous, trying to hold on to the edges and outlines. They open the ambulance door, with a nice rush of fresh air. The first thing I notice is that it's night. I am not at home. It is not noon.

I see my husband's face, the night sky framing it. I focus. I swallow and my throat feels stuffed with Styrofoam. "My appendix?" I manage in a whisper.

"Yes, honey. They discovered that it was in pretty bad shape and about to rupture, so they sent for a general surgeon and it was removed," Amory says.

Ever the optimist, I nod my head. Oh, good! I'm thinking, now pleased. So *that's* what has been causing all the trouble. Great! Now my troubles are over. Whew! He drifts away before I can ask the other three questions. Who has the baby? Where are the kids? And what time is it?

As the hospital room appears around me, I see my mom. A retired registered nurse, she also begins by answering my questions without my having to ask. This must be a skill you acquire after years of looking at patients' faces. "Amory is home with the baby. It's about eight-thirty and the kids are still out trick-or-treating. How do you feel?"

How do I feel? Always the mother, even in the fog of the anesthesia lifting, all I can think about is that somebody has to find my kids and take them home. Of course, this means a major, out-of-the-way-drive for the unlucky friend who answers her phone.

I ask for the phone. "Mom, can you dial for me?" I call my friend, Merrilee. She knows about the whole laparoscopy because we talked about it a couple of days ago, but her voice clearly says that she's surprised to see that her caller ID reads "Boulder Community Hospital" and not "Host, Amory." I give her the short version, which is that I'm not sure exactly what I'm doing here, but that my kids, along with my nephew Stover, who is spending the weekend, are out there. I ask her if she can go and find my kids and take them home.

A mother to the core, she is horrified along with me at the thought of my kids being out there unaccounted for. She doesn't waste any time asking more about me but says what makes me feel better right this second, and she hangs up quickly. She's a mother on a mission and I stop worrying instantly. She goes out to find my kids. Anyone who knows Merrilee knows that she will not fail to do so.

She leaves her two little ones at home with their dad. It's anyone's guess how long she drives in circles through her neighborhood, searching through the waves of costumes at night, to round up my two and my nephew and take them home. Once there, she offers to stay with my crew and the baby so that my husband can come back to be with me at the hospital. This is the kind of favor that you don't forget.

With each hour, I get further apart from the general anesthesia and closer to reality. I slowly start to put things together. The next thing that I want to know is why my mom is still here with me at 10:30 p.m. It is late for her and I'm surprised that she hasn't gone home. This is my first clue that more has been removed from the story than just my appendix.

"It's so late for you, Mom," I say, trying to get her to go home, staring at the huge amethyst-and-citrine rings on her long, manicured fingers.

"I'm going to spend the night. I just think I'd better stay here and make sure that you do all right," she tells me, pulling out her lipstick, tipping her head down and applying it in the tiny mirror of the Chinese silk case that holds it. I can smell the Estee Lauder all the way over here.

"Mom, why am I here?" I ask in that I-know-you're-not-telling-me-everything voice.

"Do you like this? I thought it looked great with this top," she answers, holding her hand out closer so I'll have a better view of the ring I've been eyeing.

"What *else* do they need me for? I want to go home."

"Well, there's more that the doctors wanted to check out," she says in her perfectly unaffected nurse-on-duty voice. "I thought about getting Marisa this same ring. After all, her birthstone is amethyst," she continues, trying to steer me away from my question.

"*What* more? I thought that my appendix was the problem," I mutter.

"They have the necklace, too."

"Mom, it's too big for her, she doesn't wear stuff she can't ski in. I can't talk about jewelry right now."

"What do you mean?"

"*What* more, Mom?"

"Well, I think that's all we know for tonight, honey," she says, turning her back to fill my water cup. "Now, Amory will come down here first thing in the morning and talk to you," I hear her saying.

"Call him for me, Mom."

"Now? It's so late. Let's not wake the baby."

I close my eyes. I can't struggle with words anymore. Why doesn't

Amory just...call me?... Do we...need him to come...all...the way over here to talk to me? I hear myself mentally trying to control the situation, disgruntled that I can't get people to do what I want. I hear myself mumble parts of my thoughts out loud, as sleep overtakes my curiosity.

Just like 9/11 or, for my mother's generation, the assassination of John F. Kennedy, the question "What were you doing when you first heard the news?" brings utterly clear memories to mind. Hardly anyone I know doesn't readily remember all of the particulars in relation to themselves, about either or both of those events.

Unfortunately, a diagnosis of cancer etches an oddly similar memory on its recipient. It is a catastrophic hit with all sorts of details and with invisible pain and trauma that are known only to you.

The wall clock reads 7:00 a.m. It is morning and I still don't see my husband, so I let the numbers blur and the clock itself melts into a Dali abstraction. When the abstraction comes back into view, it has a nose and eyes and is looking gently at me. My husband is sitting on the edge of my bed, and we are alone. I am quiet. I don't need to talk. He is going to tell me the truth. I hear the individual words coming out of his mouth. His subtle tone begins to sound like a rushing river.

You are on the river. You are in a boat, and it even has oars. You have the distinct sense that these simple facts are about to change. You hear the distant roar of the great falls you are headed for, as the river's current gains speed and depth beneath you.

I can barely hear his voice above the rolling waves that are taking me down. The oars are ripped away and the oarlocks are empty. I hold on to the boat but it does not hold on to me. I can just make out the word *cancer* amid the deafening roar and spray, and then the river swallows me up and every sound with me.

Silence.

You feel your boat drop away. You are suspended for a split second and then you drop away, too. You are not just slipping over a giant waterfall; you are being shoved over its raging edge while being pulled down, down hard, by its sheer gravity. You are drowning in this crashing sensation, holding your breath, tumbling with the rocks and stones.

You are still using your eyes. All of your other senses have shut down. Your eyes, full of water, are trying to focus through the wavering light. You hit the bottom and the water is pummeling you. You come up and gasp for a single breath. You're back under, below the water, tumbling in a hole. The river spits you out into its rolling waves. You grab hold of something, anything, and hold your face up to the sky. The plunge over the falls hasn't killed you, but it has crushed you. You feel broken everywhere. You see your life in pieces bobbing around you in the swirling eddies while the rest is floating away with the current. You won't need those pieces anymore, but you don't realize that yet.

The River

November 1, 2003

I t appears I'm still here. After a horribly long night, I feel solid and heavy, with an unnatural sense of confusion. I'm not asking for a mirror to see if I look the way I feel. Once again, just like a month ago, I am most upset about being here in the hospital, abruptly separated from my baby, carted off without any warning.

A doctor arrives to explain. My sister-in-law Trina, my dear friend Sara, my mom and dad and Amory are all quiet, waiting.

"If you could pick a cancer to have, carcinoid tumor would be right up there on top." This is the line I am thrown by Dr. Sitarik, my newly appointed oncologist, from the bank of the river to my bed in the middle of it. "Now, it's true, there is no cure, but it is slow-growing. Carcinoid generally does not respond to chemotherapy or to radiation the way most cancers do. Surgical removal is the standard course for most carcinoid patients. Now, with a successful surgery you can do pretty well," he explains. Just like that, "pretty" becomes "ugly."

My right hand goes instantly to my neck to touch the 18-karat gold coin which I always wear, but it's not there. Why would it be, I'm in the hospital. My aunt Florence bought this particular charm on the Ponte Vecchio bridge, in Florence, Italy, in 1963, the year I was born. Growing up, it was my favorite charm on her bracelet. It's a coin that has a beautiful woman's profile in relief. She's wearing a blindfold, her hair is flying out behind her. Tiny symbols of chance represented by cards, dice and a roulette wheel, are beneath her. On the back is an incredibly detailed etching of the Ponte Vecchio Bridge. As a young girl, I'd often finger through the charms on her heavy bracelet. When I'd come to that one I'd ask about it, saying, "What's her name again?" She would give me the same answer, "That's Blind Faith. You've got to have that in life."

To be honest, I had never really known her meaning until the day of her funeral. As she had wished, all five of us nieces were sitting in a circle in her living room. From a large brown paper sack we were to "choose" a small zip-lock bag containing a piece of her jewelry within it. Then we'd go around again until the brown bag was empty. This was so like my aunt to find a way to be fair and not to play favorites among us. There were over thirty-five pieces in that bag.

The first time that I reached in, I pulled out the charm, the one that had been my favorite. Just like that, "Blind Faith" became mine. At the time, I was shaken up by it and couldn't help feeling that my aunt had "chosen" it for me, and I've pondered over it many times since.

"Okay," I'm thinking, I will most certainly need her now, pulling my mind back into the tension. Now I'm a *cancer* patient. I've just landed here in this bed from a four-hour surgery that started as a one-hour, outpatient procedure, and he sounds fairly sure that I'll be in need of more surgery still. Maybe they'll just remove this tumor and that's it! Okay, that sounds reassuring. Better than ovarian cancer that ended my Aunt Florence's life at fifty-six, just seven years ago. I know how her suffering broke all of our hearts. She was like a second mother to me, and without her in my life, things will never be the same.

I read somewhere, later, that oddly enough, most cancer patients would not trade and be a patient with a different cancer, given the chance. Does this mean we are all individually pre-wired to bear our own brand of misery right from the beginning? Or are we simply so scared of what we've been diagnosed with that we don't dare think of anything else?

"What's it called again?" I ask, from the middle of the river.

What the pain medications from the appendectomy do is allow my brain to write short stories with happy endings. In the story I write:

> I have a single tumor the size of a quarter at most, the talented surgeon downstairs removes it, say tomorrow, and ta-da, I'm well. The End.

Everyone leaves the room looking extremely concerned, but although I feel physically thrashed, I'm optimistic. I'm good with the story that I'm telling myself, sure that I've already survived the fall. Now, I'll just swim with the current, pull myself out onto the bank and be done with this river. Then it occurs to me that they are all out in the hall reading a different story. When they come back in, I can tell by their faces that I'm right.

However, when they have all taken leave for a spell and I am alone, I continue writing myself short stories with happy endings. My cell phone rings a couple of times and I glance over to see the familiar 970 area code that indicates that it's my little sister calling, my closest friend. Oh, no, they have told her. I pick it up and slowly open the flap, sensing that this call will change everything.

"Hey," I open, trying to sound morning fresh, trying to see if she even knows I'm in the hospital. After all, I reason, last night was Halloween and she is even farther out of town than her Aspen home. She and her husband have stopped over in Malibu on their way to Carmel for his brother's sixtieth birthday party.

I'm hoping the next words out of her mouth will be a quick rundown of the creatures she saw roaming Sunset Boulevard last night, or of who wore what, or of what she is wearing to the big birthday bash tonight. Instead, there's a silence that is bulging with tears and all that she can't bear to say. We stay quiet like that for a minute, while I wait for her to get her words together.

"I'm so sorry, Carrie," she sobs. "I wish it could be me. What is this? Why does it have to be you? You have the kids. I don't have any kids and this doesn't make any sense. It should be me."

She means this, and my heart is pained by my little sister's tears of anguish and disbelief. I can't bear to hear her crying over me like this. In an attempt to cheer myself up and to keep her out of the river, I tell her the upside of things: now that I've got cancer, I may never have to go to the dentist again. She joins me in a lame chuckle and says, "Yeah, that could be a bonus." Then I hear her start to cry again.

She's kid number six in the family and while that makes her the baby, she's by far the toughest girl I know. She can convince you up, or down, any mountain in your path. Her many friends and colleagues alike would agree there's nothing flimsy about Marisa. She defines the word *genuine*. In her reliable, sturdy iron-skillet style, she can cook up your favorite dinner, or send a robber or a bear running for his life.

But now she has glued herself next to me through this tiny little phone and she is not going to leave my side. She won't let me drown; that much I know for sure. My mind flashes a snapshot memory onto the screen, a sunny day twenty years ago when I was visiting her in Malibu, California.

We were neck-deep in the surf. A lifeguard on the crowded beach began blowing his whistle in shrill blasts and motioning frantically to everyone in the water to get out. My sister automatically started laughing. Then looking at me with a crazed stare, she started "bhum, bhum, bhumming" the theme to *Jaws* to freak me out.

Two seconds later, as if by a shark, a forceful riptide grabbed us both by the ankles and yanked us under. We tried to reach for each other when we popped up, but we were already too far apart. After the first roll, I came up half kneeling, half standing and got yanked back under five or six more times. Huge heavy waves barreled down on me, crushing me into the rocks and gravel below. My head popped up, and as I grabbed one last breath, I saw her there, washed up on the beach on her knees, her eyes pasted to my face. On her feet, she hurdled a wave and fought her way back in, toward me. Then she hauled me out with what I can only describe as pure, superhuman adrenaline.

We were facedown, topless and beaten to a pulp with sand packed into our eyes, ears, noses and mouths. Both of us were coughing and sputtering..."I can't even believe it, can you?" I gasp.

"No. But I had to save your sorry ass! Damn, now I'm gonna have to teach you how to swim, too," she replied, in a voice half planning to throw me back in.

We stayed there on the sandy slope, just out of reach of the breaking waves, not saying anything for a long time. That hot dry sand felt like a new lease on life, the whistle of the lifeguard still shrieking in the background. We both knew she barely made it out. We both knew that I most definitely would not have made it out if she had not come back in. We silently agree, wincing as we examine our cuts and scrapes and soon-to-be bruises, that this is not a story I will tell Mom once I'm back in Denver. I never do.

This will be the beginning of life's memories rushing up to the front row so I can get a glimpse of them now. Is this what happens when your life is threatened? I wonder. How odd that Marisa should call from Malibu, of all places, just as I feel I am going under again.

"I can't even believe it, can you?" I offer the line fresh from my memory, careful to cover the mouthpiece so she can't hear the rushing river in the background.

"No," she cries quietly, "No, I can't."

We're both wishing that she were home, so that she could jump in her car and close the distance between us and come right to the hospital. We would be able to find some way to deal with this, but we don't say this. It's not an option right now.

"Just keep your feet downstream, and we'll make it, Bear. We'll pull you out. Trust me. Just hang on," she says in her best coaching "we're gonna smoke 'em" voice. I can't believe she hears the river and uses my childhood nickname, Bear. Immediately, I return to us at nine and eleven.

We are sweet, confident, suntanned pals, smelling of Coppertone and fresh-cut grass, on our Stingrays with those glittery vinyl banana seats, plastic fringe flying from the handlebars. We're riding down Williams Street toward the drugstore on the corner of Gilpin and Sixth, for a fresh supply of Bazooka and Pixie Stix. Misa, as we called her back then, would stuff all of our candy into her overall pockets, in full control of the goods, tearing down the street ahead of me, popping wheelies.

We are just too sad to say anything else, so we end with, "We'll talk," instead of, "Goodbye," and hang up. We call each other like this, two or three times on any other average day. We both silently know how good "average" suddenly looks right now. We'll pick this up later.

I let her hang up first. Once she is safely back in California and out of this stupid river, I quietly close my phone and drop it through the rail of my bed, into the water that is all around me. I don't care if it rings all day.

I don't have what it takes to answer four more calls like that, the ones from the rest of my siblings which are sure to follow. These calls will come one by one and make this day more and more strange and scary and less and less average. I don't have what it takes to swim for the bank, either, so I just hold on to my sister's words in a futile attempt to keep my head above water. Finally, I'm crying with full abandon, knowing my tears are merging into the current so no one can hear them, least of all, Marisa.

Trina, the saint, spends the second night at the hospital with me. This relieves my mother of her hospital shift, but in her tireless way she simply goes to the house and helps Amory take care of the kids. Trina's on the horribly uncomfortable recliner chair next to my bed. She pretends to be sleeping, between trying to keep my spirits intact and fielding those calls I knew would come, one after another.

Her voice lulls me, soft in the distance. She paces the hall, patiently recounting the details in sequential order to the caller on the other end. There's a lot of "yeah, we'll have to talk later" sprinkled throughout. Each time she tells my story, the one I didn't write, I feel more and more numb. Soon, I stop hearing her at all, but only see her lips move.

The river seems to be getting colder and deeper, as I silently float along its surface. Cancer instantly draws a dark, heavy curtain of sky down around me so that I can barely hear or see anything at all. I'm not ready to replay all the memories of my life right now, but it doesn't let me choose. The river rolls through the snapshots of my life. They're all in black and white. I quickly find that the best thing to be at the moment is numb. I'm not ready, but it's time to take stock. Everything close to me becomes a blur.

The Current

—◦∞◦—

On Sunday morning, my nurse tells me that I'll be able to go home later today. Oh, boy, I'm thinking sarcastically, now I can start thinking of how I will eventually have to tell my children. I'm hoping that "eventually" will never come and that this will all turn out to be another misdiagnosis, like Crohn's disease was. Just for this moment, I wish all three of them were babies so I could skip that part. I can't tell them that I have cancer. That's not right and it's unnatural. It's unreal. That is someone else's unreal story, not *mine*.

I go with "it's not real" and reach for the little black button. Clicking it, I allow myself one more delicious, drug-induced, delusional, pain-free moment of short-story writing. Then they remove my IV and send me home to reality.

It's too soon for me to know that this will be the beginning of all kinds of angels showing up. When I get home early that evening, my brother Steve is waiting there for me with his wife, Barbara. Their kids are downstairs shooting pool with Marco and Chanel, the clack, clacking of the balls in the distance. I walk straight into their arms and start to cry.

Barbara walks me to my bedroom and reaches out to me with a gift. It has floated beside my bed ever since, inviting hope into my heart: a pewter angel, hanging from an ivory silk ribbon, cradling a baby in her arms. Etched into one of the wings is a quote from Willa Cather: *"Where there is great love there are always miracles."*

My husband, Amory, is a man of action who makes a plan and then follows through, so I affectionately call him Planner Pants. He is a man who finds solutions to problems and gets them handled, all while others are still complaining about the problem at hand. Much to his chagrin, he is now going after the biggest problem that can be dished up—cancer.

He meets this problem head-on. He is going to find the doctors that will, at the very least, prolong my life—and maybe even save it. He draws on his many years of business expertise and launches himself into a local and national search for the right team of surgeon and oncologist.

He is on a mission, and nothing will stop him until he is satisfied with the results of his search. He just keeps pushing ahead. He is sending out complete summaries of my case, including films and test results, to various doctors, from Anshutz Medical in Denver to as far away as Sloan Kettering in New York. Then he contacts specialists in Boston, Washington, D.C., Texas, California and Minnesota, asking them to evaluate my situation. He rapidly sets up appointment after appointment with these qualified doctors.

With the Thanksgiving holiday nearing, many of the doctors we need to talk to are about to take vacations, some for several weeks. He convinces their secretaries and schedulers to create appointments for times that don't exist. Somehow, he does this without upsetting anyone, and in a seemingly breezy manner. He is a gentle bulldozer, as my father so aptly refers to him. He takes all of my films and test results to each meeting. We ask the questions, and he takes detailed notes on the answers to each one. When I get back into the car, overwhelmed with too much information, he says, "Don't worry, I'll lay it all out for you so that you can make the best possible choice."

Then, he does this. He begins to fill a large, three-ring binder with profiles on every possible cancer facility and profiles on oncologists and surgeons who have had anything to do with my rare disease.

Dr. Herbert Hoover of Massachusetts General even calls us from his home one night, in response to my husband's informative and incredibly well-written letter asking for his advice on how to proceed. Dr. Koss, a highly respected oncologist in his field, calls from New York to recommend Dr. Joseph Rubin, a leading oncologist at Mayo Clinic. Here at home, Dr. Dughi gives two thumbs up to that recommendation and adds that Dr. Nagorney, also at Mayo Clinic, is one of the most well-regarded surgeons in the specialized field of carcinoid.

My husband sets up additional interviews by phone and in person with our narrowed field of doctors, so that we can finalize which road to take. Amory knows what I know about my cancer, and more. He has been researching. I have not. I'm not ready to know every scary detail about this disease, at least not yet. I stop reading about it all together after I read the following definition of my disease from *Mayo Clinic Family Health Book*, which I pull from my shelf of general medical reference books when I return from the hospital.

Carcinoid Syndrome
<u>Signs and Symptoms:</u>
Flushing of the skin
Diarrhea

Carcinoid tumors are slowly growing malignancies, usually in the ileum, the lower section of the small intestine. These tumors may spread to the liver and also may metastasize to the lungs and other organs.

Occasionally, Carcinoid tumors can cause the flushing of the skin and diarrhea (Carcinoid syndrome). With this complication, detection of excessive levels of a normal body chemical in the urine is an important biochemical indicator of this type of tumor.

Depending on how soon the cancer is detected and where it is located, some people fully recover after surgical treatment. Many live 5 to 10 years after the cancer has spread (metastasized) because the tumor grows slowly. Death usually results from heart or liver failure when the cancer reaches these organs.

The seven words that I grab hold of are these: *"some people fully recover after surgical treatment."* These words become my lifeboat. I immediately decide to get into this boat and to hang on for dear life. Suddenly those two words, *dear* and *life*, become extraordinarily clear for me.

Cancer is like that. It can throw you overboard with one short definition, and then it can help you decide that you are strong enough to swim for a lifeline. Only you can choose to read between the lines and find one small bit of information to hold on to. Allow even the smallest bit of encouragement to be the thing that keeps you afloat. Do not underestimate your own desire to live. Hope is a powerful thing.

The Way Time Ticks

Until I began dating my husband, I had never heard of time referred to in thirty-, sixty- and ninety-day increments. But this is how time ticks for a businessman: thirty days, sixty days, ninety days; or this quarter, next quarter. Honestly, it never occurred to me that a year could be viewed as a large pie cut into four parts of roughly ninety days—not an exciting picture any way you slice it, to my way of thinking.

To this day, I find this way of seeing time as slightly disturbing, as it takes all of the romance out of life. I guess I have never been that "out there in the future" type of gal. In fact, I haven't been much of a planner at all—that is, until I am gingerly informed of how short my future might be.

I am told one November afternoon that, in my current condition with this cancer in its advanced stage and situated in or on most of my internal organs, without surgery my life expectancy may be from eighteen to thirty-six months.

What?

This is how I am tossed out of that lifeboat that I am so relieved to be in. After I hear this, I decide to read about it for myself. Now, because of my exploration into the world of cancer, on paper, I am finally forced to see time as a big pie cut into pieces. Rather than seeing time as a beautiful mystery that unfolds slowly, day by day, I see it as a threat. Now, I'm sure that I was right about never before having chosen to see time like this, compressed into finite sections. It is unpleasant.

It's true that I am not good with numbers, but this math rolls right into my head. Being optimistic, I immediately take the thirty-six-month future and add this number to my children's current ages and come up with four, fifteen and seventeen. The ages my children will be when I die. What? No, this *can't* be right.

I start reading again. I start to do the smallest bit of research in hopes of confirming my initial reaction that there is no way that this cancer can press my whole future into thirty-six short months! Instead, I confirm that this information is true, as the average case goes, and that these numbers are, in fact, the unfortunate result of more than just one doctor's random opinion.

Words, which I have considered my closest companions, have turned on me. A mutiny of words and, like it or not, I'm out here splashing around again. I'm thinking, *Be mindful of what you read. Do not trust in words—words can turn on you. There's only an* R *between* friend *and* fiend.

I try to think about my life in months, but instead I go with days, as a businessperson would: ninety days, sixty days and thirty days. It's no wonder business people everywhere are stressed out of their minds. In a poet's mind, there is no such thing as thirty days out. Why care about thirty days that aren't here yet, when right this moment the light has attached itself to the edge of that tree against a steel-blue-gray stormy sky?

Suddenly, I do.

My poet's mind is shattered. I have spent my life paying attention to nature's subtleties. I enjoy it all, from noticing the vulnerability of the tiniest flower poking its head through a crack in a parking lot to the way that a single boom of thunder quiets all of the noise in your head and for one precious second, you feel life.

I am not ready for this. No one is.

Those unadorned words that make up the medical definition of the way that this is likely to go have demolished my heart. I begin to panic. *They must know more than I do. They have been watching what this disease does to people. They have been keeping track of the results.* At once, I hate scientists and doctors, both. I hate their clinical papers and their stupid statistics. I break down in a whole new way, on a whole new level. I stop reading and I stop breathing.

In a fog of disbelief, I wedge myself deep into the corner of the couch, pulling the heavy pillows up around me so nothing else can come close. Of course, my old cat, Coal, deftly makes his way along the back ridge and drops into my cave. He looks at me with his crystal seafoam green eyes, stretching his neck up toward my face, nudging at my chin with his cool nose. Circling down, he curls himself into my lap. He begins to purr, his only sound since he's mute, a handicap that I am slowly beginning to relate to. I'm too scared to cry, so I stare at the fire until I fall asleep. The dream that ensues causes me to fear sleeping as much as waking:

I arrive where I'm going. Estes Park, at the base of Rocky Mountain National Park. I hear the crunch of the gravel as I slow to a stop in Moraine Park, a valley with the Big Thompson River running through it. My foot on the tire, I jerk the laces on my shoe, tying it too tight, yanking my hat down snug. Powerfully weightless, I'm pushing up off one rock onto the next, propelling forward, upward through the woods, exhaling in puffs of white mist. Using my foot, I clear away a circle where a campfire had once burned, mixing dirt, snow and cinders, then placing dry twigs and sticks into a small pile and lighting it. My fire snaps, pops and smokes its way to life. Sensual and alive, silky flames undulate above the frozen ground, pointing to the jet-black stream of smoke rising up, like a thin prayer. The thick silence of the forest holds vigil, while my mind weaves in and out of the amber flames. The warmth upon my face lets me know how cold I am. I begin to cry. The ground changes to stone, the pointed treetops arch into a gothic ceiling.

As my fire weakens, so does my breathing. My church of stone falls away. My body turns to wood and my bent shape becomes part of the old log. A black bear watches from a distance as I fade into this forest. Together with the glowing embers, I grow colder. Their powdery white edges, delicate over pulsing red-orange centers, slowly and imperceptibly turn to gray.

When I awake, completely drained, I'm so sure that I was actually frozen in that forest and not dreaming that I look down at my feet to see if my boots are still on, but they're not. I'm then haunted by this dream night and day. Desperate to put this somewhere, I write a poem and add it to all the others in the suitcase. I know it will be the last I will write for a while—if not forever.

My panic creates a tight, dark space around me. I can hardly breathe. I can't look at anyone I love without feeling grief over the impending loss. Not only the loss I am facing if I die, but the knowledge of how much other people are hurting at the idea of losing me. Immediately, I begin to forgive. I want to love. I want to bring peace to every situation. Ridiculous grudges and misgivings magically melt away, in light of the end in sight. I begin to cherish each person in my life, each time I see them, as though it will be the last time.

Now I see that I am down from the seven-word lifeboat of "*some people fully recover after surgical treatment*" to a boat that is barely afloat but for the one, hopeful word, "some." Yet I am getting into this boat, even if it is made of only *one* word. If I have no wind, then I will row. I will not go down without a fight. I'm now determined to embrace the intensely invasive surgery that I am so afraid of, because suddenly, surviving it has become my only hope.

I was full of aspirations for my future, and then I uncovered an unpleasant statistic that sent me reeling to the bottom. I have never felt time move the way that I do now. I'm filled with a sense of solitude, a fear that time is moving way too fast. I want to lock time up, but I know the truth. I know it will still be there, ticking. No doubt, it will take courage for me to face it down.

The Truth

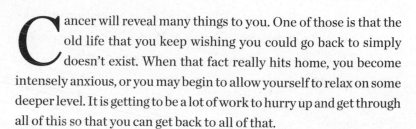

Cancer will reveal many things to you. One of those is that the old life that you keep wishing you could go back to simply doesn't exist. When that fact really hits home, you become intensely anxious, or you may begin to allow yourself to relax on some deeper level. It is getting to be a lot of work to hurry up and get through all of this so that you can get back to all of that.

Now that you are looking into new definitions of what's "normal," you begin to be more comfortable with where you actually are. You quickly learn that insincerity takes way too much energy; you drop it.

Finally, trying to settle in with yourself makes some sense, so you pull up a chair to have a chat with your cancer. At some point in the conversation you will learn that you are already a changed and better person for all of your suffering. Then there is more.

The removal of a carcinoid tumor is a tricky surgery. As one report outlines, "the tumors do not like to be disturbed." When they are, they fight back, releasing a deadly phytochemical into the bloodstream that, if not countered with an injection of the drug Sandostatin, can result in cardiac arrest. Nice.

To avoid this possible outcome of cardiac arrest as a result of my upcoming surgery, I am being pre-treated with daily subcutaneous injections of Sandostatin to my abdomen. My favorite nurse, Lolli, with the super-short, Annie-Lennox-yellow-white, spiked-up hair and her cheerful print tops and her ever-changing wristwatch collection, teaches me how to give these shots to myself. I will need one three times a day for two weeks. I have a severe aversion to needles, so when it comes to injections, looking away is how I have gotten this far. Even someone fairly stoic around needles might change their mind when faced with injecting one into their own stomach. Amory comes to my rescue and gives me the thrice-daily shots, often leaving his office to come home for the midday shot.

Now a certain solemnity sets over me as I begin to realize how lucky I was to survive the appendectomy and cyst removal. I was not treated with Sandostatin during those surgeries. There was no way for Dr. Thayer or Dr. Fox (the general surgeon who was called in) to have anticipated running straight into this rare cancer. Once the frozen biopsies had confirmed carcinoid tumor, they turned to an oncologist, now my oncologist, for advice on how to proceed. Friday, October 31, was an extremely busy day in Dr. Sitarik's office. When he received the call with questions, he made two mistakes: he told Dr. Thayer and Doctor Fox to remove more tumor than was needed for another biopsy, and he didn't tell them to treat me with Sandostatin.

"The truth is that I could have easily come to the end of my life right there on that operating table, never having had the chance to fight this battle at all," I say, when I see Dr. Thayer for my postoperative checkup at his office. I can tell by his visibly shaken demeanor that, since my surgery, he has read up on this fact. Yet he behaves as a professional in never laying blame on his colleagues but instead directing our discussion to the outcome. He calms me down by pointing out, "You have a strong heart and you made it through. That's what's important."

Hearing him say this, I feel we were all just narrowly missed by the same forceful bolt of lightning. Returning home with this image in mind, I crawl into my bed where William is napping. Looking at my baby's face brings yet another sobering fact to light. If ten months earlier I had given birth by cesarean section, I would most certainly have lost my life. They would have cut directly into my abdominal wall, which was full of carcinoid tumor.

The front page of our local newspaper, *The Daily Camera,* spins into my mind, 1930s movie style, with a December 18 headline that is definitely not full of holiday cheer:

NEW MOTHER DIES!

Doctors baffled yesterday, during a routine cesarean section at Boulder Community Hospital. A mother dies as a healthy baby boy is born. Due to complications, the mother, an apparently healthy thirty-nine-year-old, died of cardiac arrest. The exact cause of death has yet to be determined. The family grieves while waiting for autopsy results.

I know that to imagine this right through to the newspaper article is creepy, but this is what your mind does when it adds up the information that tells it that it's all but met its Maker. I push this horrible story from my mind and quietly say the Hail Mary, wishing I didn't have such a lively imagination.

I actually shudder at this near miss, which really could have hit, given the current popularity of the C-section. Could I be this lucky, or is luck involved at all? This is where my curiosity about angels begins, guardian angels in particular, as they embellish so many paintings through the ages. Where did all of these angels come from? How can all of these artists be wrong?

As a docent at the Denver Art Museum, I have used my laser pointer time and time again to direct the viewer's eye to this or that angel. Some are hidden in the clouds, and some appear front and center. These hover over another figure in the painting who, but for their guardian angel's protection, is positioned to die an otherwise unfortunate death as in the painting *St. Michael and the Bull,* circa 1650, by Sebastian Lopez de Arteaga.

I reel my thoughts back from my own imagined death and picture an angel hovering directly over William and me. His angelic light is separating me from the scalpel of a C-section so that in the end, my painting features a grateful mother and baby safely nestled together, surrounded by family and happily glowing. Of course, three more semi-transparent ethereal angels are floating over the heads of Amory, Marco and Chanel. Their wings are perfectly arched, to protect them.

When I leave this gallery of thought and return to the present, I remain there for only a second. I then revert to considering the surgical error of omission that actually did take place. I'm not sure that I want this oncologist to be my doctor any longer. I decide that I'm going to ask him directly about this mishap to see what he has to say.

This is my introduction to the fact that doctors are human, something that had eluded me until now. This is why the general public is better served by touring an art exhibit and not touring medical schools. We are not meant to see all of the current doctors teaching their future colleagues about all of the things that can and do go wrong inside the imperfect world of medicine.

Doctors are the people from whom we expect solutions. We simply want our doctors to be perfect. My doctor ought to be able to fix my problem, right? I picture the top of an application to medical school to read:

Only the bravest marvels with nerves of steel and incapable of making mistakes need apply; no humans allowed.

When I confront Dr. Sitarik with the fact that he gave Dr. Thayer incomplete advice that could have cost me my life, looking me in the eye he simply and quietly admits to his error. I am completely caught off guard by his honesty. He is humble and he is at least as unhappy about it as I am. By being honest with me, he has disarmed me. He has got me putting my pointing finger away and realizing, in a kind of panic, that even the best doctors *do* occasionally make mistakes. What? Doctors are human? Who knew?

At one point, I had wanted to take Dr. Sitarik and throw him out to sea for all the anxiety he was causing me. For continuously ordering yet another round of tests or for being too slow to read me the results, and for not being God so that I could at least put in my request to be saved while having my blood drawn. Then, he did something unexpected and was totally honest with me, when I was expecting some fancy footwork or just straight denial. Nothing pulls up a chair and sits down as plainly as the truth.

Dr. Sitarik's honesty showed me his integrity, and he earned my trust. I decide that I respect this doctor, his honesty and his brave spirit. I decide to keep him. It is this moment when I learn the importance of not giving my doctor the role of God.

The Suitcase

November 2, 2003

"So how long do you think I've had it?" I ask Dr. Sitarik at the end of my exam, already suspecting the answer to my question.

"Five, possibly even ten years."

I can see by Amory's expression that this is yet another piece of information that he is trying to deal with—he's surprised by it, but I'm not.

"It's not uncommon for carcinoid patients to have the cancer for a long time before it finally presents enough symptoms to be correctly diagnosed... it's so difficult to spot ..." But I've already stopped listening, though I'm sitting attentively. My mind has climbed the narrow staircase to my tiny writing room. I need to open my old suitcase and find a certain poem.

"Can we stop by the writing room on the way home? I need to get something," I ask Amory in a dull and distracted voice as we're getting into the car.

"Sure," he answers, not asking me why.

Cancer was there...all this time. I don't have to go that far back. The poem is here. It's *got* to be here, somewhere. "Here...we are..." I'm saying aloud to myself. Rifling through a fistful of poems, and noting the dates they were written, I deal each one into one of five stacks: 1993, 1994,

1995, 1996 and 1997. Some of the titles from ten years ago: "Solitude," "Sorrow's Maze," "Fear," "Steps of Stone," "Empty Shoes."

"Oh, my God, I knew it. I *knew.*" I whisper, with a sharp little in breath, pulling a piece of paper from the next stack. Here it is..."My Ghost"...1995...the one I was looking for. What startles me worse than my memory of its title being correct is the little note I had scrawled in the bottom right-hand corner: "I hope I never see this awful poem again, it makes my neck tingle. It *scares* me."

Grains of Rice

November 3, 2003

They tell me that over the next five days they will "stage" my disease. Up until now, I have always related the word "stage" to the theater. I can already tell that this newest definition is not for me. I want to go back to my previous understanding of the stage, the one with sets, costumes and lights. The medical world that I have slammed into is upsetting all of my sensibilities.

Could this be the reason I'm continuously creating metaphors for both the short and the long term, as a way of coping? With cancer as my reality and three children at home, I have to have a way to process the intensity of my situation that isn't a nervous breakdown. Just like my short stories, my metaphors serve me well; they allow me control of my mind.

My husband accompanies me to every test, and there are a lot. Before every one he is there to help tie my gown in the back, and after every one he is there to push me in my wheelchair or quietly help me into the car.

"I cannot endure one more torturous test!" I say, starting to cry. "I *can't* do this. I don't even feel well enough to sip a cup of tea, let alone submit myself to a radioactive injection. Are they insane?"

What I'm not saying is that I don't want to discover what nuclear medicine has to offer me. I don't want to open that door. I don't want a test that will clarify that there might be more tumors in my abdomen than they had first suspected.

"This is stupid!" I rant on, realizing that I sound just like my teenage daughter. Suddenly, I can appreciate her fourteen-year-old, delighted commitment to the use of the word *stupid,* her favorite way to describe just about anything. Then this ridiculous fact makes me aware of all the "stupids" that I might miss and opens a well of tears to which there seems to be no bottom.

Amory looks me squarely in the eye and then holds me tight, not saying a word. This is a cavern much too deep in which to venture. He knows instinctively that words will just sound flimsy. He gives me strength through his silence. He's brave enough to let me cry and cry some more.

He continues to run his multifaceted business as well as serve as president of the board of the Colorado Youth Program, the non-profit camp we founded, to connect low-income kids with nature and the community. He is managing the hectic schedules of our two older children, both in middle school, both just seven weeks into a new school year at a new school. Also, he's pacing the halls at night with our ten-month-old son who is not yet sleeping through the night and who is still adjusting to the abrupt change from breast milk to formula from a bottle. This is not just an extraordinarily loving and patient man by my side, this is an angel.

"The first test that needs to be performed to begin the staging process is an echocardiogram. It's basically a three-dimensional picture of your heart," Dr. Sitarik tells me. "We want that done right away, so we've got you scheduled for tomorrow morning at 8:00 a.m. We want to check out the valves in your heart." *Yes, we do,* I'm thinking. But I've already lost my courage to ask why. So I don't. Thirty minutes later, in Dr. Fox's office, I find out the unthinkable answer to that question.

This is how I first meet the general surgeon who removed my

appendix just four days ago and who, along with Dr. Thayer, discovered my cancer. And through this, our first actual introduction, my life falls apart completely. I have never seen such sadness, or complete empathy, in any doctor's eyes before or since. Amory and I are grateful that it was by his kind and gentle manner that we were first really told how bad things actually were. His sensitivity somehow made it more bearable.

He rolls his stool over, to be right with us, as we lean close together in our chairs along the short wall. He prepares to impart the information we can barely stand to hear. Sensing this, he lowers his voice to just above a whisper, and begins. I will never be able to remove from my memory his deep green, intelligent eyes. Eyes full of compassion.

"I need to be honest with you. The tumors are everywhere." I freeze. "Yours is the most extreme case of carcinoid tumor that I have ever seen. It appears to have metastasized all over the inside of your abdomen," he adds delicately, slowly. "This is serious. I'm so sorry, I really am," he says, pausing, trying to let us absorb just the surface of what he is saying.

"What does it look like? Can you see these tumors?" I ask, trying to get a visual, in the pitch-black that has closed in around me.

"Yes, you can. They look like tiny grains of rice, white and rubbery," he answers.

"Oh," is all that I seem to have available. It's a response I'm using a lot lately.

"I can do the surgery that you need. But there is something else that we need to talk about now," he says, adjusting his rectangular tortoise-shell glasses precisely, then placing his well-groomed surgeon's hand, thumb to temple and fingers to forehead, as though to keep any movement from disturbing his delicate thought process. He's looking post-op into the eyes of this mother of three children, on whom he's already done surgery, preparing to tell her that her life is in the balance.

His formerly enthusiastic doctor's mind must have to rehearse several versions as he sits with a husband and wife, maybe only five years older than himself, trying to find a way to say: *"Depending on the outcome of tomorrow morning's test, there may be no way to prolong what is quickly beginning to look like your short future."* So he has to hold his head still.

"It's your heart. Let's talk about that for a minute," he says, leaning on the word *talk* as if making this just about the language will make it seem less real. Just like that I hate words. Words are stupid. Talking is over-rated. Monks know this. Let's all take a vow of silence, quickly, before we say something stupid. *No. I don't want to hear this. My body's already recorded the message and is completely numb. Please let me leave now.*

"If...the cancer has metastasized to your heart...there won't be anything we can do—surgically, I mean," he informs us, swallowing, looking carefully over at Amory, then back to me.

"What does *that* mean?" I ask, starting to cry, already sorry I've asked.

"Carcinoid tumors cannot be removed from the heart. It is surgically impossible. This is why I need to tell you this, so that you understand about the echocardiogram tomorrow," he says in a hoarse whisper. He is so genuinely afraid for us, that I feel for a moment that he is about to cry. His hands are lightly trembling.

My mind goes blank and then praying comes to mind. First, I pray for mercy. Then I start trying to make deals with God. Please take me out of this black, black night. Please let my heart be clear. *Please give me a chance. Just let my heart show up clear and I'll never ask you for any more favors, ever. Well, maybe a few, but not huge ones.*

This kind of pleading runs in a circle between me and God all the way home. Walking into the house to the beguiling innocence of all three of my children's faces, eyes full of light and of love, is suddenly too much to bear. *They don't even know that I have cancer yet. How will*

I tell them? I can't. I'm not throwing them into this river, I won't. I'll have to leave them. They will have to see me being swept away. No.

Once in my room, I drop to my knees, gripping the bedpost, trying to hold on to something, anything, with both hands. Try as I might, I fall into this cold, churning and godforsaken river, where I'm yanked into its tremendous current. I try to look back, to swim back to my children, without their mother, alone on the bank. Then, God's stupid river sweeps me away, into total darkness.

Cancer is like that. It may be the worst thing that you will ever need to explain to your children. Telling them the news of your own impending death is plainly not right. You shudder internally. It shakes you to your core. It helps to read up on what the experts recommend, but in the end, you, the parent, must rely on your intuition, strength and faith to see it through. Even then, it will be a horribly painful experience, one which there is no way out of, one that you must go through. Like all storms, it must be faced directly, and headed straight for, lest it chase you down. This conversation is not a storm you can outrun.

Mermaid

November 4, 2003

The person you might not have been counting on can turn out to be the real deal. This is the one who decides how she can help you and then just does it. She climbs over her fears and yours, and just shows up. One individual's selfless act of coming to your side without your having to ask creates an unexpected space for you to get a sense for how you feel.

If you have just one friend like that, you are lucky and you have a lifesaver. If you have several friends like that, you have a lifeboat. One person's kindness feels like falling into a pile of warm laundry. Finally, you allow yourself to exhale.

My sister Wendy turns out to be one of these people. She comes to see me, without calling first, on the Tuesday night following my diagnosis. This may not sound like a big deal, but she has to fly in from California and find a co-volunteer to relieve her of her duties heading up the relief station for firefighters. She is exhausted from a week of battling the massive October wildfires of 2003 that bordered San Diego.

When she arrives at 10:30 p.m., I hear the doorbell ring and then the kids tearing down the stairs to see who could possibly be out there this late. The temperature is freezing and it's a school night. We live in the middle of nowhere north of town. I hear their shrieks of delight: "Aunt Wendy! Aunt Wendy!"

I'm in the baby's room rocking him to sleep, when I hear her loudly whisper my name from the darkened hall. I slip him into his crib and turn to see those beautiful green eyes looking into mine, through the dark, as they did so many times when we were growing up. Her eyes grow wide. "He's so beautiful, I want to hold him," she whispers. We quietly squeeze each other's hands, trying to quench our desire to pick him up. We marvel anyway, exchanging warm smiles over his sleeping little baby self. We hug, and then step out into the hall and give each other that next look that was coming, the look about my cancer, a hard look to exchange.

As sisters who shared a room for many years, we've had a lot of practice looking at each other in the dark. Every night we would lie there in our twin beds, looking across at each other, with the little oval nightstand between us. We were just summing each other up the way kids do, non-judgmental, just looking, finding safety in each other's eyes. Not really thinking about anything in particular. The streetlight casting a slice of silvery blue through our window, across our room and onto our mother's 1940s quilted bedspreads with the satin bows. The crescent of hand-painted pink roses that adorned our antique white headboards took on a grayish hue in the dark.

The memory of how much I'd loved her as a child just rushes up and engulfs me. She is right here, in the dark with me again, making me feel safe. For this moment I am five again. I walk into her open arms and we just stand here, in my dark hallway, and cry. She smells of wood-smoke from the San Diego fires, and I, in my flannel nightgown, of baby lotion and powder. These scents swirl together and send me flying back in time.

We are playing dolls on a cold winter's day in 1968, the fire crack-ling in the fireplace and our Madame Alexander dolls freshly diapered and powdered and bundled up, all lined up across the velvet sofa. As the snow blankets our house, we're pretending that a terrible storm is threatening us and our babies. Then, my big sister quickly thinks of a way that we can hide and escape from the storm. She describes an enchanted island with mermaids, one where we magically become mermaids, too, and swim away with our babies. Whispering urgently the perils that are about to befall us, her luminous green eyes wide and convincing, she saves us from the storm. She always saves me first, which makes me list her in my prayers at night for being the best big sister ever.

Back in my hallway, I don't say anything. I don't have to. She knows that I'm scared. I know that we're both afraid that this might be the one storm that she can't save us from.

We don't yet know that in four weeks she'll be coming back to take care of my three kids, while 1,200 miles away, the doctors at Mayo Clinic will be helping me weather the storm.

Cancer is like that. It takes out all of the "in between" and puts what really matters in front of you, including people. This is the time for cherishing those moments and the people inside of them. Right now you are stunned. You don't want to believe that you might lose, but the thought has crossed your mind. You want to win, but you don't know enough to get a clear sense of that, either. So you're here, just a child in the dark, straining your eyes to find something to make you feel safe until morning. If that something turns out to be the eyes that are right there looking back at you, jump in. Take shelter from this storm, even if it is only for tonight.

My Old Life

Before I drop over the waterfall without my boat, I have a totally different description of myself. I am a poet. As such, I am a hopeless romantic about life. For me, details are worth noticing. I love music and art, fine china and candles. I believe that a bath can cure practically anything that ails you, and what the bath can't cure, hot tea and music will.

I've been volunteering for three years as a docent at the Denver Art Museum, giving tours, which I enjoy tremendously. I also serve as vice president of the board of the Colorado Youth Program, where my main contribution is the planning of our annual fall fund-raiser. It is a silent-auction event that takes place in early November, in the same place where my husband and I first met, the historic Hotel Boulderado.

Mainly, I am a full-time, stay-at-home mother of three children. I love doing this job, but what I haven't understood until now is what a really big and important job it is. Until I am benched, I don't quite get just how much I do to take care of my family, or to create our home.

This fall is suddenly different. I find myself scarcely helping on the fund-raiser, and I am unhappily requesting a second leave of absence from the museum. The first was for the end of my pregnancy, when the pain began. But the big job, the main place where I am missing in action, is at home. I am stunned by how many people it takes to do the various jobs in my home on a daily basis.

It was probably a busy mom who handed Nike that successful line of advertising, "Just do it." It wouldn't surprise me if she'd thought of it while racing between the grocery shopping and picking up her kids, before heading home to knock out the second half of her sixteen-hour day. We busy moms don't waste a single minute moping or calculating how hard it will be—we *just do it.* I believe most families have little awareness of how much Mom really puts into handling the details of their lives. Now I understand that if you need to get something done—and done right and in record time—go hand it to a busy mother.

Too bad it takes getting slammed with cancer for me to truly appreciate myself. Up to this point, I haven't ever fully and confidently claimed credit for the tremendous job that I do. Until my boat drops out from under me, followed by being told that if this cancer has made it to my heart it won't matter if I have a boat or not, I haven't understood that I am the heart of my family. In fact, I have never truly taken stock of my full job description until I try to fill the position from my hospital bed. Have I said that besides being terrifying, cancer is a nuisance?

It seems that the "unknown" is becoming an unwanted category in my mind. Like most normal people, I have never considered the sizable hole I will leave if I vanish. If, like me, your primary job is managing the needs of your family, then you know how awkward, and even painful, handing over the reins can be. It's as though someone has just hit the pause button on your regular routine and you are now only a spectator of your own life. You are not even on the sidelines, you are in the stands and you are way up there where no one can hear you shouting plays. All of a sudden you can see a lot going on down on the field.

When asked by one of the professional business people who surround my husband what I do, I easily reply, "The laundry." This answer catches them off guard, because of its naked truth. They laugh and say, "No, *really.*" "Really," I reply and smirk along with that, because behind my smile is so much more. Behind my smile lies certainty. I have never been more certain of anything in my life than of my desire to be a mother.

Creating a beautiful home is important to me. I try to see to it that we eat dinner together as a family four to five nights a week. In this fast world we live in, I consider that single item a total triumph. At least one Monday a month, we have what I call "Monday-night manners." We sit in the dining room, complete with formal place settings of china, silver and crystal, candles and music. We enjoy dinner while practicing to make our best manners better. Monday nights have become our own comedy of errors, so to speak. I want my children to be comfortable in any setting, now and as adults, and I believe that polished manners are one of the keys to allowing them that luxury.

We hold hands and sing an old song of grace, a tradition handed down from my husband's great grandfather, Grandpa William Cole, to his grandmother, Elizabeth Cole Grinnell, to his parents, Stig and Jeanne. Even though the children's eyes occasionally roll, I like to remind them of the importance of recognizing that what was shared by those who have gone before is still worth sharing and that it will contribute to their lives. At the end of our song, baby William claps and sings "Ohhh...man!" instead of "Amen" to a round of family approval and laughter.

In the warmer months, we'll take walks down the road after dinner to the mailboxes and back. This is the magic hour where the lusty glow of evening sun washes over our skin and absorbs us into the landscape. Amory and I are still amazed by the billowing "cowboy clouds" that change colors as we walk, tinting the dry prairie grasses that line the way. The kids tease by imitating us, saying, "Wow, look at those clouds!" or "Look at that view." They are used to such grandeur, being raised in the foothills of the Rockies. Just as if they were looking at a landscape painting, they won't grasp the whole picture until they move farther away.

Embracing traditions around everyday life, as well as around every holiday, allows me to create occasions for my children to treasure, experiences I'm hoping that they might someday pass on to their children.

Terror pulses through my veins and pounds in my head as the echocardiogram is underway. This is so much more profound than a thought, than some random line of thinking. This is about my children, the very center of my life, my heart.

"So what kind of cancer do you have?" the echocardiographer twitters.

Knowing that nothing can fill the void I might leave behind for Chanel, Marco and William is making the idea of my death much more difficult than just something I must face myself.

"Carcinoid tumor," I say distantly, trying to discourage her from asking me anything else. The room is dim except for the shifting light of the screen in front of her.

I thought I would always be here, with the kids. They would grow up and leave me, not the other way around.

"Oh, really? Well, I've never heard of that one before," she blabs.

My mind strays around the many intertwined dynamics of my life. I'm simply overwhelmed. Also, I am becoming weaker.

"It's rare," I reply succinctly, inferring the end of this discussion that she is so inappropriately perky about having.

How will I be able to do any of this? How will I go on being a mother and holding my children's lives together? Nothing will ever be the same. This cancer is already damaging my children's lives. Oh, my God, it's forcing me to think about "goodbye." I don't want to say goodbye.

"So...how did they find it?" she asks absently, with just a thread of interest, as her gaze remains fixed on the screen, her right hand clicking away at the keyboard.

"Please. Stop talking, please!" I hear myself say, in the tone of a direct order, not of a request. The technician stops her senseless chattering mid-word and gives me an astounded stare. I shut my eyes and shut her out. I don't care how she feels; I just want her to shut up.

The slippery ultrasound gel allows the probe to glide and twirl over my skin like a carefree skater on the ice...a whimsical figure eight...then, swooping and lifting off, just for the briefest second, then touching back down, pressing into the ice and pushing along, all in one strong motion...then riding out the curve...arms outstretched. Sensing through tiny waves of sound...all that lies in the dark beneath the wide, frozen river. I know my heart is in there, but is it clear?

"Here. You can wipe that off with this," she says, tossing a small, white towel onto my hip. "The doctor will be in soon," she finishes curtly.

"Can't *you* just tell me, please?" I start to cry. "Please." *Since you like to talk so much.*

"I really can't, I'm sorry, we're not allowed to," she says, satisfied to throw her rule at me. "I know it's hard. He'll be right in, I promise," she says rushing out, her truly pathetic apology landing like a brick on a cloud.

Please, God, please let me have this chance, please. Guardian Angel, don't leave me under the ice, I'm freezing to death down here. I can't breathe. I know you don't swim, but please pull me out. Hurry, please...I can't feel anything...my heart is barely beating....

"Mrs. Host?...Mrs. Host...you okay?" The doctor's voice sounds as though his mouth is full of marbles.

I'm trying to nod my head yes, but it won't move; I'm immobilized by the freezing water. Then I hear the muted thud of something heavy smashing down on the ice above me. I hear a dull crack, the ice splitting, slow and staggered.

"Your heart is clear," he says. "It's perfectly clear. Your heart is in good shape." His voice vibrates in the air like the tone of a triangle, as I gasp for my first breath. He doesn't see the angel kneeling beside him. That angel's arms are elbow-deep in the icy water, hands firmly under my arms, thumbs pressing hard into my clavicles, hauling me out of the crack in the frozen river into the stiff morning light.

Cancer is like that. It creates moments where you're so scared that you absolutely cannot breathe and you feel as if you are drowning. In the seconds that drag, while you are trying to come up for air, you become clear about wanting to live. This sets you up for the most beautiful part of your life. Now you have taken that breath because you've wanted to. Cancer also takes you to places that you'll never really completely come back from. Sometimes, while all is still but the rustle of leaves, I'll hear that angel's wings brushing the ice, and feel that strong pull, lifting my heart from the cold, dark, water, and I'll weep.

Frozen

———❦———

November 17, 2003

I decide that nothing would be worse than telling Chanel and Marco at home, in our house, where their memory of hearing of my cancer would be forever sealed. So I try to decide on a location where I can drop the bomb and later it won't matter. The setting needs to be a background for the dialogue. Writing has trained me to understand that the "where" can be as memorable as the "what."

I think about a park, or riding in the car, or of the three of us in the car, parked on Flagstaff Mountain. No, that's too dramatic. I need a place with some built-in distractions. It needs to be a place where they can mentally jump into and out of what I am saying, a place which is familiar yet to which they have no major sentimental ties. We love Tom's Tavern way too much to drop a bomb there. So I settle on a different hamburger place to tell the kids, Red Robin, a chain none of us is sentimental about.

It takes calculated energy to appear the opposite of the way I feel. This is something which a parent with cancer knows well. It won't always be possible. I know this, but while I'm still able, I want to give my smile to my children. It's because I know that it will not be long before my charade is through. It may not be right, but it's what a parent does and it's what I'm doing to feel that I'm still in control of some corner of my shattered life.

I take just Chanel and Marco for an early dinner by myself. We order burgers and chicken strips in a basket with fries, with a side of ranch dressing for dipping. I'm well aware that I won't be able to eat what I'm breezily asking the waitress for, but I order it anyway to put the children at ease. Also, I need something to hold on to and to cheer me up, so I order a chocolate malt with sprinkles on top. Marco follows my lead and orders vanilla, and Chanel has strawberry lemonade.

Too many tacky framed posters on the walls are just the right amount. The eager-to-please waitress is just the right bearer of good-tasting things. A booth at the top of the stairs in its own little corner is just the right location to hold a somewhat captive audience. Just as I planned, the only voice I can use to carry over the bustle and music is a fairly clear and ordinary one. No whisper or brooding note will be heard in here. What I'm going to say will be intense enough without a still and solemn atmosphere to magnify it. Yes, this feels right, as odd a choice as it may seem. Here goes.

"So kids, you know that I've been pretty sick lately, so I want to tell you a little bit more about it," I start off easily enough. They give me their full attention. They know things aren't right, and they want to know exactly why.

"Well, on Halloween, when they kept me in the hospital that night, it was because I had my appendix removed. People have their appendixes removed all the time, and your appendix turns out to be one of the organs that you don't really need that much, so that part is okay. The only thing is that when they did that surgery on me, they finally figured out the *real* reason that I haven't been feeling good. You remember how I had a lot of pain before I had William and they couldn't figure out why, and then how after I had him my face kept turning red all the time?"

They are nodding in unison. They are in sixth and eighth grades. They are on board. *Keep an even tone. Don't cry. Take a sip of the malt, appear relaxed.* I swallow the sip and keep telling myself, *you can say this and they can hear this.*

"Well, it turns out that I have cancer." *There, I've said it. Their eyes just opened wider. They are fiddling with their drinks.* Lifting the straw out of my malt and picking up some sprinkles, I eat some from the bottom end and keep talking. *Try to really believe what you say next.*

"Now, I don't want you to start thinking about all of those movies and stories where the person dies of cancer. That's a different kind of cancer. I have a really weird and rare kind called carcinoid tumor. The kind I have grows *really* slowly, so *that's* good. Things can turn out well for me." *Smile.*

"Can you die of your kind?" Marco asks astutely, getting to the only point that matters, making my thighs go numb and my esophagus press back into my spine.

"Yes. But that's not my plan. I plan to beat this cancer up and throw it off a cliff—how's that?" They both smile. We all smile. The food comes. *Thank God.* We start salting and dipping. I take a wide flat fry, dip into the ranch dressing and put it on my plate instead of in my mouth, knowing that I won't be able to swallow anything.

"I don't know if Dad's had a chance to tell you that we won't be going sailing next week because I need to be here for this operation."

"Yeah, he did. He said we might go this spring instead," Chanel tells me, blowing on a chicken strip to cool it down. She's completely focused on her food and not on my face. *Thank God.*

"Oh, good," I answer. And trying to make positive conversation, I announce, "Well, we're going up to Aunt Marisa and Uncle Jack's for Thanksgiving in the cabin, so that'll be a lot of fun." *Smile. I didn't just really tell my kids that I have cancer. No. I want to go back.*

"Can I bring a friend?" Chanel asks.

"No, honey, not this time. I doubt that anybody's going to let their kids go somewhere else for Thanksgiving."

"Oh, yeah, that's true."

Apparently, they are satisfied with this level of information. They've shifted gears and are finished talking about this, but I still have a few things to say.

"So about this cancer business, you know me, kids—I'm not the kind of person who gives up. Plus, you know Dad—he takes good care of me, so you don't need to worry. I may be in bed a lot—you know, getting better—but Dad's ready to help you with your schoolwork and with taking you to do fun stuff with your friends."

"Okay. But who's gonna cook?" Marco asks.

"Well, Nonie for one...and Dad."

"Dad?" they ask skeptically, in unison.

"Okay, that may be stretching it, but he can take you out to dinner and you know he will." *I'll never buy another house where I can't even get a pizza delivered.* "Even though he does make the world's best scrambled eggs, I'd have to agree you can't live on those." They nod. "He's already found the best doctor in the world for me, so I'll have the best chance of things going right."

"What will they do?" Chanel asks.

"They will do a surgery and remove all of the tumors. Then I should be all right. It might be different seeing me in bed so much. I'll probably look pretty bad for a while, and being *practically perfect* in every way, that part *is* hard for me to face," I say smiling in my best joking tone. "But seriously, I think it'll all come out the way it should. So let's try not to worry too much and just see how we can all get through this, all right?"

Yes. Nods all around. Good job, Mom, you did it. The worst part is over. Eat a fry. Thank the Lord. Oh, yeah, one more thing.

"There's one more thing. If you have any questions or you get scared, or if you hear people talking at school saying things like, 'Oh, those poor kids, their mom has cancer,' please come and tell me about it and don't go searching the Internet to find out about my cancer. I've already done that. It's really depressing. They tell you all of the bad stuff that scares you. I didn't really like what they had to say. Just come and ask me or ask Dad, and we'll talk it over. I'll answer your questions for you, okay? No private searches, okay?"

"Okay, Mom."

"I love you both so much."

"We love you too, Mom," they answer together.

"I'm sorry that we have to go through this, but let's stick together," I finish, signaling for our waitress.

"Okay, Mom."

"Can we have the check please?" *And a good stiff drink?*

"I think Aunt Wendy's coming out to take care of you guys while I'm in the hospital. Won't that be great?" I ask.

"Really?" they ask, both breaking into huge, sincere smiles.

Good, that's the only answer I need. I knew she was the right choice.

"Yep, really." *Thank God.*

On our way home, we stop off at the grocery store to buy mechanical pencils and cookie dough. While we're there, we buy the bus passes and lift tickets for the Eldora ski area. I make it all the way home without crying, by making small talk and asking them a lot of questions about school. I know a whole lot more that I could have told them, but it felt like enough for the first round. I've primed the canvas. The details will begin to get clearer with each layer that I'll add. Over the next couple of weeks, I will have many more conversations about my cancer, but this is the best I could do tonight.

"Eldora's opening on Friday, so you can go up this weekend. Maybe when I'm in the hospital, Aunt Wendy can bring you downtown to catch the ski bus on Saturday or Sunday morning, whichever you want.

I'll remind her to have you call some friends to meet you, so that you can all go up together."

"Okay, cool," Marco answers.

Once we pull into the driveway I let them out, saying nonchalantly, "Tell Dad that I'll be right back. I need to drive back down to get the mail." What I need is the space to have a complete breakdown. By the time I reach the row of mailboxes, I'm crying so hard that I can barely see through the tears. I pull over and get out and begin to walk down the frozen dirt road, overcome with the grief of having told my children that *I have cancer.* Knowing that their lives will be forever changed by it and that in some way the pure innocence of their childhood is now gone is too much to feel right now.

Walking across the small ditch to the split-rail coyote fence that lines the road, I lean against it for support, tears falling on my knuckles and running between my cold fingers and into the rough wood. *My God, what has happened to my life? What will happen to my children without me? Help me, please, please, Mary, I pray to you as a mother, I ask for your light, for your Grace. Please.*

There's nothing that I can think of that is as hard to face as the conversation I've just had with my kids. I don't know how I got through it. I'm only just beginning to feel it. My cancer is already becoming a burden to my children, and this hurts me deeply. I'm trying to look to nature for all of the subtle places that I need to calm myself. Closing my eyes, I take a deep breath and see where it leads me.

Turning around, I sit down, putting both hands on the ground, trying to feel something, anything but this sadness. Lifting my gaze, I see a dry, dead stem of milkweed, its three pods open and empty. *My three children open to fully believing in my recovery, empty of the ability to understand the great tragedy that my death will become.* Reaching out, I easily snap the stiff brown stem in half, pulling the top half with the pods on it toward me...*the trinity...the divine...the past, present and future*. This is a message. Walking slowly back to my car, carefully setting my treasure on the seat beside me, I turn for home.

"Did you get anything in the mail?" Chanel asks from behind the homework clutter at the kitchen table.

"Yes, I did, honey," I answer her from the stairway.

"I got *exactly* what I was looking for," I say aloud, mainly to myself. I gently set my milkweed stem on my nightstand, just below my angel, and go back downstairs to bake the cookies.

Snapshots

T hanksgiving in Aspen with Marisa and my brother-in-law Jack is just what I need. I'm not well enough to cook, and I need a little break from the landslide in Boulder. I can't wait to be in the cozy cabin with Amory and the kids. This is William's first Thanksgiving and also the day he takes his first step. I'm grateful that I'm here and not in the hospital again, missing this moment.

Marisa's snapping all the pictures: William's first steps from Chanel to Marco in front of the fireplace...William holding his first turkey leg in his greasy little fist...tied to a wooden kitchen chair with a dishtowel...eating a slice of pumpkin pie while sitting on top of a stack of books. Her dogs are nudging at his feet and ankles, hoping for mistakes. I'm thinking that these will be our happiest memories, treasured for a long time.

Then it happens. Anxiety rushes through my body, my hands feel like two thick sponges, and I can't swallow. *Oh, my God, are these the last pictures that anyone will take of me with the kids? Will the children have only pictures of me, or will I be there in their future, pulling a turkey out of the oven?* These thoughts utterly topple my sense of composure. I try to imagine myself well enough to entertain the whole family for Thanksgiving with flair the way I once did. I notice that I have involuntarily backed out of the kitchen.

I go to the bathroom and sit on the edge of the tub; it's cold porcelain, smoother than my thoughts. I used to think nothing of posing for a picture with my children. Now, I'm simply awestruck as I try to fathom how I may no longer be in those photo albums. How will my job as mother get done if I am no longer here to do it? Cancer is taking me off the field and making me a spectator. I'm watching the game I once played in and finally see what it really looks like. I don't like this. I no longer have control. I want to scream, but all I can do is cry. I am too tired to scream.

Standing, I pull out a lipstick from my makeup bag and touch up my lips and cheeks. This makes sense. I'm going to make an effort to at least look good in the pictures that are being taken. If indeed they are the last to be taken, at least they'll say, "Mom was so pretty. How could she really have been so sick? She didn't look sick—she's happy in all of these." *Yes, kids, I was sick, but smiling for you because I love you so dearly. I want to leave you with pictures that capture that resilient part of my spirit.*

This is the first visceral moment, aside from the day I first told them, where I'm acknowledging inside that knowing that I have cancer while raising my children is breaking my heart. And it's going to break my heart again and again. I can't believe I'm looking into my makeup bag to try to tame the fear that is running off with my mind.

Men don't know this, but lipstick is what most women reach for to give them the sense that everything is right with the world. Half of the time, we don't even know we're applying it. This time, I am acutely aware of the irrational aspect of this moment, making a simple thing like putting on my lipstick unbearable.

Later that night, Amory washes all of the big pots and pans, and then my sister and I finish the last of two tons of dishes. We graze on leftovers while she pours us each a cup of tea from the big red kettle. We then take to the couches, lying down with our feet pointing toward the corner of the L that they form.

"This reminds me of Mom and Aunt Florence. We're turning into them already," I say, staring up at the pine log ceiling.

"Oh, my God, *we are,*" she agrees. "So how are you doing?" she asks, looking at me.

"I don't know. I'm just so glad to be here with you," I answer, reluctant to meet her gaze.

"Yeah, me, too, so glad."

"I can't stop thinking about how this all just *happened,* you know? I feel like I was just up here last month, hiking and enjoying the colors. You were telling me how great I would feel after my shoulder got fixed, remember?" I ask.

"That's right, I forgot about *that.* How is your shoulder?"

"Great. Just like you said it would be," I answer succinctly, content to be quiet for a few minutes.

"It's like my life had just taken such a good turn with having had William, and now, well, I just can't believe that I have cancer. They just don't go together, you know? A baby and cancer," I think aloud, dragging both of us out here on the edge, with the truth.

We simultaneously look into our cups. There's a kind of silence that neither of us wants to break. We both look up, knowing it's not something we can alter. It's the same silence you have when you're a kid and your best friend, ever, is moving away. The world is taking her from you. You stand there barefoot, in your cutoffs, your hair falling over your shoulders in its midday tangle. You're there, in all of your ten-year-old summer magnificence, with nothing that you can do but be really quiet when the doors on that faded yellow Town and Country station wagon with the fake-wood side panels slam shut.

You know that this stupid car is going to drive away with your best friend, but you are hoping differently, so you just keep looking at each other. You're hoping beyond hope that one of the adults in charge, whom you now solemnly swear to hate, will have a change of heart about separating you. Your friend's face is looking back at you, wedged in that open window, and your toes are gripping the cool grass as they drive out of sight.

I look at Marisa's fingers gripping the handle of her tea mug and feel my hot tears boil to the surface. Then our eyes meet, and because, like children, we both know that this isn't fair, we start to sob.

Fortune Cookie

November 29, 2003

I n the past ten months, I have welcomed and nursed a new baby while still caring for my older two. I have undergone shoulder surgery to remove a bone spur that had plagued me throughout my pregnancy, forcing me to sleep sitting up. I have been hospitalized three times, twice with unexplained severe pain, and again when I had my appendix and two ovarian cysts removed by laparoscopy. I have undergone a painful lung biopsy, partially conscious so that I could respond to direction from the doctor. He explained that he had to go between two ribs to get the sample, while trying to avoid puncturing my lung. I have had three vaginal ultrasounds, four CT scans with both oral and injected contrast, five octreotide scans, which include a radioactive injection that is given the first morning and is then attracted and absorbed by the tumors which then "light up" as my body passes through the scanner each of the next four days. Instead of being in a machine that emits radioactive waves, now I am radioactive and the machine is harmless. It's taking daily pictures of the tumor mass in various locations, which increase in clarity everyday.

Every night, I pray that those pictures will stay the same. Yet each morning as I lie on the long tray and pass through the scanner, I crane my neck to the right and look over the radiologist's shoulder at what I can see of the screen. Each day, more is glowing white. *No.* I want my eyes to deceive me. I want to get off of this table and go back to the old me, the one with no radioactive substance being absorbed by the cancer that is growing inside.

My bowels and abdominal cavity, including my liver, are full of cancer. This, coupled with the plain fact that I am on chemical overload from all of the medications and the tests necessary to gather information for my surgery and make an exact diagnosis, makes for a highly abnormal and most uncomfortable physical state.

I am experiencing all of this while suffering the unpleasant effects of "Carcinoid Syndrome," the symptoms caused by the cancer in its late stage. To say that I now have a new definition for the term "full plate" would be an understatement. This is the condition I am in as I head for surgery.

I'll be flying to Rochester, Minnesota, to meet the two doctors who I think will help me fish the pieces of my life out of the river. Before I meet them, I only know that both come highly recommended from several sources. My primary source, Dr. Dughi, who was once a student of Dr. Rubin, has already told us of Dr. Nagorney's tremendous reputation at Mayo Clinic.

Ultimately, I will have to decide if they are the team to work with. I realize that if I choose them, I will be farther away from my family. But in order to buy some time to be close to my family in the long-term, I might have to venture outside of Colorado.

Before I leave on that mission, my dad calls me to ask if he can take me to lunch. I say yes, and we meet downtown at the Orchid Pavilion, my favorite Chinese spot. I can't remember ever having seen this kind of earnest look in my father's eyes. The moment we're seated, he wastes no time getting to the point, the point about my living versus my dying.

"I want to tell you something, honey. You can make it through this. You've got what it takes. You're one tough cookie!" he's saying. I'm wondering if he knows something I don't, like how to leap buildings in a single bound. But although my father refers to himself as the Western Distributor of Kids, being the father of six still isn't the same as having the babies yourself. I don't think he can possibly know how tired I am. I'm nodding in a barely visible way.

"Now, I'm serious, honey." He regroups, tilting his head and taking my bird-thin hands palms-up into his old but strong ones. I fix my stare on his smooth-edged triangular wedding ring snugly worn on his pinky finger. I'm not ready to look at him yet. Holding my hands, he pulls gently but firmly in his direction. I have no choice but to look him in the eye. When I do, he gathers me up in his soulful gaze and takes a deep breath.

"Of all of the kids...out of all six of you...you're the toughest. You're the strongest. I've always said so to Mother," he says with a slow drag on each word, trying to back his story up by slowing it down, in case I think he's augmenting the truth especially for this occasion.

Being the fifth of six kids has trained me to be leery of enormous personal compliments, no matter the source. You learn early on, in a big family, that it's not all about you. He lets go, and we continue eating our meal, comfortable without further conversation, since there's nothing left to say that matters. Sipping our tea, we're content with looking up now and then.

"Now, I just know you're gonna make it, Carrie, and don't let them put any other idea in your head when you go out there on Monday. You'll get through this," he finishes, waving the flag at the finish line.

As we stand to leave, the fortune cookies arrive. We each pick one up, but after looking mine over, I decide not to open it. Instead, I hand mine to my dad, and smile an impish grin. He knows what I mean.

On our way out, I stop just before the door and ask quietly, as would anyone about the possibility of the impossible, "Do you really think so, Dad, *really?*"

"Absolutely! Ab-so-lute-ly," he answers in a booming voice, startling the other diners, crushing me with a big bear hug with exactly the strength that he would if I were strong and the picture of health, not custom-tailoring it the way someone else might.

I don't think of my father as a man who prays, but at least he's eager to deliver me to my appointment with God. He drives me to St. John's Episcopal Church, where I'm meeting Father Rol, who is waiting to pray with me before I leave on my trip. My father being punctual, we enter the chapel a few minutes early, take a seat, and wait in silence.

"Hello, I think you've met my dad, haven't you?" I say to Father Rol as he enters through the side door, precisely on time.

"Yes, of course. Welcome, welcome," he says sincerely.

As he reaches out for me to come closer, I'm looking at the Navajo silver-and-turquoise cross hanging over his vestment from a chain around his neck. I like that this unusual cross indicates that he may have considered Native American wisdom on his spiritual journey.

"Shall we pray?" he asks.

I walk forward as my answer. He takes both of my hands, then dropping one, reaches out to my father—who he knows is not a big subscriber to God's word—and without asking, pulls him to us anyway. Putting his arms around our shoulders, he pulls us closer still.

He begins to ask God for many things. "By Christ's glory, cleanse Carrie's blood and heal her, Lord God. We come here, asking for your miracle...wherever two or more are gathered in your name..." Near the end of our prayer, I look across at my father, and he is crying.

"Amen," my father says, with us, wiping his eyes. *Amen,* I'm thinking.

Cancer is like that. Somehow it sifts out the small unspoken details, and you feel and see as you never have before. It is as if all of the subtle messages that you may have missed have become gigantic in a world of diminishing hope. There's nothing you need to say; just go ahead and give that friend of yours with cancer a great big hug. One good, tight hug, backed up by total love, is more than enough to convince even the most uncertain person that they have a chance. I learned from my father that afternoon that it is better to crush a person with love and words of encouragement, than to tiptoe by and watch her drown in her own fear and uncertainty.

Muddied Waters

December 1, 2003

On this cold Monday morning, my husband and I cross the street from our hotel and enter the Gonda Building, just one of the numerous buildings that make up Mayo Clinic's campus. This is the beginning of our introduction to the most advanced and efficient medical environment that we have ever seen, much less experienced.

Immediately, I'm struck by the odd juxtaposition of downtown Rochester to Mayo Clinic. The town looks and feels as though it were left behind in 1953, never to be touched again by anything remotely current in terms of modern-day culture, while the medically advanced world of Mayo Clinic, and the more than 1,500 doctors who contribute daily to its already giant reputation, runs at high speed in its center.

The downtown is dotted with mom-and-pop shops and diners that have served the same two fried eggs to the same customers for forty years. The locals have the easygoing manner of people who appear to be pleased with where they are, people who would never consider leaving a town full of their friends and families.

"Mayberry Meets Microsoft" names the feeling I have as I am swept into the expert hands that make up Mayo Clinic. The Gonda Building is an architectural delight, with its massive marble, glass and steel lobby, complete with an art collection that absolutely stuns me.

A huge glass sculpture installation by Dale Chihuly graces the ceiling of the "Nurses Atrium," an area dedicated to the devoted nursing staff, past and present. A series of works by Andy Warhol line a corridor where I am practically running into people due to my lack of ability to focus on where I'm going, which is down to the lab area to have my blood drawn. Five minutes later, it has been drawn and sent off to be analyzed so the results will be available to me for my appointment three hours from now—rather than next week.

I now have time to linger over the Joan Miró works. I stand astounded in front of five substantial pieces. The art that surrounds me is a welcome relief to all that I am trying not to worry about. I find myself thinking about how much time I'll have between my other scheduled appointments, so that I can take the guided tour that is offered daily. From what I can tell, all of the people employed here are attentive and informed in their specific areas. I have a general sense of security based on the apparent intelligence that surrounds me.

First, we are introduced to the oncologist, Dr. Joseph Rubin, who specializes in my rare cancer. He enters the room, shakes our hands, then takes a seat in front of us. His desk does not separate us from him. It's placed against the wall, the same wall as the couch we are sitting on. He wears a smart, gray gabardine suit, a handsome tie, and Italian shoes, which lace up and are polished to a high sheen. His long fingers are folded neatly, church-and-steeple style, with the steeple positioned just under his chin. He gazes down through perfectly clean, chic glasses at the notes in a crisp stack on his desk.

Based on his appearance, I imagine that this man does not like anything out of place, which is a good feature in an oncologist. Conceivably, this is the reason he is drawn to study cancer and has made a career of understanding the one phenomenon where a single cell goes haywire and will not be put in its place. I don't know.

But what I do know is that he specializes in my cancer, an odd bird, out on the farthest island of the "rare cancer island chain." I find that even stranger still.

Beyond this, it is difficult to read him. He clearly pays attention to detail, and though adequately friendly, he doesn't appear to be in the market for new friends. According to his reputation, he has seen a lot of cancer and has had many successes. He appears to be serious and quiet. This suits me perfectly; I'm in no mood for jokes.

He reviews with us my scans and test results to date and explains, slowly, yet succinctly, his understanding of my whole picture. "Mrs. Host, the upshot is that with the disease having widely metastasized to include your ileum, the small part of the small intestines, your colon, liver, spleen, gall bladder, abdominal wall, and having pretty much fully taken up residence in your abdominal cavity and upon nearly all of your major organs, including the one spot on your left lung, I recommend that a major tumor 'debulking surgery' be done immediately."

He seems clear on my current condition being serious, yet he appears unable, or unwilling, to promise anything about my future. I don't press him for more after I can't get a definite yes to my question: "Do you think that I can make it five years, because what I've read says eighteen to thirty-six months?"

He hesitates, hesitates in that "I know a lot that I'd really rather not scare you with right now" kind of way. I can't believe his hesitation. He *has* to say yes to five years. He has to say *yes*. If I stay really quiet, he will say yes....I mentally fill in the black hole where his yes should have already been. I write the following script for him with lightning speed: *"Of course, you will definitely have five years, not to worry. You'll probably have a lot longer than that."*

He's still not talking. I know that he has to say yes soon, since it's me we're talking about and the alternative answer couldn't be for me. Since I'm no longer breathing, I'm as quiet as is humanly possible without being dead. I'm keeping my mind sharply focused on the answer that I'm waiting for, which is when that will be. We are only two seconds into his eight-second hesitation. Seconds become lifetimes when you're waiting to be let off the hook. I tell myself to remember this the next time I'm fly-fishing and to have more mercy on the poor trout.

He must see that all of the blood running through my body has turned to ice. I sit here staring down at my hands, which have turned a lavender hue except for my knuckles, which are white. While I'm struggling to imagine not even seeing my baby boy start kindergarten, the surface of my eyes begins stinging with how much I want my *yes,* but I won't cry, because he's *going* to say it.

The longer he says nothing, the more I want to tear the stupid, high-tech, flat-screen monitor from in front of his steady gaze and hurl it out of the window. I don't want him to calculate any more information, or to keep looking at all there is to see, which is lots and lots of cancer everywhere. There's no window. Six seconds ... okay, he's taking a breath in through his nose and here it comes. He tells me what I already know.

"Dr. David Nagorney is without a doubt the best surgeon for carcinoid, Mrs. Host. He will be with you here in just under an hour. If you'd like to wait here, you're welcome to, or y'all can go for a walk then come on back," he says gently, trying not to fracture the ice sculpture sitting across from him. I hear his subtle South Carolina accent awash in whatever he says to me. Oddly, the sound is comforting, the way only a Southern accent can be.

With everything else all muddied together, one thing is perfectly clear to me at this moment: Dr. Rubin has had to do this same routine many, many times. He has had to decline many desperate patients requests to be told their future. Telling people their futures is not a logical thing to do, and that is why it is done by fortune-telling gypsies and not by oncologists.

Instead, he has to go with what he knows, which is a lot of statistics that tell him the way my story is likely to end. He'd rather not tell me that story right now, so he stalls by stepping aside. Meanwhile, I wait here to meet the doctor in whose hands I will place the balance of that quickly diminishing future.

When that surgeon has netted some time out of this raging river for me, he will send me back here to Dr. Rubin with it, so that he can add up all of the parts. Then he'll nod, and say, in that rock-a-bye Southern accent, backed by razor-sharp intelligence, "You're doin' great. Hang in there."

My eyes are fixed at whatever angle they were when he didn't say yes and I'm barely breathing. Dr. Rubin pushes back from his desk, smiles with closed lips and stands up. He is picking something up off of his desk and leaving. I want to do the same, I want to leave, but I can't move.

Amory and I are unable to find our feet, much less take that walk the way carefree people might do. The only thing we *can* do is look at each other. Slowly turning toward each other, our eyes connect in that best-friend way for the first time since we sat down with Dr. Rubin.

I find that just looking into Amory's eyes is by far the hardest thing to do. It is unbearable to gather in a single moment the sum of the greatest love I've ever known, but it happens. It's as if I'm slowly being pulled out to sea and never coming back. I'm looking in a whole new way. I'm memorizing every beautiful line of his face, every lovely imperfection, promising myself that I will keep it with me forever. I want to promise him, again, that I will stay with him till we are both old and gray, as I once did back when we were innocent of cancer.

We don't like that death is coming to get in between us so we instinctively *pull* each other so close, we try to meld together. We hold on so tight that nothing can rip us apart and we stay like that until the next doctor knocks on the door to see if anybody is in there.

No, no one is here. We're not here. We've left and we have gone far, far away from the mouth of this ever-widening river that is carrying me out to sea, carrying me away from the people that I love.

The hour we were told we would have to wait has passed in a blur, and Dr. Nagorney and his entourage of three residents have shown themselves in, since we weren't there to answer his knock. Clearly, he is used to scouting the river and fishing people out of holes. And like any reliable river guide, he is also here to bring us back off the river. His delightful smile floods the room with light—and you feel the way you do when getting one last picture-perfect cast in as you come to the take out.

He is warm, sincere and full of pep. No, it is more than pep, it is creative energy. It's the kind of energy an artist radiates when he has just completed a masterpiece and is breezily stretching a new canvas with delight at the prospect of starting on another. This surgeon is not in any way unclear on the subject of my cancer, and it shows. He has apparently read my case history in its entirety and is prepared to remark on any aspect that my husband and I bring up. He's completely informed, able and available in every way. Wow.

He asks me all about my kids and wants to see a picture of my baby. Of course, I am instantly cheered up by showing one to him. He notices my custom "Stallion" cowboy boots—my lucky pair, in a cognac-colored leather with fancy flames of triple stitch work. He says, "Those are some good-looking boots you've got there. Where'd you get those?"

"Thanks. A boot-maker friend of mine, Pedro, down in El Paso, Texas, made them for me," I say, feeling a mischievous smile inside, because as irrelevant as it seems, it feels like my lucky boots may be starting to kick in.

Bringing yet another light and uplifting question to the table, he asks, "So how's the skiing out in Colorado?"

"Well, I tried to ski over Thanksgiving with my sister. Two short runs were all that I could manage, but it was wonderful."

"Well, let's get you feeling better and you'll be all geared up for next ski season," he replies, pasting my eye to the keyhole of my future. Just envisioning skiing with my family again melts the ice in my veins and puts the color back in my cheeks.

"On that note, I'd like to see you have this surgery done right away, so that we can get you back home with your kids. I feel that you can do well with this surgery," he says, his voice, words and mannerisms all exuding his confidence in a successful outcome. "I'm enthusiastic about your case and I feel strongly that I can help you. At forty, you're young relative to the average carcinoid diagnosis, which is sixty, and aside from the cancer, you are in every other way an extraordinarily healthy person. I will do absolutely everything in my power to help you get a good outcome here." He finishes with fireworks.

Since I've just flown in from another state, I imagine that I will be walking him through my case history. I expect to have to look up every so often to see if he's catching on, or to have to stop and clarify the results of this or that hospitalization or test. That never happens. This whole experience is the opposite of begging a doctor for attention. Apparently he has done his research and is interested and prepared to take immediate action to help me. Here at Mayo Clinic, there are people taking care of me, not the reverse. I feel that my interest is the only interest at hand. I feel truly cared for. I see talent everywhere I look.

This doctor deals in futures and is able to help me see mine. It stretches itself out in front of me, unfurling from the tangled-up little wad that it was five minutes ago. Getting there will be rough, but there is absolutely no doubt in my mind that Dr. Nagorney is the surgeon that I want to see me through.

When I ask when he wants to do the surgery, he says brightly, "How about tomorrow?" I'm taken aback. I'm not ready for this. While I'm intrigued to have become this doctor's number-one priority, his answer underscores the level of trouble that I am in. I wasn't expecting to have surgery right now. I thought I would be sent back to Colorado with a date for January or February at the earliest.

I am quiet at this prospect. Amory does not answer for me. I mentally retreat to my home where I know that I want to put up the Christmas tree. Normally, decorating the tree with the children is a big, delightful ordeal where we reminisce about each ornament in our collection, while Amory sits in a big easy chair reading. Looking up every now and then, he'll check our progress. Then at the end, he hangs all of the ornaments which we have saved for way up high, where we can't reach. Finally, he places the star on top, our personal "Bumble." We turn off all of the lights except for the strands draped on the tree, then we all stand back together in admiration.

It's not just the tree that I want to decorate, but the rest of the house as well. I want to bake some cookies with the kids. I need to plan out their care while I'm gone. Any mother knows that it takes a *lot* of note-writing to leave three kids for two to three days, much less weeks, and that December and May are the two most hectic months of the year, in regards to school parties, tests, final projects and holiday activities. I have a lot to do to prepare to be gone. While my own life has come to a screeching halt, the lives of my children have not. I have to orchestrate a ton of details for other folks to carry out, which is a lot more complicated than I would like.

The kids know how much I personally enjoy the Christmas season. Knowing this, I need to picture my kids in our house, with my motherly touches, for the many weeks that I will be hundreds of miles away in recovery after my operation. Sheepishly, I tell Dr. Nagorney this, fully expecting him to make light of it, with my husband nodding in agreement, both telling me that I should opt for the tomorrow-morning plan, and agree to have surgery in eighteen hours.

Instead, he leans forward and says, "Absolutely. It's important for you to feel secure about your kids, and that things are going to be well taken care of. You go on home and do that. I want you to come into this feeling settled, as settled as possible given the circumstances." He scans his Day-Timer and asks, "Would next Monday, the eighth, seem appropriate?"

"That's perfect," I reply. At once, I'm relieved and feeling optimistic about my future for the first time.

Cancer is like that. It makes us quick to fill in all of our blanks with our own disturbing answers. As I am learning, it is so much more productive to fill them with constructive questions.

Moments

December 4, 2003

It's Thursday morning; I'm back in Boulder, sitting on the end of the examination table in my oncologist's office. I'm full of angst, terrified of my impending surgery. I'm waiting to see him, once more, before I fly to Rochester, Minnesota, on Sunday afternoon. I am emotionally drained. I've been forced to feel way too much in such a short period of time.

My hospital gown has become far too familiar. The thin layer of paper covering the examination table beneath me makes a crinkling sound every time I shift. It begins to grate on my nerves, of which I have very few left. This ingenious layer of disposable white tissue is there to keep me safe from germs. This annoys me further because all it really does is serve to remind me that I no longer have the word safe at my disposal, the way I once did. Even though I know better, I indulge myself and think, "I want my old life back." Just then, the same doctor whom I've been running from in my nightmare comes in, wearing a pastel-pink shirt with the splash of a Jerry-Garcia tie and an upbeat smile. I just can't buy into anything even remotely cheerful. I am angry. I wait for my zombie stare to be pinned on him before I let the hammer fall.

"How can you do this job? It's depressing; your patients are all dying. How can you stand this every day?" I blurt out. I am serious, and I am ready for an argument with this man who has been trailing me in every nightmare, wrecking my sleep.

Caught off guard, he takes a moment and leans against the wall. Looking curiously upward, he turns his gaze to me and says calmly with conviction, "I can do it...because I see wonderful things. Sometimes I see things that defy medicine."

"What, like miracles?" I suggest.

"Yes. Occasionally, I even see miracles. And *all* of my patients are not dying," he corrects me sincerely, the right corner of his mouth pulling back toward his ear. In a sort of half wince, half smile, his brows knit together to form a friendly scowl, while he's unconsciously nodding his head in a yes.

"So, am *I*...going to be one of those miracles?" I venture timidly, barely audible.

"I'm counting on it!" he says without a single second of hesitation. His voice is full of honest enthusiasm. His words become the net that breaks the descent that I didn't even register was happening.

Just the way it feels when you're falling in a dream. Some unseen thing scoops right in below you, jerking all of your senses to a sudden stop, informing you of the previous speed of your fall. Then you float down easily, the rest of the way.

With those words, the grim reaper's cloak dissolves. Now this doctor looks more like the man who, with a sparkle in his eye, gives you that double scoop of ice cream. When you're a kid and you only have enough money for a single. Now he has a name and eyes that look back at you, and you notice that he even moves like a regular human being.

The best thing about these types of doctors is that they often choose their staff, meaning they tend to work with like-minded and mannered nurses. And as most cancer patients quickly find out, a nurse can save your life. Nurses walk and talk us through everything. The best doctors know that they would be nowhere without the talent of good, solid nurses to back them up.

You may be walking down an empty hallway where you're listening to your own steps, drowning out the sound of your pounding heart as you head for some injection or procedure you are dreading. Then your team of nurses is there to welcome you, to help you suit up for the marathon. Their presence can calm your pounding heart. "Okay, I can do this," you tell yourself. It will be the first of many moments when you hear yourself agreeing with something inside that tells you that you will make it.

Cancer is like that. You will need these moments. They will be the tiny cups of water that are swiped up by you, the runner, at the various aid stations on the course. Most of the water will spill onto the sizzling pavement, but one swig will power you on. The enthusiastic nurses, reaching out to hand you the spilling cups, cheer you on, as will some of your doctors. These are the doctors to run with, whatever course you are currently on; they will encourage you to the finish line.

Friendship and the Map

One of the hardest burdens to bear can be the one involving our friends. Cancer means that there will be emotional, physical and mental suffering. You know this. There will be scars, literally and figuratively. Yet only you will know what has truly gone into the formation of each one.

There will be old maps and new maps. Our doctors are on this new map, and they stay put. We automatically believe that our friends are going to be on it, too, since they were on the old map, but they may not transfer over. Some roads on the old maps that were drawn in pencil may fade and even disappear. Other parts were drawn with indelible ink. You were handed this new road map for your life and made to read it while your friends are still free to choose what they are comfortable facing. This is where the road splits. Your friends have to renegotiate their own emotions in relationship to you. Whatever your presence in their life once represented has now changed. Certain people will come with you, others will not. This doesn't automatically sort people into "bad" and "good" but it does sort them into "absent" and "present."

It's difficult to understand completely the strange phenomenon around friendship and cancer. We can choose our future doctors, but we have already chosen our existing friends. We don't even question if our friends will stay the course. We believe that their strengths will grow with our own and that they have access to this new map. This is where cancer comes in and charts some unfamiliar territory.

There might be giant voids where certain friends or family members once were. There will be people you have confided in, trusted and felt you could hold on to, but just like your boat, they drop out from under you. They must have a reason for their withdrawal, but it is unlikely they will ever share it with you. Apparently, it is hard enough for them to understand their feelings, much less to communicate them honestly to you.

It seems as if with cancer you have become less desirable. It may be that, at the beginning, the cancer makes it hard for your friends to see you and talk about anything else. On some level, you're able to understand this, so you agree that it makes sense in order to not feel as let down. You are no longer a convenient friend and now require their emotional honesty. You don't mince words the way you once did. You now say what you mean. This, as it turns out, is uncomfortable for some people.

You might also have physical issues, which may limit your ability to be the person they want to see looking back at them. That scares them. The fact that you may be facing your death forces them to consider facing it, too, as well as the idea of their own deaths. With death comes fear—fear that they may have of potentially watching you waste away before their eyes, fear of facing the unspoken parts of the friendship and, possibly, fear of having to take care of those you will leave behind.

Cancer does affect more than us, it deeply affects those who love us. We're not primed for how unprepared others may be to accept our situation, so we become distraught when they leave. To be fair when we judge them, if we actually had the option to run from the situation ourselves, would we not consider it? We should not expect them to understand our needs, as we are barely able to understand these ourselves.

You may initially be hurt by their sudden disappearance from your life, but interestingly enough, you may find that you can forge a new relationship with yourself through a courage you hadn't known that you possessed. You can find the strength to create a full life in spite of the emptiness of having lost some of the people in it. We can choose to see what is available, rather than what is absent.

The heart has the capacity to generate love, and choosing to give love in your time of greatest need feels a lot better than choosing resentment. You might find that once you experience giving the love that you yourself may have so desperately needed but have been denied, you will be able to return there again and again. You get better at giving love as with anything else, by practicing often. Only love can heal. You can stick with being right, or you can experiment with being at peace.

One of the things that your friends may lack is the knowledge of your pain in prematurely having to say goodbye. This is another reason you find yourself torn apart. It's terrible to mourn the loss of someone you love who is still alive, who could still be with you if only this person had the courage to stay. You think your close friends will be with you for life. But cancer, like the river, can and does pull things away. It runs in currents that are not always visible on the surface. Certain people may not have what it takes to hold on, so they simply let go and are swept away.

Auspiciously, you will discover that friendships exist in places that you didn't know about, with people you weren't counting on. This is an unexpected sweet spot in the cancer deal. Because of cancer, you actually make some new friends. You become a more understanding, loving and authentic version of yourself. These traits make you the kind of companion a friend would want to have. Your new friends recognize that you bear the burden of cancer, but they choose you anyway. Isn't that wonderful?

It is touching the way some of your most genuine friends come closer and don't need to do a lot of talking. You get to be quiet with them. You also get to share precious laughter about how awful things are while your eyes well up. You let your guard down and together discover humility. You have some middle-of-the-night chats with them where you're on the phone together in the dark, speaking freely of your deepest fears. It's with these friends that you access a camaraderie that can only be gained in the trenches.

What I learned is that the friend who's been brave enough to remain has chosen to become closer to me. That's incredible. I rejoice that she has *chosen* to stay by my side, to stay on the map and go with me wherever it leads. Together, we've discovered that cancer is not necessarily where the road ends, but precisely the opposite: where it begins. My friend's presence is a hallelujah for the way things are. That is the gift of friendship.

Forgiveness

If you have not previously discovered the benefits of forgiveness in your life, cancer will give you an opportunity to do so. Forgiveness is like finding the right lid for a jar. It is not complicated, but it is satisfying. Our capacity to forgive is an extension of our ability to love. It is a true asset.

There is tremendous relief in discovering that you can choose love at any time. It's human nature to gravitate toward love, independent of any other circumstance. Love provides a peaceful place to reside. It is a sound place in which to heal your body and more important, your heart. Forgiveness is a choice.

Many people have tried to explain forgiveness in this world. Personally, I had struggled to understand why I should give something to someone who had wronged me. My anger felt like something I should hang on to, to even the score. Deep in my heart it didn't make sense that it was possible to forgive. As I'm now beginning to know, forgiveness is one of those things that I have had to experience repeatedly to fully grasp. It is simple beauty. To comprehend it, and even as I try to explain what I'm learning, I must first submit that until you have truly forgiven someone, you will never actually know its healing power. It's a kind of catch-22.

Ironically, forgiving someone else is not giving him something at all, but it may be the most generous gift you can give to yourself. Some holes cannot be patched and some damage cannot be glossed over, but I've found that the *cause* of that damage can be viewed differently.

Ultimately, that hurt, that piece of the past, is negative energy which equates to an extremely heavy burden. We keep the weight of this hurt tied to us by the attention we continue to give it. We can choose to drop this burden. For me, this *is* forgiveness in its most basic form.

By choosing forgiveness, we free up our energy to heal. We allow ourselves to breathe. Holding on to anger is like holding on to a cement block while jumping into a lake. There is no advantage to it. When we release it, we spontaneously surface. The thing that holds negative energy in place is attention. When we place our attention on the negative, we give it the energy that it needs to continue to plague us, energy that we could use to heal ourselves instead. How much more of our energy should we submit to negativity?

We don't have to try to change the past, which obviously cannot be done. We have only to move our attention to the present, which we can do. Rarely does forgiveness involve a dialogue, because we are the only ones who have to decide anything. Just like setting down something heavy that we're carrying, we don't stand there forever analyzing it; we do it, because we can.

Forgiveness, more than anything else, seems to be a profound place of understanding. Yet it does not involve complicated strategizing. It's not an art. Its very essence is a form of self-preservation. Anger is unnatural. Like holding our breath, it becomes more debilitating the longer we do it. Love comes naturally, like the urge to breathe. Forgiveness is the extension of that urge. It's taking that breath. It's that satisfying.

Fear

December 6, 2003

Immediately, I decide to deal with their fear first, so I come up with reasons why my family and friends shouldn't worry. Not because I'm that generous, but because I've learned that the easiest way to deal with my own fear is to start with someone else's.

Your own fear is another story. It is a lot harder to comfort yourself than someone close to you. You will randomly tell yourself that you'll be all right. You'll want to believe this and some days you will. Other days, you'll get the distinct feeling that you are leading yourself down the garden path.

You are aware at this point of your personal fear, of the stakes you are facing, but you have probably put it in a cage like any other wild animal that might unexpectedly show up in your vicinity. That first day, when you see him crouching, ready to spring, you lock him up in the far reaches of your mind where there is no room for escape. "Yes, indeed, I have got my fear under control, right where I want him," you tell yourself. Your fear is definitely pacing back and forth, a tiger in a cage much too small. Once you've locked him up, you'll convince yourself that you do not need to visit this tiger at all, because he's not really there.

Occasionally you will feel his hot breath on the back of your neck and you will turn to look at him. Quickly you realize that he is bigger and stronger than you and that you have a tiger on your hands, so you had better keep him locked up tight and deal with him later. Cancer is the one case where later comes sooner.

Later has become a mental luxury that you will no longer partake in. It is a luxury reserved for people who are enjoying their good health. It seems unfair that these folks should have both their health and the luxury of "later" but the two seem to go hand in hand.

I used to be one of those lucky people. I start to realize tonight, just two days before my surgery, that I should go and pay my tiger a visit. I really don't want to. I can hear his low, sinister growl in the back of my mind, the mind that I have tried to fill with positive thoughts so that it doesn't have room for things that growl.

At this point, after so much hardship and so little sleep, I am weak. As day becomes night, and night becomes the long and tedious part of day that I don't enjoy anymore, I lie awake staring at the moon. I'm listening to the quiet rhythm of Amory breathing and I know that it must be done. Tonight I need to deal with this fear that continually paces so close to me.

I creep into the baby's room and just watch William's beautiful face. The picture of tranquility, he's lying with his arms open and back so that his little hands are resting on either side of his head. I want to scoop him up and hold him to me and smell his sweet new-baby head. I want to hide us from the world, so that nothing can take me away from him. I sit by his crib and gaze at him longingly through my tears.

I can barely stand to leave him for even a few hours, but in the morning I will have to leave him for several weeks or more. A successful surgery is my only chance of seeing him through his childhood, yet I can barely swallow the thought.

I've asked my sister Wendy to take over my life for me at home. It will be a huge sacrifice on her part, as she runs a business and it is the holiday season and she will have to leave behind her own husband and three teenagers. She will be arriving from San Diego tomorrow. We will just miss wishing each other well in person, but I find peace in knowing that she will care for all three of my kids the way I would. She will hold and love my new baby with all her heart. She'll never let him cry.

Closing William's door, I walk to my daughter's room. When I reach her door I smile at the wooden letters painted like clowns in different poses that spell her name C-H-A-N-E-L. We bought those in the Bavarian town of Tegernsee in Germany when she was five years old. Now she's fourteen.

I quietly turn the knob and step in. She's my eldest child and only daughter. I feel the tears rise up as I gaze at her exquisite face. She is curled up in her fluffy bed of pink, her fat white cat nestled beside her feet, purring. I fight back the thoughts that are impossible to run from. Will I stand by your bed again on a cold winter's night and dream of your future? Will I see the milestones of your life? My lovely bird, I don't want to leave you. Remember all those songs you sang for me? All the Robert Frost poems you recited so sweetly? I want to see how wonderful your life will be. I want time to stop here, so I can watch over you and hold you in my arms forever. Reluctantly, I step out into the hall. I press myself against the wall to keep from crumbling to the floor in grief. I am weeping, trying to hold back my fears until I can gain the strength to go and look at Marco.

His giant green eyes are closed and his eyelashes are so thick and long that, kneeling down next to his bed, I can see them in the dark. This makes me smile, since Chanel and I often boldly brag on about his lashes to anyone who will listen. Of course, he inevitably rolls his eyes and looks upward pleading for deliverance from our ranting.

I watch my twelve-year-old son sleeping pleasantly, and once more I am filled with the horrible fear that if anything goes wrong during the surgery, I might never look upon him again. I want to see him graduate from high school and from college. I want to see him become a young man. I want to see him design his first car or motorcycle or fulfill his other passion, to become a great chef. I want to see his future unfold. But the future unfolds a day at a time. I can't hit fast-forward and take a peek. I need to be there. This might not happen.

It hits me hard. I have to deal with this fear. It is immobilizing me. It is forcing me to think scary thoughts and is eating me alive. Heart thudding, I head for the front hall and pull my ski pants from the closet. I pull them on over my pajamas, then add my jacket, hat and gloves. I step into my boots and out of the house. It is about nine degrees outside. I go crunching across my yard. It is quiet, in the muffled way that only snow provides.

Sadness floods my soul, like the toll of an ancient bell. I want peace with everything in my life. I don't want to be facing the end of my life at forty. I see that later has come. The time to deal with my fear is now. Crackling with terror, I start seeing everything.

I start with the stars glittering over my house which is situated at the base of Left Hand Canyon. The dark, sacred night stretches out over the snowy fields in front of me. A deep-blue velvet sky that turns to black and holds the brightest stars I've ever seen. These stars are piercing my heart as they do the night sky, because I am afraid it will not be that long before they may become the last dazzling stars that I will ever see. I may not see them later, so I gaze intently at them now. I realize that ever since I put that tiger in his cage, the world around me is on a twisted form of auto-focus, zooming in on things without my direction.

I lie down on the hill that borders the side of my house. It feels so good to vanish into the landscape of gray shapes, rocks and trees, a frozen yucca plant now a strange ice sculpture, long-dead prairie grass frosted white, arched and still. The stars lift my heart, while my body settles into the earth below. The fresh powder cradles me, quiet as down.

Out of habit, I first make a snow angel to postpone really feeling anything besides the snow. I absorb the quiet that enfolds me. Filling my nostrils with the crisp air of winter, I begin to feel the darkness that surrounds my soul, the darkness that is my solitude. Eyes closed, I'm watching my fear. I see him pacing in his too-tight cage. I start to approach him. He is not purring but growling dangerously low. When I muster up the nerve, I look directly at what I've locked up. I look now at what I was going to look at later.

I feel the hot tears that rim his eyes rolling across my temples toward my ears, the bristle of fur on the back of his neck, across my own. I want to turn and run, but fear's intensely controlling eyes, full of fire, demand that I stay. The longer I sit and look, the more I am able to see him for what he is. He is the opposite of love. I sit close enough, long enough, so that I finally know what I need to do about him.

First, I will have to breathe deeply. I find the slow raspy sound of my breath calms him down. As its rhythm becomes smooth and even, it quietly invites him to stop pacing. Finally, I watch this hot, angry tiger lie down, panting with exhaustion. It is time to let him go. Guarding him has worn me out. I reach down deep and find that without my fear, all that I have left is love, the key to his cage.

It is with pure love that I look fear in the eye, and simply put, we fit together. There is no me versus him. *We* are only what I see. I open his cage. He does not devour me, as I had once supposed. He does not need anything from me, now that I've let him go.

Cancer is like that. You become so afraid at one point that you are immobilized. Then, while focusing only on your breath, you might be able to allow yourself to approach your fear. You might try to get just close enough so that you feel that if you let it go, it will not completely devour you. You also may discover, as I did, that all you'll have left is love. None of us really has more than the present. It's just that before we had cancer we rarely questioned that we had a future. We do have a future, and the picture of that future is made up of a bunch of tiny dots called "right now." Take a moment to wrap yourself up in that.

The Closet

December 7, 2003

Amory is already in the car. The front door is open, and I'm on my way out. I'm only intending to quickly choose a coat to wear as I leave for the airport. I don't know that, besides my hats and coats, the closet holds a monster. So I casually open it.

Instead of seeing the coats and shoes as they are, I see the emptiness they will represent if I do not return. This sadness makes me so afraid for my children, for Amory, for my sisters and for my parents that I feel my head tingle and fill with pressure. Looking down at my shoes, I wonder who will have to pick them up and put them in a box if I don't make it through the surgery, if I don't make it back. These are things I've never thought of when looking at my own shoes. These are the thoughts of someone who is closer to death than to life.

I cannot bear looking at my shoes sitting there, so I settle on the coats. I pass by the long black double-breasted. It's too morbid. I may never wear black again. The deerskin hip-length with fringe is too hippie. The leopard swing coat with the shawl collar is too bold. The cream brocade with raglan sleeves is far too heavy. Finally, the fitted knee-length burgundy velvet is too delightful altogether.

I'm beginning to regret the fact that I have a coat fetish at all. I can't stand looking at these stupid coats. I want to rip them from their hangers! I want to give them all away, so they won't become a row of sadness from which my daughter will have to choose. I take my ice-cream pink tweed from the middle and put it on. I can at least take one away.

"Are you ready, honey?" Amory says kindly from the front steps.

"No. I'm not sure that I am," I answer, looking miles into the closet and then up at him.

Part II

The Current

Letting Go

—❦—

December 8, 2003

Watching as my mother slides my wedding ring snugly onto her pinky finger while the nurses prepare to roll me away to the surgical prep area really hammers it home. I am about to undergo a major five-hour abdominal surgery, a search-and-destroy mission. I'm signing consent forms that release my doctors in case of the worst. I figure that it's okay because back at home, in the top drawer of the sideboard in my dining room is my Last Will. This is the will that I had featured myself writing at, say, seventy, in case I didn't make it to ninety. Instead, the time is now. I do have a smile for my husband and my mother as they start to roll me down the corridor, away from them. I have to just go with this, I'm telling myself.

When I am wheeled to my final pre-operative area, I cannot believe the sheer number of gurneys with awaiting patients on them. Being from a relatively small community with one medium-sized hospital to serve its members, I have never laid eyes on a scene as big or as intensive. Both walls and even the middle of this cavernous basement room are simply lined with pre-operative patients like me, and it's only 7:00 a.m. on a Monday. Thin curtains hang between us to impart the idea of privacy, but in fact, there is little.

While I'm waiting, two IV technicians show up to do their job. I've never known a place where just the business of inserting IVs into people is a full-time profession. Here, it is. They have a two-tiered cart and are apparently familiar with every little box, needle, tube, clip and stopper on it. They check my full name, address and birth date three different ways, making sure all three references, one of them a verbal response from me, exactly matches the data on my wristband, before proceeding.

Smiling, they place my IV so swiftly and elegantly that I hardly notice that they are finished and smoothing out the tape that goes over the needle in my arm. There is no miss, second time, problem or pain, just, "Well, there you are, Mrs. Host." And with another smile, they've moved on to set up shop with the person on my right. These two are serious about their job this morning, and their professionalism imparts a sense of security, something I want to cling to.

I am waiting to meet my anesthesiologist. This is not routine, but yesterday I requested this through my surgeon's office so I can meet the person who is going to preside over my life today. Dr. Gurinder Vasdev arrives at my side in full surgical scrubs and cap and introduces himself in a soft, melodic Indian accent.

"I've been doing this for over forty years," he says in a not-to-worry kind of way. Good, I'm thinking, one year for every one that I've been alive and an extra one for good luck. He politely informs me of his background in India and of his long and impressive education at Cambridge and elsewhere, with humble respect, as though he were addressing the most important person he has ever met. When he finishes, at the risk of offending him, I ask him my question. I want the truth from this man.

"I know that this is a complicated surgery. Will you lose me in there, or will I make it back upstairs and back home to my kids? I'm just so scared." My eyes fill with tears, and he takes both of my hands in his and holds them good and tight, pauses, looks me straight in the eye, and says with a sweet smile, "I won't lose you. I promise."

As soon as he is gone, my nurse tells me, "In a few minutes you'll be heading to surgery." In those three minutes, I return to a conversation that I'd had with Dr. Gottlieb, back home, before I left for this place, at the height of my anxiety about having this surgery.

I'm telling him, "I'm just really scared, I feel like they're just going to slice me open like a fish. It will be so violating, in every way. My solar plexus...well...I'll just be lying there, cut wide open, totally exposed in the worst way."

As usual, Dr. Gottlieb is not in a hurry to rush for words. Instead, he extends his neck, seemingly floating his head above it. He takes a long, slow, rich breath through his nose, half closing his eyes. He does this in such a leisurely manner as to wordlessly invite me to do the same. In doing so, I immediately begin to feel the chair beneath me. As he slowly gathers his response, I look over his left shoulder, letting my eyes rest on the stone sphere fountain. Water bubbles softly from the top, running smoothly over the rough sides. Calmly, he proceeds to describe surgery for me, as only he could.

"Actually, during a surgery where they are working to save a person's life, it can be spiritual in many ways. The operating room itself is bright, clean and quiet. There is light everywhere. Your body will be meticulously draped to cover everything but the area that they will be working on. Every tool and necessary object is in its place, waiting to be used. The doctors and nurses are standing in a kind of circle around you, with the anesthesiologist at your head, all focused on the same goal. It is a powerful and moving sight. I invite you to imagine that when Dr. Nagorney opens your abdomen, it will then be flooded with light. Then still more lights will be added to that. I have observed a number of surgeries and many of them are really beautiful."

That's it. In a matter of minutes, I now have a new painting of my surgery. This is a precious picture, an image of healing, as described by Dr. Gottlieb. I leave his office and take this new picture with me. I'm not sure that he realizes the gift he has given me. I frame it, and hang it on a prominent wall in my mind. I look at it often, especially when my brain returns me to the gallery of El Greco-style paintings that feature me, amid deep-red blood and gore, face gaunt, tinged with green.

I didn't get to choose to have cancer drop me over the falls, but I can choose not to become a slave to the ranting of my fearful mind. I can choose to focus on images that please me, and I should. I do not need to see myself as a victim. I must only accept where I am as a transitory state. Acceptance brings peace.

In the few minutes before I am rolled into the operating room, I close my eyes. I enter the gallery where Dr. Gottlieb's painting is hanging, and I consider it. The word *allow* comes to mind as I gaze at the image of radiance he's painted. I sound out this word and crawl into it like a hammock. I feel the word gently supporting the weight of my fear as I say it over and over, letting it rock my mind and body to sleep as the first injection is administered.

Twelve Hours Gone

I should have known that, as a mother of three, the only possible way to get twelve uninterrupted hours of sleep would be surgery. One thing about sleeping—if I can call it that—during a surgery, is that I have no sense of time passing the way I do in my own bed. Some twelve hours have disappeared, and it is now roughly 8:00 p.m.

Finding and removing all the cancer that is there has extended my five-hour surgery into nine hours. Sadly, this fact leaves my mother and Amory pacing in the waiting room for an extra four hours without word of my condition. While I'm unconscious, they have the really difficult job. It isn't easy to be the one who is sitting there waiting. I can only hope that answering all of the continuously incoming calls from my five siblings, not to mention in-laws, friends and relatives, kept them both occupied. Luckily, being Italian, my mother, Elma, loves to talk. She makes the perfect "surgery-update relay point" for the rest of my large family that stretches from coast to coast.

That's how they probably remember it. My first postoperative memory is of me sliding off a giant blue-plastic-spatula thing onto a bed, like a fish from a Teflon pan onto a plate. The weight of my body bears no significance as they easily move it from one surface to another. Amory's standing right there at the end of my bed, a giant archangel from a Renaissance painting. He is a vision at six foot four: handsome, healthy, bold and glowing against the backdrop of the drab confines of this tiny hospital room.

I'm wondering in a fuzzy way whether Amory is really here with me or if I'm in Heaven, because just over his shoulder I see the profile of Jesus. Then I make out that it's in a frame on the wall, so I figure I must've made it. I'm still here on earth, which reminds me to thank the Father, the Son and the Holy Ghost for the favor I had bartered for.

There are nurses on both sides of me, as well as others coming and going, clipping, snipping and rearranging. They are checking the tubes that are running in every direction, and adjusting things in general. Apparently, there are a lot of things to check on in a person whose abdominal cavity has been completely disassembled and then put back together again.

My eyelids weigh more than my thoughts. Like shutters, they open slowly, then close, capturing only single frames: Amory leaning over me...sliding my wedding rings back onto my finger...squeezing my left hand with both of his. Without a word, he restores my sense of belonging somewhere, to someone.

"Good night, my love. I love you, Carrie," he whispers past my closed eyes. His deep, gentle voice climbs over the wall of sleep. I hear him, though, because no matter how faint my conscious presence may be, I can permanently recognize the sound of love.

Missing Pieces

December 9, 2003

The morning arrives and four doctors, led by Dr. Nagorney, come to see me. Dr. Lee and Dr. Heidenburg check my incision, which the latter has personally stitched and is obviously proud of. They tell me and each other that it looks really good. I'm glad for their summary, because I've never seen anything like it before and "good" would be the farthest adjective from my mind. I hazard a look down at it myself. I've never been a person who wants to see anyone's remarkable stitches, and I do not feel any warmer about it now that they are mine to inspect.

Dr. Young is then introduced to me as the pelvic surgeon. He was called in when they came across tumors they weren't counting on. These tumors were deep inside of places that required a completely different type of surgeon to excavate. A less-experienced surgeon might have easily left me with a colostomy. I am deeply grateful for his help and expertise. Later we are told of his professional reputation and of how lucky I am that he was available to scrub in when Dr. Nagorney called for his help. This is what I mean about feeling taken care of at Mayo Clinic. They are prepared to handle a lot, and they do so expertly. I am waiting to hear the results of Dr. Nagorney's work.

"Well, good morning, Mrs. Host. How are you doing?"

"Pretty well, I think."

"I got 98 to 99 percent of it!" he says, as easy as can be.

I am so happy that I can barely speak. Amory, my mom and I exchange a three-way smile.

"There are two small tumors that I had to leave behind. One is in the center of your spleen, which could not be removed without removing your whole spleen, which I wasn't comfortable with," he explains. "The other is the spot on your lung, which you know about. That will have to be removed later by a thoracic surgeon, when the time is right. I think, over all, that we were successful." He finishes with a smile, his entourage standing proudly in their jackets and ties beside him.

This is the first really good news that I've heard since this all began. My good news will have scans and blood work to verify it. My eyes are full of tears, but these are tears of gratitude.

"Thank you, Dr. Nagorney, thank you so much." This is all I can say to the man who has just saved my life?

"Don't mention it. It's my job. I'm just happy to see you doing well." That's what a real hero says, with a pleasant demeanor, when he's spent a full day pulling me out of a raging river. "No problem!" he adds.

Once they've gone, I begin to get a sense of what day it is. Is it Wednesday? No, Tuesday, it's only Tuesday. Monday morning was my surgery. That was yesterday? How does a twenty-four-hour day only have a beginning and an end, but no middle? Where do we go during that part? Was it really just a night ago that I was imagining myself post-op, back in my room, having a great big steak and baked potato with the works? I was envisioning some fancy restaurant in town delivering dinner to my room: "Room 517, thank you."

Now I'm finding out that not only will there be no fancy steak dinner coming my way but that I will not be fed anything solid for at least a week. All food is solid, I'm thinking. Wrong again.

I adapt to their plan at once. I'm completely willing to forget about the food part of the deal, if I can just have a drink. Lesson number one, about tolerating an onslaught of physical suffering, is that thirst is far worse than hunger. Number two, a drip line in my vein doesn't count as a drink, although my nurse repeatedly assures me that it does.

You start to count the days when you're really thirsty.

I know this firsthand, because it will be exactly six more days, on December 14, when I finally have the luxury of a single sip. For no apparent reason, I start lusting after Riptide Rush Gatorade to satiate my thirst. It's a less sweet and slightly salty version of grape Kool-Aid. Acting like my twelve-year-old son, I beg and plead with every adult I come in contact with, *to just go down to one of the vending machines and get one for me.* I can't get it out of my head, which I find odd, since I don't recall having ever previously craved a Gatorade in my life. Not one person will cooperate with me.

Too weak to hold a phone to my ear for more than one minute, I strictly reserve my telephone energy for my children. All other calls are taken and relayed to me by my mother, the communication expert. She enhances and expands all of my one-word answers to include all sorts of detail, so that the caller on the other end feels satisfied that they have actually spoken to me. Italians not only enjoy cooking and eating, but they like to talk about what someone else had to eat. Since they're not feeding me yet, she can't tell them what I've had to eat. This makes her even crazier than it makes me, so she tells them what she's had to eat and at which restaurant. Also, she'll tell them what Amory's had or will be having for breakfast, lunch or dinner.

Did I say that my mother makes friends in the same time it takes other people to say hello? Well, she does, and by the second day, she's already got two new friends lined up, one lady on either side of my room. She lunches with these new ladies and then keeps me abreast of all of the new developments in relation to their loved ones' progress, as well as what everyone's had to eat. This makes me sure she's confided my daily progress to them, in blow-by-blow detail. When I'm inching along the hall three times a day, holding on to my rolling podium, they wave to me as I pass, and smile an informed smile, nodding a nod that wishes me well.

I tell myself that it's a good thing that I have her new friends waving at me, because being so far from home, I won't have any visitors of my own. Speaking of home, at my request, Amory is heading back there tomorrow to be with the kids. I am relieved to know that they will have their dad back for a week or so and, since I will have my mom here, I won't be alone.

A hospital room isn't the best place to spend the night. Night after night, it becomes particularly grueling and lonesome. Because of this, you discover some new things about yourself, things that you couldn't see until you're stripped down to the bare essentials. Then those things just sit right there for you to notice.

Being alone at night is definitely what I notice. This is when I have the deepest desire to be at home, standing by my baby's crib. I want to watch him sleeping, or pick him up when he cries and hold him close to me as I rock him back to sleep. This thought alone opens up an incredible longing for my children. I become a wreck at night, every night. I miss sending my two older kids off to bed with a kiss and a chat about tomorrow. I miss going to sleep with "all my birds in the nest." Being so far from my children in the middle of the night, missing them is the hardest thing to cope with. Fortunately, Amory gave me a stuffed animal the day after my surgery, and while a small thing, it helps me tremendously. It's a ridiculously soft and silly-looking frog, wearing a red-and-white stocking cap and scarf. I hold on to him every night and prop him under my sore neck every day.

Adults will rarely admit to it, but a stuffed animal is a cozy thing to have in the hospital, no matter your age.

I discover pain on a whole new level as my post-surgical battle begins. I thought the worst was over by the third or fourth day. As it turns out, there are so many layers of pain that go along with a surgery this involved, this deep, that I am hard-pressed to find new ways to cope. Morphine is helpful; it closes the door marked Pain. But this kind of pain stomps in and kicks that door down. Demands are made on my body that I did not expect. For one thing, I'm given a blood transfusion, which I quickly add to my list of things I never want to experience again. Mainly because I can't bear the thought of someone else's bodily fluid merging with mine, even if they do clean it. I mean how do you "clean" blood? No. Don't tell me.

When I'm in agony, scared, sad or missing my kids, experiencing this terrible kaleidoscope of feelings where I'm stuck pretty much the all of the time, I'm grateful that my mother is sitting in that chair next to my bed. She is there to meet my gaze, and when she does, in that quiet, complete way that a mother can, she gives me the feeling that eventually there will be an end to my misery.

December 12, 2003

Around the fourth or fifth day, I am feeling a new brand of loneliness set in. I hear the sound of the river starting to creep back into my ears, setting me apart from the rest of the world. Like an island in a stream, Marisa surfaces into my dim little room, her long, honey-colored curls indiscriminately tied back, sunglasses on her head.

She's here in all her girl-who-can-rescue-you glory, ready to cheer me on. She's got a bag full of presents and tons of stories to tell. I can see that my mother is thrilled to have her here as well. We're both starved for a change of scenery. If there were music to accompany Marisa, it would be "She'll Be Coming 'Round the Mountain." She's a modern-day Annie Oakley, and it feels as if fresh mountain air has whirled in with her.

Our first excursion is to the shower. She pushes me in my wheelchair down the hall to the bath station, which is all set up with a salon-style sink. While I'm in the shower, I'm shocked to find out that I can't raise my arms up past my shoulders. Afterward, I'm grateful that I can have my long, thick hair washed the easy way in the sink, with me sitting in my wheelchair, neck back, and my sister doing all the work.

Three good washes and one deep conditioning later, I feel like a queen. Nothing since my arrival has felt as delightful as that shampoo. Washing my own hair, once a simple task, is now a great luxury. Forget washing my hair, just *having* my hair seems to me to be a gift. I haven't had to bear that particular insult of losing my hair, as most cancer patients do, since chemotherapy isn't part of my treatment. Still, I empathize with those who have lost their hair, some more than once.

Our thirty-minute excursion exhausts me, but having my sister help me scrub up allows me to regain a sense of personal dignity, an aspect of privacy I had generally taken for granted. That privacy has been slowly diminishing, as my personal hygiene has become a public affair for my nurses to handle. But right now, I am catching a glimpse of sunshine in my sister's healthy face and, as I continue to learn, this moment is all that counts.

A couple of days come and go, and then, as she must, so goes Marisa. My mom keeps hanging in here with me. She stands close by and helps me discover that I'm strong enough and brave enough to take more of whatever it is that I'm sure I can't take.

I feel like I'm spread out like some kind of community jigsaw puzzle. Everyone on my team is taking turns looking at me with a slightly skewed sideways glance to see what piece they might put into place. I'm a person in pieces, hoping that one day I will be a complete picture again. Right now, I'm just happy to find my "corners and edges."

At night, I'm mainly on my own. Most of my daytime team has gone home, exhausted from searching through the pile for that one piece. Then my night nurse comes in, covering me with a warm blanket and a quiet smile. Nurses know the suffering of pieces everywhere. They have seen a lot of unfinished puzzles.

Drought

December 13, 2003

I once had a door slammed in my face. That door was pretty much all that I could see for a while. Pain is like that.

The assortment of physical sensations I'm beginning to feel is unappealing. Thirst is one of these. It goes from being a sensation to being pain. It will inevitably outweigh all of the others so that I can't think of much else.

The last time I had anything to eat or drink was five days ago, at four o'clock on the night before my surgery. Suffice it to say that I would have certainly savored that drink, had I known how long it would be until I would have another. A drink becomes all I can think of. I vary the types of drinks that I imagine. A long, cool drink of water is the desired beverage of the moment.

My nurses are trained and accustomed to turning a deaf ear to this particular brand of misery, and they have their answers all ready to pull out in case they have to respond to my lame plea for just one sip.

"You might be able to have chips and sips in a day or two. We'll have to see how you're doing," my night nurse tells me. *Chips and sips?* Ice chips are what she is referring to. *She might allow me to be the beneficiary of the tiniest possible piece of ice?*

"What? How about delivering a small lake with a personal straw?" I'm moaning sarcastically. This starts the third day of the Drought.

The next four days remain the longest and driest in my life, except for my tears of frustration which, like some desperate frog, I stick my tongue out to catch. Then, remembering the uncanny fact that frogs don't drink water—they absorb it through their skin—I start to cry ridiculous tears of rage.

I am sure that they have lost their minds. I'm sure that they can't be serious about not giving me a drink for this many days. As it turns out, on this particular ward of this hospital, where virtually every patient has undergone an abdominal surgery of a significant nature, they are. Very serious.

"I just don't understand why I can't have a drink!"

"Your intestines have 'closed up shop' and until they are open for business, nothing goes into your stomach," my nurse says, putting it gently.

"When will that be?" I ask, already knowing that the number will not be one that I like.

"Well, now, it's normally about one day for every hour of surgery that was done."

"But that's nine hours...nine days. *Nine* days?"

"Let's get you fixed up here. It's time to check on that incision," she says, dodging my question by changing the subject. "As long as I'm here, I'll just take your blood pressure and your temp as well. That way I won't have to come and bug you for a while," she chirps.

"But that's three more days."

"Would you like another ice pack for that?" she asks, staring at my incision.

"I want a drink. I can't stand this for even one more day," I say sullenly.

"Let's get your blood pressure here, and then I'll get you that ice pack."

While my nurses are kind and courteous in manner, it becomes abundantly clear that they are not open to my suggestions on the routine that must be followed in order for me to recover. The lack of an actual drink isn't where the torture ends. In order to make sure my sense of thirst is heightened, my nurse routinely comes in and swabs out the inside of my mouth with a fine, rough, purple sponge in the shape of a star mounted on top of a sucker stick. This sponge is more the texture of a pumice stone and thus is barely damp.

In the days that follow, I amuse myself by mentally writing absurd analogies for this procedure whenever my efficient nurse comes in with the purple star. My personal favorite becomes: *Swabbing my mouth, the Sahara, with a pathetic little sponge, is like trying to humidify the inside of a cathedral with a teakettle.*

Finally, I'm driven to start thinking like a teenager. There must be some way to outwit these annoying adults who seem to have total control over me, including my mother, a registered nurse. Due to the nature of her medical alliance, she feels compelled to nod in agreement and strictly adhere to the rules of the nurse on duty. I go back to the old standby: sneaking out.

I plan to slip out of my bed in the middle of the night. Around 2:00 a.m., holding on to the side rail, it takes me roughly thirty minutes to manage to scooch myself to the edge of the lower third of the bed, an excruciatingly painful move. But with the bathroom sink only six or seven feet away, I'm motivated.

It's only now I realize that somehow I have to get my IV stand rolled around from the left side of the bed to the right side, where I sit, helpless. Using tools, like an ape in the zoo, I grab the TV remote and use it as an extension of my left arm. It just reaches but, to my horror, my arm is barely stable enough to remain elevated, much less to push the stand.

Just then Didi, the most wonderful night nurse of all time, pops her head in, which is easy to do as the nurses' station is just five convenient feet from my door. Sizing me up, she asks sweetly, "Are you ready to take your walk?" then proceeds to answer her question for me, "Well, good for you." At the same time she's leaning into the hall to roll a podium in.

"Sometimes the middle of the night is best. We like to see you pushing that podium whenever we can. Sooo...let me just get you all untangled here..." she thinks out loud, in her strong Minnesota accent. With the flick of a wrist, she's got my IV stand right where I'd wanted it just forty-five seconds ago.

Ten seconds more, and she'll have every bag and tube transferred and hanging from the lower half of that podium, my escape vehicle. Just as soon as she leaves the room, I will walk over to the sink. I'll turn it on full blast and slurp down as much water as I can hold.

"Okay, let's get you through the door here." She leads, squarely positioning herself smack in front of my goal: the bathroom door. Her sturdy foot, clad in an even sturdier thick white nursing shoe, props open the door to the hallway. Leaning my forearms on the brown vinyl panel, I dutifully start the slow shuffle down the long hall. I'm the busted teenager, my angelic nurse seeing only my good intentions and not my actual plans. But like an unyielding teenager, I remain focused on my plan, vowing to double my effort if I must.

I'm making a mindless study of the geometric layout of the linoleum tiles, and their late-night, freshly polished gleam, as I begin to fashion part B of my failed plan for a drink. At the mere thought of running water, I make a dull stop and push left to a full about-face and work toward my room. Good, they are all away from the desk...I'm g-e-t-t-i-n-g there...*please* stay gone...I don't *want any help*...I *want* a drink... I don't care if it makes me vomit...I don't care what you're all thinking...I...don't...*care*...about anything but *water!* I'm thirsty. I'm forty years old and, damn it, I'm going to get a drink...right now, thank you very much. I talk myself in.

Once through the door marked 517, just three feet short of my destination, I'm stopped cold. But this time it's by the podium, which is too wide to angle into the miniscule bathroom. I stand still and try to think hard through all the medications that are clouding my vision. *If I let go, could I reach for the sink and walk in? Yes. Yes, that will work,* I'm telling myself. Looking down at my slippers, I'm thinking, *slippers are good, they won't let me slip, yes...thank you God, for whoever invented rubber-soled slippers. Okay, it's only about four steps, five at most.* I continue to calculate, as my eyes catch sight of the three evil bags hanging upside down like sleeping bats, just above my slippers. Each bag has a tube. And each tube is running into or out of my body. *Oh, my God, I'm attached!* Not one of the tubes is long enough for me to get to the sink from here.

At once, I'm mortified. I recognize that I'm not going anywhere! I can't get to the sink. My body is attached to this four-legged monster. I'm the goddamned prisoner of a podium! Suddenly I'm nauseous and feeling faint. This whole excursion has been far too much for me. My abdomen begins throbbing, the stitches that are holding it together start to burn, and my mind goes up in flames along with them. *I'm trapped in a body that can't do what I tell it to do. I'm trapped by this stupid podium! I'm trapped in this stupid hospital!* Leaning my head forward, I feel a trickle of sweat run from the back of my neck around the outside of my parched throat and over my sternum.

"Didi? Are you there?" I hear my voice crack like a weak spark from a bonfire. The flames are too much. I break into a cold sweat all over. I start shaking violently, which makes me sorry for cursing the podium, the only thing now keeping me from total collapse onto the shiny speckled floor below my prized slippers, where droplets of perspiration are pooling.

"Didi!" I try to scream through chattering teeth, and she arrives right as I can't stand one second more.

"What happened here, honey? I'm so sorry, I didn't see you sneak by. You got right back here, didn't you? Sometimes we think we're up for that walk, then—" with a pop-snap of her gum "—we're just not as ready as we thought, are we, honey?" She puts a strong arm around my shoulders and backs me up to the bed, where I have to be changed like a child from my soaking wet gown to a dry one.

When I'm in bed, Didi covers me with a blanket fresh from the blanket warmer. She makes sure to tuck it snugly under my feet, genuinely smiling at me all the while. My chattering teeth slow to a stop. I am totally spent. Pain crawls in under the covers and settles in around me. Tears stream in rivulets across my temples, curl around my ear lobes and run toward the nape of my neck, soaking the pillow below me.

Pain jacks up its right to be heard over the constant whining of thirst. Ironically, both are obliterated by the sound of rushing water. The river drowns out all else.

William's Candle

December 17, 2003

I t's 5:30 a.m. As hard as I try to keep from crying as my nurse stands close to me asking me if I'm okay this morning, I can't do it. I'm not okay, not today.

"Well, my baby turns one today, so I'm just really sad that I can't be there. I don't want to miss his first birthday, you know?"

"What's his name?"

"William...William Amory Host," I expand, to hear the sound of his name.

"That's sweet."

"Sweet William...yes."

My voice is cracking, as I whisper through my tears so that no one will hear, including me, "I was hoping that I'd be home by now, but I didn't make it."

She squeezes my shoulders and hands me several tissues. "I'm sorry, I really am. I know it must be hard. I have two kids myself, so I know."

"I miss him so much," I cry. "He's just a baby. He needs me."

"Is anyone there to celebrate with him?" she asks, helping me look at the positive.

"Yes, my sister's there and my older kids, Marco and Chanel...oh, and my aunt. So he'll definitely have a lot of attention. It's just that I want to get him out of his crib and say happy birthday to him first, you know," I say through my tears. She nods her head yes. She does know, I can tell.

Amory has returned, and he and my mom come in together around eight o'clock. They help me call home to talk to the baby. This is the first time I have talked to him over the phone, or even heard his voice in ten days, days that seem like an eternity. I have been worried that, at his age, it would be confusing for him to hear my voice but never see me walk through the door. While this may have protected him and been for his benefit, it has been difficult for me.

Wendy answers and enthusiastically relays every tiny detail of every precious birthday-morning minute to me. She talks me down the stairs, while taking William to the kitchen table to look at his round cake with a snowman on it, which she describes, hoping that I like it.

"That's just exactly what I would have picked out," I assure her, trying not to cry.

"Don't worry. You know me, I'm taking lots of pictures. When we have his cake later today, I'll call you so you can hear us sing to him, okay?" she says. Just hearing all of his little coos and baby sounds in the background makes me feel the kind of biological desperation that a mother feels when she's too far from her infant. I want to get there as soon as I can. I want to go home now. I want to rip out this stupid IV and run from here.

I'm afraid that William won't remember me, or that he won't come to me. I'm afraid that he'll have replaced me with his "new mother," my sister. She looks and sounds enough like me to be confusing to a baby. I know that my sister is talking about me and telling him that I love him, but I still feel like I'm losing. I'm losing my children.

After I hang up, I slip back into the river. Its ice-cold water begins to replace the blood in my veins. I'm being pulled under into a type of grief that becomes a powerful current, heavy and slow. It's only 8:27 a.m. How will I get through this day?

There is no cheering me up. Neither my mom nor Amory can eke out a single response of any kind from me. They take leave and head out to regroup their efforts over breakfast. They sense a raging river downstream and they are right.

I'm done talking. I'm done with this whole horrible experience. I'm done hearing about my life over the phone, as it goes on without me in it. I'm done.

With my thumb, I click my painkiller button, six times in a row. Unhappily for me, the technically correct—and, might I add, stupid—medication-dosing machine limits the supply. It only dispenses enough to make me stare hard at the unadorned corner of my room without blinking for a long, long time.

While I stare, I block out the machine's incessant beeping and click the button again, refusing to read the flashing green message on its screen to my left. Now the machine starts screaming! It's alerting its able nurse to correct this disruption to its steady activity and to advise its angry patient on its proper use. I know what it says. I know without looking: DENIED.

In the early evening, while I'm alone, my nurses come through my door singing "Happy Birthday," and place a tiny little cake with one candle in front of me. Of course, it's not lit—this is a hospital—but I'm overjoyed! This kindness truly lifts my spirits.

"Thank you so much. This is too much. Thank you!" I say, with a real smile.

"You're welcome," they say in unison.

When Amory comes back into my room, he finds me with a little birthday cake and a big smile. The cake's sitting on my tray. It sits on a paper placemat that says Happy Birthday William, and is decorated with balloons in primary colors. He sits down on my bed right next to me, puts his arms around me and pulls me close.

Being in a hospital this long has made my olfactory gland razor-edged. I find out that every tiny scent has a whole world of memory immersed within it. Because he's just come in from a long run in the cold Minnesota winter air, he smells like a Christmas tree. He still has a trace of the icy air on his collar. I lean my head into his shoulder and, closing my eyes, savor every cool, clean bit of it.

"Thank you for giving me a beautiful son, thank you," he whispers.

"He's a miracle, Amory, he really and truly is."

"His mama's a miracle, too." He kisses my forehead.

Then he pulls a small pine bough from his overcoat, puts it in my hand and says, "For our winter baby." We cut the little cake and Amory eats a piece. I take a tiny swipe of sugary frosting, just to be in the spirit. This moment is the first that resembles a return to my life outside of this room.

Cancer is like that. A nurse can save your life. Or it might be that she simply saves your day and, within that, a certain part of your soul that you need to start healing your body. There are most likely many cancer patients who have tried to escape the moment at hand, knowing full well that escape isn't an option. But as we will continue to discover, our souls keep propelling us into this precious moment, today. This is all we have right now, and it is therefore worth having the courage to save.

Staring

—◦—

December 18, 2003

I t is a real art, taking up with a person who is hanging on by a thread. Someone has to find the meaning in my life for me and then lead me back there every time I start to fade away. It is a job for someone who loves me deeply.

To say that my insides feel as though they are shredded and dripping with battery acid would be a lame attempt to describe the vilest pain after a surgery such as mine. It is a stubborn type of pain that occasionally creeps out of its holding cell. Breaking free, it rushes to my brain to tell it the bad news: "Hey, they cut you up inside—pay attention!" Until the pain finds a pathway to my nerves, the morphine is keeping it under control.

Morphine is a good thing, until it enters my dreams. Each time I close my eyes, strange things happen. Faces begin lifting up and peeling off the surface of a smooth pond, one after another in succession, each one emerging out of the other. It's a super-slow, eerie slideshow of the people in my life, their faces clear, yet distorted by the ripple on the surface, the surface of my farthest recollection.

I open my eyes to escape the past, and I see a real face, the dearest sight in the world right now: my mother with her geranium-pink lipstick. Her chartreuse silk collar pokes out from beneath a chocolate cashmere sweater like a crocus in spring. Her dark brown hair is set with hairspray in short waves above large, square eyeglasses, framing eyes that have seen plenty. I thank God for her, the saint He's put at my side. I'm hoping that He hears me.

In the middle of the night, when she's not here, I say a prayer that my mother might sleep a peaceful sleep. I pray for a guardian angel to watch over her the way she's watching over me, day after dismal day, with every cell in her body.

Two long, dull days, full of extreme longing for my children, have somehow passed. I'm filled with anxiety at the notion that William may not recognize me or has forgotten me. I'm afraid that he will turn away when my sister tries to hand him to me.

All of these fearful feelings started to come up yesterday after my mom left. She went home ahead of us to pave the way, as it were. Today, Amory will help me begin the journey home. Carefully and lovingly, he makes every possible effort to have the arduous journey be as painless as possible.

I can only walk unassisted the distance that I can go in a slow shuffle for about two or three minutes. This is how I move between bed and wheelchair, wheelchair to car, car to wheelchair, wheelchair to airplane, and the reverse. Piece by piece and slowly, I successfully make it all the way from my bed in Minnesota to my bed on the second floor of our house back in Colorado.

People stare. It's human nature. They've got the princess and the frog picture—but this reversed version, they aren't so familiar with, so they stare. They have to gape at the prince and the frog and who can blame them? When you see a sight like Amory, a tall, muscular tri-athlete, classically handsome, health radiating from every pore, pushing a smidge of a lady the size of a child in a wheelchair, you gawk.

I'm wearing my light pink tweed overcoat, and a velvet hat that frames my large brown eyes whose sockets are far too deep. Other than wincing, I have no facial expression, and I am barely able to keep my bowling ball of a head centered upon my spindle of a neck each time the wheelchair starts forward or stops. My large hands are spread across my lap. My long fingers, once graceful, even lovely, are now a heinously bruised collection of knuckles and bones and look completely out of proportion and barely attached to a pair of miniscule wrists.

If those staring people had seen me just eight weeks ago—strong and athletic, five foot seven, 135 pounds, olive skin, long chestnut-colored hair, big smile—I'm convinced that they would not believe it to be the same person sitting here. I was confident, animated, and had personality to spare. Now I'm twig-thin and in such a weakened condition that I'm unable even to walk through the airport.

The longer I sit here in this wheelchair, a pitiful sight, the more I see that this is the beginning of my merging back into the world. While I am being stared at, I promise myself never to even sneak a stare at someone, ever again. Instead I'll try to offer the nearly invisible nod of compassion that I am beginning to learn from others. Every so often, I'll receive one from an elderly person, with enough life behind them to know better than to just stare.

While my current appearance *is* deceiving indeed, I simply decide to enjoy looking like a frog in a pink coat. Frogs are creatures I've long admired, as anyone who knows me will tell you. Now, although I'm sitting here emaciated and broken, on the bright side, I'm telling myself that when I arrive home, I'll be the largest frog in my collection.

Cancer is like that. Without your permission, it will take what you're made of, melt it down, and remold all of the parts, dropping any that you won't need anymore. Then it will construct something stronger, simpler and utterly exquisite. It is a painful process, being rebuilt. In exchange for your tremendous suffering, all of your senses are washed clean. All of the extra stuff you once filled your endless time with disappears. This makes room for your soul to expand to its rightful location, front and center, where it radiates like never before and begins to heal you.

Amory's Ring

December 20, 2003

Opening my own front door allows me inside more than just the house; it reunites me with my life. Feeling my thumb pressing down on the frozen brass handle, the old familiar motion comes back to me, a simple thing that I took for granted. Today, it resonates in a way that it never has before. I enter feeling triumphant. I've made it! I'm home. I'm walking through my front door and into the arms of my family, a welcoming committee: Marco and Chanel, Wendy holding William, my mom and my Aunt June who has flown in from Santa Barbara to help. Also, there's a new face, Teri, the woman Amory has hired to help us with William. Having never met me, she stands aside, yet offers me a sweet, compassionate smile. Instantly, I appreciate both her discretion and her quiet. We are going to be a good team, I can tell.

Marco and Chanel run to hug me, but stop a little short, the way you do when you are going to hug someone old and frail. They pace their motions and hug me carefully so as not to crush me to smithereens. This is my first unspoken message as to how I appear to them. There will be a lot more of these messages from all sorts of people, so I accept it right away as a fact, nothing more. At little more than 105 pounds, I must look like a scarecrow at best. While holding on to Amory's arm, I drop to my knees, where Wendy meets me on hers to hold William out to me.

"Hello, darling. Hello, my William. It's Mommy, do you remember me?" I coax softly. I smile, willing back my tears, watching his face. His big, dark, coffee-brown eyes begin to search. I let him take his time to try to put the sound and the sight of me back into his world.

"Remember Mommy, William? It's Mommy." Marco and Chanel, now on their knees, urge him separately, yet together. In those precious seconds that pass, we are all holding our breaths, because we all want the same thing. We all want William to recognize me. I reach out and take his fat little hands and walk him to me. As I pull him close, I make a sound that I've made many times before as I've held him, nursed him and rocked him. I sigh a deep, soft, *uhhhmm* with my exhale. This is a secret sound that only he and I know.

Instantly he remembers and immediately starts to cry. It's a cry that is angry, happy and sad all at once, but it's his cry. That wonderful sound is music to my ears. Then, he pushes his sweet head into my skinny neck and cries some more. I hear all of the involuntary oohs and aahs above us, the same sound we make when a rainbow appears—one can't help making sounds of appreciation at this simple radiance.

"Mommy's home. William, I'm home," I whisper in his ear. I know now that he *knows* it's me. He didn't completely forget me as I had feared.

My sister Wendy and my Auntie June have done a wonderful job of taking care of the kids. I know that I am truly the luckiest person in the world. The kids are showing me the ornaments that they've been making, and then they each show me the silver-tinsel Christmas trees in their bedrooms. Marco's is lighted in apple-green, modern, of course, while Chanel's is all pink. When I finally enter my room, I find they've decorated a special one just for me, in a dazzling purple.

After so much time in the hospital, each of my senses springs forth at the slightest invitation to do so. In my absence, the housekeeper has taken to ironing everything in her path. Thus, I am treated to a long, white, cotton nightgown which has been pressed in a manner reminiscent of a time long gone. After my mother helps me out of a shallow bath of rosewater soap and hot water and dries off my back, I step into my freshly pressed gown. She braids my hair and Amory helps me climb into our big pine bed.

I lie there absorbing the lofty white bed and its well-worn, delightfully cool, clean linens. Amory pulls the sheets up over me, along with the feather-light down comforter. "You're home. I'm so glad that you're home, Carrie," he says with tears rimming his eyes. Wiping them away with a corner of his shirt, he opens the window above the headboard just a crack. The cold, clean mountain air laced with the scent of pine washes over my face in a tiny stream, a sensation so delicious I'm moved to tears.

December 25, 2003

Few things are nicer than Christmas in Colorado. Just waking up in my own bed on this particular Christmas morning is luscious. I've made it home. My kids and I are together and nothing else is on my mind. After stockings, breakfast and presents, Amory comes ambling down the hallway in his plaid flannel robe tied lazily off-center, tossing what looks like a poorly wrapped tennis ball from hand to hand. As Marco gives Chanel a happy but scandalous look regarding his father's gift-tossing antics, Amory sits down close and gently hands me his unforgettable little treasure.

Eternally the conservationist, he's obviously pulled its wrinkled red paper from the growing pile on the floor. He's taped it together any which way and scrawled *To Carrie, Love, Amory* across it in barely legible black permanent marker. Smiling in appreciation of his sweet wrapping, I tear open the messy package to find a much fancier, square blue-leather box. I lift the lid and my breath at the same time, stunned by the sapphire-and-diamond ring inside. I know the deep, clear, cushion-cut blue sapphire in its center. This is the stone that Amory gave me a year ago, just after William was born. Now it has been set with a brilliant white diamond on either side. One represents Marco, the other, Chanel.

For me, it's so much more than an exquisite piece of jewelry. It's a deeply personal message from my husband that he believes in my future. I can feel all of the love that he's put into creating this quiet, sparkling promise. I slip it over my far-too-skinny fourth finger of my right hand. It spins around loosely, to which he says, "Well, it's *your* size, so we'll just have to fatten you up! Right, kids?" What he didn't say was that he would go and have it made smaller. This unspoken part is yet another silent invitation for my healing.

This ring represents my deepest hope of someday getting well. Each time I glance at its loveliness, I see my husband holding our three children together, side by side. I see them cheering me on. Once again, Amory has bravely come to my emotional rescue in a way in which no one else could have done—in his bathrobe.

Listening

—◦∞◦—

December 27, 2003

I am in so much pain that I lose sight of all reason. I can't talk or listen to anyone or anything. Pain can be a tricky subject. It screams through every nerve. Percocet makes me nauseous and Vicodin gives me nightmares. I try unsuccessfully to wean myself off both and onto Motrin or Tylenol. This turns out to be one of those useful ideas, at the wrong time. I haven't yet fully learned the way to manage my pain outside of the hospital, without the little black button to click.

I call Marisa and get my brother-in-law Jack on the line to see what wisdom he can shed on my seemingly hopeless situation with regard to pain. He has survived cancer twice. He says, "Pain is a train, you have to stay on it. Never let it get ahead of you or you'll never catch up. You have to take your meds just before the window is closed, so that you stay ahead of it." *Oh, that's great.* I'm thinking: *Good advice, too bad I didn't ask sooner.* Now I'm informed too late; the train has gotten away and I'm in agony.

This particular level of torment is completely off the little chart that the hospital gives you with the faces to help you describe your pain. If pain has a ceiling, I am hovering above the roof. This agony is what I will blame for clouding my ability to tell one sensation from another, thus leading to my physical decline.

There are hundreds of tiny strings of pain all crisscrossing in different places so that it's become one indefinite sensation. Like Gulliver the giant, I'm held against my will, staked to the ground beneath me, pinned down. I can't tell that my body is about to nose-dive in a spiral toward death. I can't tell anything else, apart from the constant searing pain. I feel as if I am burning alive from the inside out. I should be taking my temperature four times a day, but I stopped taking it a day ago, or whenever it was that the pain took center stage, demanding my complete attention and ruling out all else.

The next two days pass in one jumble, and short-sightedness rules. I'm about to fall out of my boat again, but this time into a narrow strip of the river, one that rages so hard between two tall and bare canyon walls that nothing can be heard but the sound of nature roaring down her own path and demolishing anyone in it.

December 29, 2003

At 4:30 a.m. I choose. I choose whom to wake. Should it be Amory, who was already up at 2:15 a.m. with William, or my mom, who didn't get to bed till about 1:00 a.m. for all her pacing and fretting and late-night radio talk shows, or my sister-in-law, Trina, who had arrived earlier to see if she could break the world's record for the most loads of laundry done in a single night? I choose the last, since the newest arrival on my scene seems oftentimes the most rested. I seem to wear people out these days with my revolving needs and draining presence.

I hobble down two flights of stairs, thanking God for the handrail, an item for which I'd formerly had little appreciation. Peeking into the guest room where Trina is sleeping, I creep in and sit on the end of her bed.

"What's the matter?" she whispers.

"Something, I don't know. I'm sick. I have a fever, I'm freezing," I tell her.

"Here, get in," she directs me into the bed, as she rolls over and gets out of the other side. She heads for a thermometer and more blankets to pile on top of me.

"103.5—that's not good," she's saying to herself, squinting at the thermometer's glowing light, while involuntarily shaking her right foot as she sits on the end of the bed .

"I need to see Dr. Dughi. They aren't there till eight-thirty," I groan.

"We should go to the emergency room," she says, seeing a simple solution.

"No. No way. I'm too sick for that. I can't deal with that place again," I counter, realizing at once how illogical that sounds. It takes someone really sick, who has been through the worst, to know what I mean.

Getting myself motivated to go to the E.R. for help is like trying to convey a relatively easy principle in a foreign language. It's like I'm trying to explain the way I feel in Russian without knowing a single word of the language. Before I even begin, I'm exhausted. The thought of trying to express myself makes me close my eyes and swallow hard. The same is true of trying to explain things that doctors can't readily see. It is too much to attempt, so I don't.

"Let's call Dr. Dughi and see what she thinks," She tries again. "It's not even five o'clock in the morning. Do you think she'll call us back?" she wonders out loud.

"Yes, I do."

Once again, the angels are with me. Not only do I get a call back, but it's Dr. Dughi on the line, as she happens to be the doctor on call. I am relieved that she knows each twist and turn to my case before the surgery I had three weeks ago, so I won't have to do much explaining. As for what she thinks: "I want you to get to the emergency room immediately and I'll meet you there."

The underlying feeling I have about my body is difficult to assess. It's as if the volume is being turned up in a direct, yet imperceptible manner. By the time I find myself screaming to turn it down, I'm already drowned out.

The emergency convoy has been awakened and assembled. My mother's in the kitchen making a pot of coffee. She has thrown in the towel on any further sleep and will stand guard over children and house until Socorro arrives.

Amory is already dressed and scraping ice and snow off the car, shoveling a clear path for me. Before I can even get my coat from the closet, I hear the engine turning over as he attempts to warm up the brittle car. He's moving quickly and quietly. Sadly, he has become accustomed to my waking him at all hours. Like a fireman or anyone else trained to respond to emergencies, he snaps to, with compassion in his eyes, and is ready to take action. He's never annoyed or put out, he's just constantly bailing out my boat as it begins to fill with water.

Jersey-girl Trina is ready in a flash and helping me get my boots on in the front hall. There will be no leaving her at home, she's coming with us. This is the drill, the emergency-room drill, which my whole family has gotten far too familiar with in the past fifteen months. All the doctors and nurses at Boulder Community Hospital know me by sight, a fact that is beginning to concern me. Each time they see me, I am in a state of further-diminished health. Now, at 105 pounds, it seems there's not much left of me to see.

At the hospital, they take a CT scan, abdominal X-ray, blood draw and a sterile urine sample. I cry with each test because I can barely manage the additional discomfort that each one presents. Dr. Dughi takes my emaciated hand and, holding it tight, gives me a good looking over.

"Tell me what's happening here, friend," she says.

"I don't know, but it's not good. I'm so nauseated...it's too much pain...it's not good. I'm not okay. Not at all," I whisper to her in a tight groan, through a stream of tears.

"Yeah, okay, buddy. Hang in here. We'll get this figured out, okay?" she replies, tipping her head to the side, in the same direction as mine, while closely looking into my eyes. She's waiting for my barely visible nod to let her know that I've agreed to stick around while she gets more help.

My body is in too much pain to bear. It simply can't do anything more to contain me, so I let the angel who is at my side lift me softly to a nearby perch while I look on. When you're floating, you hear everything.

I watch all of their faces: first Trina, then a nurse, then Amory, then Dr. Dughi, all appearing then disappearing. They all come and go from the hallway, that crucial place that affords family members a moment to hide their fears, to huddle and whisper things they don't want you to hear about your condition. This is also where they keep a lookout for a particular doctor to turn up, or get on their cell phones to keep everyone else informed.

It turns out that, no matter where they are or how quietly they speak, I can hear them. I hear them because of what I already know. I know that I'm dying. I want to tell to Amory my immediate fears about that, but I can't, as I am barely able to talk. This scares me—to think that I might slip away from him. I might float away, like a helium balloon that has gotten loose from a child as he stares up, mouth hanging open, stunned by how quickly and quietly it happened. I'm afraid that Amory may not be able to see that I'm in much bigger trouble than it may appear, or that there is only one thin length of twine between here and gone.

When the fever reaches 104.5, I begin to rely on eye contact as my means to communicate. I think that Dr. Dughi knows this secret about patients in dire straits and that is why she looks so adamantly into my eyes every time she speaks to me. She is looking for life and by seeing it, she helps adhere me to the present.

Now I hear them talking about flying me to Mayo Clinic. I want to see my children first, but there's not time to go home. For all of the action and noise around me, I am getting quiet. I am pulling in, so I can focus on what is most important: love. That's all that is worth my attention at this point: feeling the love that I have for my children, for Amory, for Trina, for life.

Life is flowing through me, but at a trickle, and that trickle will become a slow drip by the time the sun goes down today. My mother rounds the corner into my little cubby and stops just short of my bed. The expression on her face is the one that tells me that she can see the angel who is next to the gurney, holding me gently. She is struck with the sight of her daughter being taken away. A barely audible gasp escapes her lips, but I hear it as I do every other whisper, like the distant tinkle of a thin glass wind chime on a thick, hot summer's day. A mother has this kind of filter on her vision, allowing her information about her child long before a medical team can produce a clear-cut answer. I guess that only my mother can see now what everyone else will see later.

Dr. Dughi is calling for Mayo Clinic's plane to come for me. She's told that it's out on another mission until much later this evening.

"Later is not optional, Amory. Let's get her on a commercial flight right away." I hear Dr. Dughi say to Amory and Trina in the hall.

As is often the case with cancer, it seems that "later" is the word with which we no longer mingle. I already know that this river has no later to it. There's only now. There's no floating along in this one. I need to be airlifted out, as Dr. Dughi has recognized. Right now, it doesn't feel to me as if anyone will be able to negotiate this terribly narrow gorge and its wild, unruly waters.

I know that this river will not answer to anyone, and I'm more afraid than I've ever been before. As I lie on my side, my mom squeezes in next to the angel and slowly rubs my back, reminding me with her touch from whence I came, reminding me to stay with her, that I'm still here. Without thinking, I silently begin to say the the Lord's Prayer, asking

God to bless me and my family. I ask for peace, and immediately I begin to feel it washing over me.

Twenty minutes later, Amory has reappeared, having driven home to get our things. Fortunately, my bag is always packed and sitting in my bedroom, ready to go with me at any time. We have learned, in our new life with cancer, to be prepared. Meanwhile, Dr. Dughi has signed my discharge and arranged for me to be admitted to St. Mary's Hospital at Mayo Clinic, and Trina has coordinated with our travel agent for a flight.

As I stand up to leave, quicksand grabs my ankles and I practically fall forward. Unable to pick up my feet, I shuffle into my mother's arms and whisper, "I'm so scared, Mom. I don't know what's wrong this time." I feel the panic in my voice as I hold on to her shoulders and step into my shoes.

"Now, don't be scared," she says.

"I'm scared I'll never see you again, Mom," I say, my face crumpling. I see that she, too, is full of fear. Her tears roll to the edge of her lower lids and drop off, missing her face, like a steep cliff.

"Yes, you will," she says, looking into me. "Now, don't worry, you will," she says again, this time pulling me close, hugging me more tightly and slightly longer than she normally would, the way you hug a person you know you may never see again. As we walk toward the doors of the emergency room, I notice that my feet are so cold and thin that they're slipping back and forth inside my loafers, which used to be a snug fit. No lucky boots this time.

"Will you stay with the baby, Mom?" I ask her, as she helps me into the front seat of the waiting car. She holds what used to be my elbow; it now feels like a boney hook.

"Yes. I will. I won't leave him for one minute until you're home. Now don't you worry, you'll be all right," she says, trying to convince herself and help me to believe what I can't see, trying to help me find blind faith in this vast unknown. What I can see is the total love in her eyes, and from the side-view mirror of the car, I watch her until she disappears.

I quietly begin to beg God to *"Please, bring me back home, please."* I notice that for someone who promised not to ask God for more favors, I've been asking Him for a number of them lately. To accept what I don't know and to have faith in what I can't see is the key to staying quiet and focused on life, even if it is hard to see my way to the river banks. Thrashing about won't help.

Angels don't swim. They hover. The angel who has come to the river to guard me in the midst of the water's fury is hovering right above the spray and the deafening sound of rushing water that cannot be stopped. Unable to take to the water, the angel's holding fast to me with his presence from above. I'm clutching on to life in gasps, getting glimpses of hope hovering above me, as the river below takes me where it pleases.

Looking

Together, Dr. Dughi and Amory have decided that I will be on the flight to St. Paul, Minnesota, leaving in fifty-seven minutes. Amory's driving, trying to keep ahead of the storm. Trina's in the backseat, pulling shirts off hangers, packing Amory's bag. When she's finished, she puts her hand over the seat onto my right shoulder and keeps it there. She's helping me hold on.

I can tell that she's got the feeling that this might be the last time she will see me. Without looking, I can sense her tears behind me. To imagine Trina crying is a near impossibility, as anyone who knows her can tell you. She's a little stick of dynamite, deceptively small for the power she packs. She's not the type to break down. She's capable of facing any storm, but this one appears to be brewing out of control.

Forty minutes later, we arrive at Denver International Airport, pulling up to curbside check-in, and Amory disregards his strong principles regarding being rude, pushy or confrontational in any manner. He jumps out of the car on a serious mission, cuts in front of a long line of already frustrated holiday travelers, and checks us in. He's intensely anxious and large to boot; no one tangles with him. With icy glares, they just fix their stares high at the back of his head, whispering low.

In less than six seconds, a traffic officer is already heading our way, pointing and shouting that we can't be where we are, but there's not a thing, including a cop, that can stop Trina from opening my door and helping me to my feet as she tosses a bag onto the curb and waves a skycap over for a wheelchair.

The focused officer marches up, shouting at her, "Stay in your car, ma'am, you can't stand here! Get *back* in your car!" Huffing steam from his nose, he makes himself taller and puffs out his chest as he takes out his pad. Making a show of folding back the top pages, he begins writing us a big ticket. My innate optimism trying to rise to the occasion, I'm thinking, *Good. There's a vote for me. Go ahead, write it up.*

For the first time in my life, I'm actually thrilled to see a traffic cop writing me a ticket. *I'm not sure I'll be here to pay it, but since you seem to think so, I'm with you.* To my dismay, he takes one good look at me and stops casting his vote. I can see all kinds of things cross his mind, as they cross his face. Then, I look so deeply into his eyes that his right hand drops to his side. Pocketing his pen, he pulls out a whistle, which he blows in several sharp barks, while waving the security guard in my direction.

Now I know that I must be the picture of death and misery, to be able to stop an angry, eager, ticket-writing cop in his ticket-writing tracks, at the airport, no less, and during the holidays. Just like that, he's now on my side of the equation. A security guard arrives, and they help me into the chair, placing a tag of some kind around my neck. "I still need you to move your car, ma'am," I hear him say calmly, politely, almost regretfully to Trina. I'm thinking that *now I know we're in trouble.*

Amory takes my wheelchair from the security guard, nodding for him to lead the way. The man's jogging ahead of us, radio in hand, verbally taking down barriers before we even get to them. Now with only five minutes until the plane departs, they are running me through the terminal, cutting through all lines. We pick up an armed guard who whisks us past security and onto an elevator which an officer is holding open. We head down to the tunnel, where his armed presence automatically orders passengers out of our way. As we approach the gate, I can see by the expectant look in our direction from the agent that the airline has gotten word, likely from Dr. Dughi, and held the flight. Once again, this doctor is out there, pulling for me. She never drops the ball.

Outside, alone in the cold gray morning, Trina is driving the round-about over and over in an absolute panic, waiting to hear if we've made it on board. Amory calls her from the jetway, out of breath, saying, "We've made it, we're on." I feel her relief and fear as he hangs up.

Meanwhile, I can see the whole story in the other passengers' faces the moment I enter the cabin. Some have been getting worked up and angry that all of their well-timed plans are dashed. They are through waiting for some idiot who can't set an alarm clock! When they lay eyes on me, their expressions change instantly, from frustration to sympathetic terror.

I must look much worse than I did just four hours ago in my kitchen. People are clearly afraid that I might sit next to them and be contagious. A flight attendant picks up on it, too. Halfway through the cabin, she taps Amory on the shoulder and invites us with a beckoning finger to sit in first class where there are two empty seats. It may be generosity, but I believe that it's so they can close the curtain on me, the sideshow. They, too, appear scared that I might not make our destination, and they would rather not involve all the passengers. I'm not sure I want to fly first class after this, now being under the impression that it is the preferred place for a passenger to die.

No one says this, no one has to. All you need are a pair of eyes with average vision to see that this doesn't look good. I wish someone could tell the passengers that they can't catch the life-threatening sepsis that I have. What I have is locked up inside of me and is too busy trying to kill me to harm anyone else.

As we will learn at Mayo, I have a liver abscess and several separate pockets of fluid have formed in my abdomen. Within these are growing an overwhelming bacterial infection. I don't know this yet, because back in Boulder they only saw a single large abscess, one which they were going to puncture and drain. I was saved by Dr. Dughi's bold decision to nix their plan, based on her opinion that my CT scan had not been read correctly. She was right, as the doctors at Mayo Clinic quickly reveal that the abscess they were planning to puncture and drain was, in fact, my full bladder, while a staph infection in my liver, along with the sepsis, was the actual cause of my fever, pain and severe condition. This potential mishap is fully documented and is even now hard to read and come to terms with. It has become abundantly clear that staying in Boulder, a town that I love, for a single day longer would definitely have cost me my life.

I'm admitted through the emergency entrance of the Mayo Clinic's Saint Mary's Hospital. A wristband is quickly attached, I am placed on a gurney and an IV is put in place as I am swept downstream. This is how I'm pulled out of the river. The radiologist in charge of fishing me out has got an ultrasound device in her hand and is "looking" at the various abscesses that need to be drained and tested.

I thought I had already earned my doctorate in pain, but it turns out I was wrong. I am not sedated when the first of three syringes, each the size of a turkey baster and fitted with a large and frightening needle, is inserted straight through my lower abdomen, still tender from surgery, into a pocket of yellow fluid that is now being sucked back out into the syringe.

Nothing in my growing list of miserable procedures had prepared me for this experience. I'm thinking *that they can't seriously be doing this to me straight out, with no painkillers.* The high-tech procedure room that resembles a spaceship has just transformed itself into a medieval torture chamber.

I will myself to pass out or die, but I don't get my way. I'm screaming to the nurse on my left, "Oh, my God, are you *kidding* me? I can't do this! No! No way!" as though she will somehow put an end to this procedure. Instead, she helps the nurse on my right to hold me still, while giving me a true look of empathy, as the third nurse prepares the second syringe. In my weakened condition, like a gutted fish with a fresh set of stitches running straight down my center, it doesn't take much to restrain me. The searing pain that has just been imparted to my lower abdomen does part of the job, while the two nurses easily do the rest.

"Can't we give her something?" one nurse, seeing my agony, anxiously asks the doctor.

"Not right now. I need her with me, so she can hold her breath for that last draw. I need that needle placed right between those ribs," she replies. Turning a quick glance my way, she says, "Hang in here with me, and I'll get you through this as quickly as I can, all right?"

"I'd rather be *shot*," I answer, half crying, half moaning, but totally serious.

"Sorry, we don't keep any guns around here," she says, while remaining focused, with tremendous intensity, on her ultrasound screen.

The insertion of the third and thickest needle is the final frontier in pain, as it requires my cooperation. When it has, at last, made it between my ribs and into my liver, I glance across and down at the thick needle and the huge, clear syringe sticking out, and I think of the shaft of an arrow, just like in the old Westerns. I imagine a cowboy on his knees, gritting his teeth, sweating bullets, just like me. He's trying in vain to pull the arrow out, hoping that someone will have mercy on him and just shoot him out of his misery. No one shoots me; instead, they grab the shaft, pull the arrow out, tape me up and drop me back into the river.

I continue downstream, face up, ears under, mouth closed. I'm listening to a strange mixture of sounds: the quick, even huffing of my exhales through my nose, the occasional slow and labored swallow, the gurgle of gurney's castor wheels rolling beneath me. And I hear the ever-bubbly current, churning, its impartial voice taking the lead as I head in the only direction I can: down.

Finally drenched, shaking and exhausted, I'm hauled out of the water. I'm placed on land, but all that I can see is the tumbling current. They've left me way too close to the bank for my liking. I watch as large hunks of mud and rock break loose from the edge and disappear into the rolling water. I have to wonder if I, too, might vanish, when the precarious ground beneath me finally falls away.

Then, I look across the water at Amory, loving me. He is so terribly afraid, afraid that I might be carried away forever this time. He's sitting close to my bed; his wide, strong back angled forward, his elbows on his thick knees, both of his hands holding one of my limp ones. He wants to pull me away from this unstable edge, but he can't and it is hurting him. Watching me fade is hurting him. He's a strong, able man, but he sits bound to a stake, watching as his closest friend is slowly slipping over an edge that drops into eternity.

I don't like the story that seems to be unfolding in front of us. I don't like the story, or its tragic ending. So, closing my eyes, I write a new one.

My new team of doctors, safe inside a warm, dry cabin, somewhere close to my river, has begun to work up their diagnosis. Working with the fluid they've drawn from all suspect sites, lanterns burning deep into the night, seraphim hovering, they experiment with a series of combinations of antibiotics until the winning one is found, then administered. I am saved. The End.

In the story I write, I don't let them stop to do anything rational like sleep. I'm not even sure that I have totally sold myself on my latest story.

Although it seems to have promise, I can feel the cold, damp silt and gravel beneath me shifting toward the water with every hour that passes.

Each of these potentially final hours, I spend with my back to the thin curtain which divides my small room in half; behind it is a young girl my daughter's age who's given her kidney to save her mother. In contrast to my situation, she's heroically rescued her own mother and is happily recovering in her half of the room, which is packed with balloons, cards and flowers.

I'm failing to spare my roommate the sounds of my agony. Due to the sensation that a grater is being pulled from my throat while my abdomen is ripping apart each time that I vomit, I'm making a racket. I'm aware that she's over there doing her best to block out the horrible sounds of my intermittent vomiting and wailing. The volume of her TV goes *way* up.

The time that falls in between, I spend silently, looking deeply and steadily into Amory's eyes. My beautiful friend, my love and my most trusted confidant, the father of my children, has tethered himself to me with all the love he has. I'm hanging on to the invisible line that he has fastened around me and knotted, as only a sailor can, expertly.

This is when I consciously decide to make it. I can't let him watch this infection take me away, after the fight we've put in against the cancer. I don't want him to lose, too. I can't stand the thought of him without me and of me gone. I start to really hold on tightly to his love and to the fact that I'm still alive, right here, right now.

Looking at my Amory and all he represents, I know that I need to stay by his side. I imagine the hurt that he will personally have to feel if I don't make it. Worse still, I imagine the hurt he will feel for our children if he fails to bring me home this time. Then, as if my emotions for Amory are not enough, I peek at the thought of my children suddenly being without me. This combination is so profoundly painful that I close my eyes and go inside. I subject myself to a place even one level deeper. Within this place, I find my will.

I huddle there until I find my voice. Finally, amid the rubble, I find myself. Keeping my eyes shut, my focus tight and my intention clear, I say to the infection that is taking my life from me, "I *won't* let go. I *won't* give up. You *will not* beat me, because I want to live." The voice at the center of my spirit is my being, both thunderous and velvet soft. This is how one more time, this time with little hope and no energy, I decide to fight.

Cancer is like that. It takes us down to our final moments, then lets us come back, to look at our lives again. Our will to live is what we have. That will is ours to hold on to, so hold on. Hold on tight. Cancer develops character in us, the type of character which cannot be had by ease and good fortune. We learn that love is stronger than fear. We learn, once again, that we have to be torn down before we can be rebuilt.

A New Year

December 31, 2003

Until my introduction to hospital life, I had only previously seen these little plastic cups tucked inside the brown bag with the chopsticks that held the to-go dinner from my favorite Chinese restaurant. They were usually full of hot mustard, or sweet and sour sauce. Now, my 600-milligram pill, Flagyl, and an even larger antibiotic, Bactrim, are both sitting obediently on my tray in these same cups, waiting for me to make a move.

I'm more of a "one at a time" type, which is how I swallow all of the large pills I am given to take. The problem is that I can't manage to swallow even one of these horse pills tonight. I'm doing a perfectly good job of ignoring my meds, until my nurse pops into my room. He finds my blank stare squarely fixed on the tilted TV screen hanging from my ceiling. I'm waiting for the ball to drop in Times Square.

It's Tom, and he wants to know when I am going to take these two pills and actually swallow them. To my dismay, he doesn't look like he's planning to leave. So this time, I put both pills in my mouth at once and reach for my giant water cup with the Gumby green lid and the fat plastic bendy straw. Keeping my eyes on the screen, I boldly imagine myself gulping both pills down the hatch while not actually swallowing them.

My nurse is the biggest man I've ever seen outside of a boxing ring. But instead of his size being imposing, it lends him more of a gentle-giant aspect. "Big Tom," as I have come to refer to him, helps me at my lowest with tender grace. In the middle of the night, he'll help me out of my sweat-soaked bed. He will change my gown and then sit me in the recliner chair while he changes the wet sheets to dry ones. Never annoyed, he wraps a dry, warm blanket tightly around me. He tucks it in behind me, never allowing me to get chilled, while I wait for him to finish. This sweet gesture of making the effort to keep me warm touches me even now as I think of it. In a single night, he does this calmly, patiently, as many as three or four times.

Now, he's standing here and nodding large and slow. He's trying to encourage me with the satisfied smile that nurses get when their patients are about to take their meds and not just stare at them. A nurse likes checking things off the little list that he keeps folded up in his pocket.

Optimistically, as Dick Clark begins the countdown, I'm thinking to myself that *these are the last big pills that I will have to take this year.* "Ten, nine, eight," gulp, "seven, six, five," gulp, "four, three, two, one," swallow. "Happy New Year!" Amory chimes in along with the crowd in Times Square, ceremoniously holding up an unopened bottle of champagne. "We'll save *this* for a celebration in the future," he says, knowing that the Grande Dame and Lord Bactrim will have a deadly argument.

When Big Tom leaves, Amory lowers the rail of my bed and squeezes in beside me. Taking my frail skeleton of a body in his huge arms, he hugs me to himself. I feel his tears push his chest out and drop onto my forehead. I don't look up at him, because I know he'd rather I didn't. Anyway, I know why he's crying. We've actually *made* it to 2004. All of New York City seems to be cheering for us.

January 1, 2004

I used to just stand up and walk out of a place when I wanted to leave. Now, leaving is a five-day process. I've been through several combinations of antibiotics, and at last, the doctors think they have the right one. It takes a series of major events, and all sorts of doctors and nurses nodding in agreement with their own assessments, and signatures, lots of signatures.

Today is only the second day of taking all of my medications orally. I have to be able to do this for five days in a row before I can be partially discharged to the Khaler Hotel across the street. Once there, I'll have to manage for two more days before I can be released to fly home.

Now, everything that goes in enters the old-fashioned way, by mouth. No more anything through the nifty little tube leading to my vein. Until they remove my IV, I don't realize what a happy little device it really is. Now, instead of being left in relative peace, I'm provided a non-stop annoying parade of pills and liquids.

Big Tom brings in short cans of Boost and Ensure for nutrition. *Do they actually think that I will be fooled by these robust titles?* Anyway, these are for old people. Apparently, now that includes me.

"You can get vanilla if you want," he says. *I don't even want chocolate.*

"You can just take them." I counter.

"Well they're yours. You're payin' for 'em, so you might as well take 'em home with you."

"Okay. Just put them on the windowsill for me, will you?"

Big Tom does as I ask, leaving one behind on my tray along with a concerned sideways look that says, should I come to my senses, there'll be one to drink.

Upon closer inspection of the labels of the can he left behind, I find that it is full of sugar. I start to cry. *Don't they know, here in the hospital, that sugar feeds cancer as well as disables the immune system?* How can anyone recover his health?

From the paper menu that they send me in the morning, I check off tea, orange juice, rice, oatmeal, bananas and two scrambled eggs, for all three of my New Year's Day meals. Water is my main beverage, bottled, please. I don't bother to check a vegetable, since I've never seen a vegetable in here that even remotely represents the real thing. They are all poor imposters that come on the tray in an off-shade of the color that they're meant to be. The only exception is corn, but I don't order that since it's the hardest thing on the face of the planet to digest—that's the reason that God gave cows one stomach with *four* compartments.

My meds are so tough to tolerate that it is hard to keep anything down. Eating is not as easy as I had earlier imagined it would be. Back when I was self-righteously checking off this choice and that from my menu, I was saying to myself, *I'll never drink one of those.* Yet, now, every so often I look over at the cans of Boost that are collecting on my windowsill and the one on the end of my bed tray with a slightly more accepting attitude.

All I can think about, between running interference on pills and food, are my kids. I miss my kids so intensely that I don't think I can possibly make it through one more night here without them. I flip through the photo album of their pictures incessantly. I fall asleep with it opened in my lap or hugging it to my chest. I want to go home, right now. But I'll have to do what it takes to get my hall pass.

These two pills don't play well with others, so I take them fifteen minutes apart from each other. Cold water does not get along with anything, so I drink it at room temperature, or warm. Saltines are friendly. They become the staple of my dining pleasure. If a Saltine is suddenly too salty, a comforting graham cracker becomes my new buddy. This is the unraveling of the new code for putting things into my body. Mine is a body on strike, a body tired of continuous invasion by one thing or another, a body not wanting to co-operate. It becomes a game, directing my body to do as I will it to do. It is a game that I intend to win.

This is when I start talking to my pills. The disobedient ones that won't stay down don't count, as I soon find out the hard way. I will have to take them again. I realize that, as with anything that has a mind of its own, I have to tell my pills, and my body, what to do. I stare at the little pill cup. I stare at the clock. 8:01. I stare at the cup. I tell myself, at 8:05, *I will do this.* I take the pill from the cup. I hold it up and have a look at it from all sides. It is way too large to be called a pill, and too chalky. It doesn't have the pretty shiny coat, like a new sled, in a bright color, which makes it slide down your throat. I put it back in its cup on my tray, and start to talk to it. Clearly, I've not only lost a quarter of my body, but of my mind as well. I start to make a deal with this pill.

If I take you, you will stay down there and do your job. You will not make me vomit so that I have to take another one that looks just like you in thirty minutes. You will kill everything that is bad, okay? You will also kill everything that is good, but you will help me to get well. You are my friend. You are my friend.

"Flagyl, lawnmower of antibiotics, you are my friend," I say out loud. Placing it as far back on my tongue as it can go without making me gag, I suck up a mouth full of water. Face like a blowfish, I look up.

Amory's standing there, ever the romantic man, holding a white teddy bear and a red rose. He's peeking around the half-drawn curtain, the one that protects the wandering eyes of visitors from seeing a live skeleton on display. He is smirking, half laughing out loud at the conversation he has obviously just overheard. Water about to burst from the corners of my mouth, I gulp fast, half laughing, as I choke it down. I spew water all over anyway.

"There's no other way," I say, trying to explain my madness.

"Hey, tell your medicine anything you want," he says, relieved to see my sense of humor, if somewhat skewed, returning to me on this New Year's morning.

My desperation to get out of this hospital and home to my kids is making me do crazy things, but I'm finding out that crazy can be good and even healing. A heavy, month-long silence has just been broken by our laughter. Sitting here laughing with Amory is delicious.

It's still okay to laugh. In fact, it's better than that, because now I can hear the sound of my laughter for the beautiful music that it really is.

Now that I know laughter is a treasure, I'm going to dig it up and spend it on myself. If it heals one single moment for me, it's worth finding. It's also healing for the people I love to see me smile my real smile, if only for a moment.

The Fabric

"Y ou've never seen me like this, seriously. I just want you to know, so you won't freak," I'm telling my friend Kirsten, trying to describe my current appearance to her over the phone, trying to prepare her for the sight of me. Amory's gone home to the kids and to work, while she is flying out here to help me get through all of my tests and to take me home. By the time she arrives tonight, I'll be across the street at the Khaler Hotel, beginning my final days of being formally discharged.

"You always look good. I'm sure you're just a little thinner, buddy. Don't worry, because I'm not worried," she lightly replies, letting me know that either she's not listening or is simply unable to imagine that what I've told her is true. Either way, I know that she is definitely not ready for the sight that awaits her here in Minnesota. What she clearly doesn't know is that the friend she is coming to get is a different one from the person she last saw a month ago, both inside and out.

I can hear the other world in her easy tone, my old world, the one where everything works and nothing is a problem. This is the world where your friends look reasonably good even when they look bad, the world that I left behind when I flew out here hanging on to my life, the world that no longer includes me, the one I'm looking at through a frozen window, the one I'm just barely creeping back into.

I hear her knocking lightly while inserting the plastic key card and pushing the door open. I raise my right hand in a hello, since it isn't possible to raise my voice enough to reach across the small room. Her bag drops in a heap on her left foot as both of her hands simultaneously fly up to cover her open mouth. I can see the giant tears rimming her eyes as they fill with the painful sight of me. She looks across one empty double bed, in total shock, to the other one with what little is left of me lying in it.

"Oh, my God, buddy. Oh, my God," is all she can say before she pulls her bag in and lets the door slam shut behind her. Tentatively, she crawls up next to me. My bruised, emaciated arms are too hard to look at, so she takes my hand in hers, carefully, as if she might snap the tiny bones. Then she lays her head on the pillow next to mine and simply cries like a frightened child, refusing to look up.

"I tried, I tried to tell you," I'm saying quietly, setting my toothpick of an arm across her hip.

The night that ensues is rough. One minute Kirsten's helping me empty the vile container at the end of the drain that is coming from my liver. The container and tube are clipped to my nightshirt like a child's mitten. Next, she's running for the ice machine down the hall to fill my ice pack. In between, she's filling the bathtub with hot water where she sits me on the edge, to soak my feet in hopes of warming the shivers out of me. I cannot actually get into the tub due to my still freshly stitched front side.

We both know that, if tomorrow they decide to remove this pigtail-shaped device connected to a clear tube that is protruding from my torso, I can go home. We are both silently willing it to happen. She's adamant about giving me my pills on schedule, while also trying to coax me to get more than a cracker down my throat. This goes on all night with neither of us ever really sleeping. No friend should have to work this hard. I'm discovering a different aspect of Kirsten: the ability to power through a trying time with utter kindness.

"You missed your calling. You should really be a nurse," I tell her.

"I'd wanted to be," she says.

"Yeah, well, good thing you're not. You're so gorgeous you'd be giving the male patients heart failure and the women a complex." She rolls her light topaz-blue eyes, raising one eyebrow with that closed-mouth Kirsten smirk. She knows I'm absolutely right.

She calls room service almost every thirty minutes for some item that she thinks I can get excited about eating. I smile from my vantage point as each young waiter eagerly arrives, clearly having been informed by the one before him of the gorgeous blond babe ordering all the trays. I'm wondering by their thrilled, stunned expressions if they think the Cameron Diaz look-alike in the room under the name C. Host is in fact the actress. This becomes the most amusement I've experienced in a while. After three trays have gone cold, chocolate ice cream finally stands out as a great idea. She orders.

Seven minutes later, the waiter from tray number one arrives, out of breath, to deliver tray number four, and takes an unashamed gander at Kirsten as she leans over the table and signs the bill with an illegible flourish, further proof of her probable stardom. I can tell by his catatonic expression that Kirsten is probably the best thing that has ever happened to the room-service waiters in the history of the Khaler Hotel.

With the first spoonful of ice cream, I discover that I'm hungry, really hungry, and that I need to eat, but I'm trying to maintain some balance to keep each horribly strong medication staying down versus coming up. I finish the first dish of ice cream and find that I'm still hungry, so I discard my pious talk about not eating any sugar and we order a second round, a fifth tray.

"Buddy, you have to eat something real now, now that you've had dessert," she's telling me.

"Okay. If they pull this thing out in the morning and say that I can go home, I'll eat the biggest breakfast you can order me," I promise her, partly lying, just knowing that the smell of an egg will make me recoil from my word. Of course, she immediately brings up eggs. "Eggs. You need protein. Do you promise to eat eggs?"

"Yes...I will. If they let me go home, I'll eat eggs," I qualify, hoping that this snug bedtime story will put her to sleep, so she'll stop talking about eggs. I glance over and she is drifting off. I wish I could trade places and wake up in her body. I stay awake like that, wishing for different things, stupid things, for about another hour, and then I give up my childish game and fall asleep.

January 6, 2004

Kirsten's pushing me—and the body I woke up in—in a wheelchair, through the subway that connects our hotel to the Gonda Building. She gets me to each of my three appointments, and along the way, we find time to buy angora hats for our daughters, who are also best friends. It seems unreal, Kirsten pushing me in a wheelchair because I am too broken down to walk. In my old life, Kirsten is my hiking partner. We'd be tearing up the trails daily. I used to be that strong and able. This is definitely out of the ordinary. It's a wonderful thing to experience a friendship expanding, when so much else is falling apart.

Finally, the corkscrew of a device is going to be removed by a Dr. Leroy, an amusing man.

"I hope he knows how to get this thing out," I say in an aside to the nurse to my left. She starts to smile and says, "Well, he invented it, so he ought to do just fine."

"Seriously?" I ask.

"Yep," she answers proudly as he enters the room.

Another round chalked up to the doctors at Mayo Clinic. Dr. Leroy starts asking a lot of questions about where I'm from. Then he casts a distraction in my direction by telling a story to me about fly-fishing near Edwards, Colorado...I go for the bait, and in that same second when he sets the hook, he deftly removes the drain from my liver with no pain, just a little tension. I can finally breathe and move without wincing.

When they wheel me back to the waiting area, I'm smiling. I've got the closed-lips, satisfied grin of someone who knows she is about to get what she wants. Kirsten gives me a high five as I nod yes to the question that her raised eyebrow implies: "Are we going home?"

Once again, it's a long way from Rochester, Minnesota, to Boulder, Colorado. Somehow the miles and minutes pass, and finally Kirsten's helping me step out of the car into the driveway. It is painful for me to straighten up after sitting for so long. We move slowly, arm in arm, through my open garage and up two wooden steps into my laundry room. Amory's at work, and Chanel and Marco are in school, a fact that saves them from another of my pathetic entrances and gives me time to refresh myself before they get home. My mother is right there, holding open the door and smiling, shaking her head. I immediately scan the kitchen for William.

"Can you even believe this whole thing?" she says to us.

There is so much we aren't saying, my mother and I. We're on the same side of this emotional seesaw and cancer is on the other side. Our last moment together, where she was holding open the door of the idling car outside the Boulder emergency room, we were down, close to the ground, looking up at cancer. Right now, at this moment, where she's holding open a different door and I'm walking back in, we're up top, looking down at cancer. Can it be? Did we really go from up to down and from down to up, with that long, narrow plank teetering between us?

"Here's your mommy!" my mother chirps to William. I can tell that she's probably been preparing him for several hours for my return, and I'm grateful. He looks over from his high chair where he's picking up peas with his fat little forefinger and thumb. Automatically, he starts kicking his legs and smiling.

"Ma-ma-mama-mama," my baby says. I'm overjoyed, but beside his exuberant baby face, my mom, Kirsten and I all look exhausted and slightly regretful. We're the friends who are left to face the huge cleanup the morning after the big party. I look past the mess and exhaustion that my cancer has made and zoom in on William.

"Thanks a million, Kirsten, I can take it from here," my mother says, granting her permission for instant departure. Kirsten pulls out of the driveway with the forlorn look of a parent leaving a sick child at home. I try to call out to her but find that I hardly have a voice, so I give her a steady, thankful look.

I turn back toward William. He's bright-eyed and reaching his chubby little baby arms out and up to me. Pulling the tray out and lifting William from his highchair, my mother begins to try to hand him to me. Then she immediately calculates that, as I'm holding on to the counter for support, I won't be able to hold all twenty-four pounds of him while I'm standing up. I kiss his forehead and then the little roll on the back of his luscious little neck while she holds him close to me. I put my arms around him as though I am holding him while my mother supports his weight. Together, we both hold him like this for a few more seconds. Taking a conscious and deep breath, I begin to feel the meaning of this moment. My lower spine uncoils and relaxes.

"Well, here we go, I'm back," I say, like an unwelcome guest who's run out of gas one hundred yards down the road. I use the edge of the counter and then the backs of the kitchen chairs as my railing and slowly make my way to the couch where there's lots of padding. Taking a seat, I hold open my arms to William. He reaches for me enthusias-tically. This is the universal miracle of the bond between mother and child.

"Well, you said I'd get back home, and you were right," I finish. After that single sentence I am out of breath and of things to say. My mom's standing here like an angel over us, tired but satisfied that all of the missing pieces have been found and put into place, my puzzle once again complete. She sets her ninth and youngest grandchild, my plump healthy baby, into my lap. Then she tucks a blanket around both of us and I begin to cry just for being here, smelling his sweet baby head and feeling his silky hair beneath my chin. Sweet William is in my lap, back in my arms. For this precious moment we're all right where we belong.

Small children do not rely on words, but instead read all physical messages. Since they can't talk, they pay attention. I've begun to do that, too, in this foreign country of serious illness. William reminds me through his touch that actions replace all the words I'm looking for but can't find. He presses his head into my neck, his face toward mine, and rotates his left shoulder into me so that his arm is hanging straight down. The back of his hand is flat against me with his palm facing out, pushing away from the world and sealing us in together. With his other arm, he holds on to my left shoulder. Then, I feel his little fingers patting me just as I have done so many times to him, with an "It's okay...it's okay" in their rhythm.

My eyes, two sunken ships, glitter with a treasure of tears for the sweet, uncomplicated love of my baby.

Seeing

January 7, 2004

Possessing a passion for art and for writing, one thing I'm good at is looking. I have trained myself to observe, and I believe that I see quite a lot. It seems to me that there are two main ways to understand art. One is by visual analysis; the other is by trying to absorb its content through the history that surrounds it.

Once inside the privacy of my bathroom, after showering, I do what I have been so afraid to do: I look at my reflection. First, an impressionistic image appears through the steamed surface of the mirror. I push open the window a crack and the mist slowly begins to dissipate. At once, I'm grateful that I haven't seen a full-length mirror in about six weeks.

I do not recognize the body I now inhabit. I try to do a visual analysis of what I see, just as I would with any painting I am not familiar with. Next, I try to understand what I'm looking at, by methodically noting the history to which it is tied. Standing there, I take a look at what fighting cancer has done to my body. Now I know why there are only small mirrors in hospitals: Someone merciful was in charge.

I see a body just like the pictures in magazines and on the world news, a body that has been ravaged by starvation. I once saw a picture that was just that, a picture of someone else's skin and bones and misfortune. But *that* body was only a distant image, and while I felt compassion, I was not truly able to empathize. Now it's *my* cheeks that are sunken, my cheekbones high and prominent. I see a narrow neck holding up a head that appears far too large and completely out of proportion to the frail body supporting it. In fact, when the nurse weighed me, fully clothed, at Dr. Nagorney's office yesterday before I was discharged, I looked down at the ever-so-accurate digital readout and saw only two numbers: nine and seven. It reads ninety-seven pounds? Is that possible? That's how much my fourteen-year-old daughter Chanel weighs. *This is how ninety-seven pounds looks on my formerly voluptuous self?* No, this can't be. I promise myself that I will never obsess over losing ten pounds again. Now I would give practically anything to slap those ten pounds, plus another twenty, anywhere on the emaciated body I see in the mirror.

I can see not only my clavicle, but every tiny rib in what now appears to be an empty cage. Over the past few weeks, I have glanced down at my incision, the one that's been made to save my life, but I've never looked at it straight on. Where my ribcage slopes above my sternum, an incision begins. It is fifteen inches long and is being held together by twelve thin white strips of tape three inches across, running horizontally. Frankenstein's monster comes to mind. The newly added slanted double strips of tape over the incision above my liver, where the drain had been, does not help this image at all. Then, there are the bruises on my lower abdomen that were left by the syringe episode. These illustrate the beat-up way that I feel, with their unattractive display. My hips are no longer smooth, soft Botticelli curves but sharp, angular protrusions. My legs, once muscular, strong and defined, are now stick-thin rails with two round doorknobs where my knees used to be. There are three inches too many between my thighs.

Steadily, I continue observing my way along, tipping my head unconsciously, slowly, from side to side, as if preparing to sketch a nude model in a Fundamentals of Human Form drawing class.

My advanced course in skeletal structure begins here. No point in looking for muscle form or luster of any kind; it has all gone into hibernation. I begin by really looking at my hands, once long and slender, and I see an odd collection of bones, knuckles and veins. I was never one who wanted to see the complex vascular system that circulates my blood, but here it is on display.

There are innumerable bruises on the tops of my hands and on both forearms from twelve weeks of IVs blowing up and just IVs in general. I wonder if they will ever go away. The skin covering them is a mess of colors, various shades of yellow, rimmed with brown, green, blue and purple, that tells the tale of far too many procedures. This is a horrific study in color, so much so that I amuse myself and title it *Rebellion of the Veins* by Random Needles.

I leave those parts and follow the line from my elbows up to my shoulders. My once-elastic skin appears to be loosely draped over long, thin bones. Not only do I *feel* eighty, but here is the proof. My toothpick arms dangle, apparently attached by some means or other to form my shoulders, but they no longer look reliable the way they once did. I look away. When I think I can stand another round, I look again, now turning to the side, craning my head around to look at my backside. My shoulder blades now fit their name. I've never before seen my rib cage in back, nor the notch of each vertebra, now clearly visible. My God, the back of my pelvis, just the way I'd seen it in a college anthropology course. I am a skeleton...enough of that!

Stepping a little closer, I lean toward the mirror to take a better look at my face. I see my own eyes looking back at me and take comfort in their big, round shape. I see softness in an image where everything else is pointy, angular and unrecognizable. I see that the most intimate and lovely feature of all, my eyes, are still full of life, so I keep looking. Leaning closer still, now I can't believe what I *don't* see. There's no red. The whites of my eyes are just that, white—white as the white of two poached eggs. I've grown so accustomed to my bloodshot eyes, along with the rest of my carcinoid symptoms, that seeing the whites of my eyes absolutely stuns me. My heart leaps with unexpected joy. Yes! Yes! Yes!

Yes, I look like hell on two bony feet, with my frog-like hands gripping the edge of the sink for support, but my body must already be on the mend or my eyes wouldn't look this clear. Stepping back, I marvel again, in a horrified kind of way, at the train wreck of a body I now inhabit, reflected in this god-awful mirror. And I think, "Okay. I'm a bag of bones, but I'm still here."

Frankly, I look so terrible that I have to laugh. I laugh at my reflection a little, involuntarily raising my hand, covering my mouth, hiding my smile from myself, as if to spare my own feelings. I'm saying out loud to myself, "Oh, my Lord, you've *got* to be kidding. You look so bad, it's beyond trying to categorize, title and work with." Realizing the complete absurdity of this whole moment, I start laughing, I mean really laughing.

I'm laughing so hard that I have to sit on the side of the tub, which hurts my bony bum. Sitting there laughing, trying to hold my ugly stitches together because they feel like they're ripping apart. Then, the momentary thought of those coming apart and how ugly *that* would be just throws me totally over the edge. I'm laughing hysterically, in that "adolescents-together-with-the-cousins, eyes watering, mouths open, heads nodding up and down, no sound escaping but the random snort" kind of way. It hurts to laugh, it hurts to sit, and it hurts to look. Then I find everything about the way that everything hurts *funny*. Out of nowhere my mind jumps back to the final scene of a Monty Python movie that as teenagers we used to howl at. Somewhere in my deranged head, I start to hear the whistle of the funniest song of all time, "Always

Look on the Bright Side of Life." I can't stand it. More laughing...I try to stop...it *hurts*.

When I have finished laughing like a lunatic, teetering on the edge of insanity, I swing one bony leg over into the tub, then the other. Sliding down into it, I put my bath pillow under me for padding, since I have none of my own. Sitting there in the empty bathtub, I settle down and get really quiet.

I'm looking out of the window at the bare aspen and cottonwood trees. They all look dead. But they are merely waiting for springtime to come and invite them back into the world. Do the trees mean less to me, here, in the dead of winter? No, they mean more, so much more. For within those frozen branches, held within their brittle appearance, is the promise of supple leaves of bright apple-green which will shiver with the slightest breeze. I start to cry. Then I cry myself a big fat river of tears.

I'm still a woman. I'm a mother, a wife, a daughter, a sister and a friend. And, I'm even better at being all of these than I was before. Above all, I'm an inspired soul. While I may look barren, or even nearly dead to some, I'm alive inside; I am a spirit, as is all of God's nature. I can see by my museum-trained eye that somewhere, on a microscopic level, I am healing. Yes, I *am*.

Chef Marco

January 11, 2004

I t's only my fifth day home, and already I can see that they have figured out how to manage without me. This fact both amazes and hurts me. *They can get along without me?* Temporarily being in the body of an old person gives me a glimpse of feeling eighty at forty. Simply observing everyone else, mainly because there is little else that I can do, lets me in on why Grandma knows a lot more than we think she does.

Oddly, regarding my three children, I am feeling more like their grandmother than their mother. This seems like an emotion that goes along with feeling eighty. I adore my children, but there is little that I can do to keep up with them, so I watch with love and admiration as they run circles around me.

Kids stop forgetting things when no one's standing there to remind them. Marco and Chanel are taking on more and more responsibility daily, some of which, at twelve and fourteen, I wish I could spare them. Waking up by setting their own alarm clocks, making their own breakfasts, and then walking down the frozen road at 6:55 a.m. to catch the school bus on time is how they start their days. Amory has his hands full diapering and feeding William, then showering to leave for work. I miss being part of their morning routine, but I'm still so weak that I can hardly even creak down the stairs to say goodbye. As a once-capable mother, I hate this is feeling.

Because I still can't drive, I miss all the good stuff heard only by us, the parents who drop off and pick up. We get a lot of information from the backseat when the kids think we aren't listening.

When the school bus drops them off in the afternoon, I wait for them to come walking up the road, but by the time they reach the house, all of their after-school chatter has been spent. Even though we're together, it's too quiet. First off, I notice that they sit down and do all of their homework unassisted and without prompting. This fact alone makes me feel like an invisible parent. Will we ever have good times again?

Chanel inevitably has more homework than Marco, so she continues to work in my office at the end of the hall, while Marco often helps me make dinner. Marco can actually cook well, not just open a can of soup. Emeril goes "Bam!" and Marco goes online to Food Network to get the recipe. On one hand, I'm proud of his ability. On the other hand, the fact that he is cooking dinner makes me feel totally inept. I began teaching him to cook when he was six, but now the chefs on TV are taking the reins. With his natural gift, he has developed an impressive talent for his age.

Although I lay out the ingredients, I take an ice pack and lie on the couch, while he does the rest, and I call out the answers to his questions from there. Some nights, I'll sit at the kitchen counter and talk him through a pork-chop dinner, biscuits and all. When Chanel comes in, she puts William in his high chair with finger food, then sets the table. Since I actually need their help, I accept it.

I want to hug them both tightly, but with stick-thin arms and a sore incision, I can hardly take a plate from the cupboard. So I pat them on their backs, as any really old lady would do, looking them in the eye with love and appreciation.

Together with Amory, they clean up the kitchen after dinner, first arguing, like all siblings, over who did what last time. Then one or two nights a week, they will do all of their own laundry and their own sheets and towels. I call to them when either the washer or dryer has buzzed. It hurts me that I am unable to switch the loads, but they are simply too heavy. Folding is one of the few things I can still do proficiently. So I luxuriate in folding the laundry, which I accomplish with impeccable skill. What has happened to my life?

As I'm laying out the baby's sleeper and diaper on the changing table, Marco runs William's bath. I peek into the bathroom; Marco's pushing his sleeve up to test the final temperature of the water, swishing it in a circle with his hand and forearm. He's only twelve, yet I can see a man emerging from his gentle attention to William's safety.

"The bath's ready, Bird," he calls to Chanel, using her nickname.

"Come on, Bunny, let's take a bath," Chanel tweets to William in her porcelain voice, which is how she came to be called Bird from her first crystal cry at birth. She bathes him expertly, lifts him out, dries him off, then lotions, powders and diapers him, while I stand next to her playing "This Little Piggy" with his toes.

Down in the kitchen, Marco is making William's bottle, being careful to measure and mix the formula just right in a tall glass, warming it in the microwave to the perfect temperature and finally pouring into a bottle. Knowing he's doing this reminds me all over again, that if I didn't have cancer, after cooking dinner and giving him his bath, I would be nursing him.

I sit in the rocking chair and lay a folded fleece blanket across my belly to protect my incision, and Chanel sets William in my lap. Giving the bottle a final shake, Marco hands it to me. Sitting here, watching my children take over all of my jobs—something that I, Miss Super Capable, would never have dreamed of before cancer entered our lives—makes me speculate: Will having to roll their sleeves up and become part of a team at such a young age make Marco and Chanel able to handle life more competently? Or will these too-early burdens simply make them resentful?

I rock and wait patiently, hoping that Amory will take a long time getting things ready for morning before he comes up to lift William from my arms and put him in his crib. As I rock, I listen to Amory scrubbing the last of the pans then walk around the entry hall putting his things to the right side of the front door and locking it. I memorize William's forehead...eyebrows...closed eyelids and lashes...his soft baby hand wrapped around my index finger of the hand I'm holding his bottle with.

January 15, 2004

I cannot speak in a voice much above a whisper, so I am forced to wait for a lull in any ongoing conversation in order to ask about something or even to be heard at all. Once I have the floor, I notice that I can be involved for barely five minutes before I am completely drained. Then I use both arms to push myself up, as I stiffly rise from my chair.

Slowly making my way toward the staircase, I look up, recalling how a one-hour trail uphill to the Royal Arch used to be a reasonable hike; now these fourteen steps look like a major climb. Holding on to the banister, I pull as I take each step. This is a completely new experience: I used to bound up these stairs two at a time to grab some last-minute forgotten item. Once at the top, I shuffle slowly toward my room. Sitting on my bed, I decide which side to lie on, because once I am down, it will be painful to turn over or to get up.

Having eased myself down onto my left side, I let go. I'm exhausted. How will I ever make it back to my old strength? When will I be able to take care of my children the way I used to? I'm cold. I want to cover myself, but the blankets are bunched up at my feet, and it would mean me first pushing myself up and then trying to bend forward to retrieve them.

Here we go again. I'll have to call one of the kids to help me. Opening my mouth, I try to call to them. It is too difficult to raise my voice enough to get to the top of the stairway, where it would then have to drop down into the noisy living room into the middle of their card game and catch their attention at just the exact second of silence, which comes only rarely, between bursts of laughter and loud betting.

Instead of the sound of me calling out one of their names, I hear a deep, low, painful moan escape my lips. I begin to weep. This is another kind of weeping altogether, the kind that any mother who has had to come to rely on her children will know the sound of. I want to take care of my kids, not have them taking care of me. I'm *so* angry, I *hate* this stupid cancer! I don't want to call my kids to *help me* anymore; I would rather lie here freezing. So I do. I cry myself to sleep.

Cancer is like that. It teaches you humility. If it hasn't happened already, you might find that this might be a good time to put your ego away. Doing this is going to lift a big burden from you. It is better to accept the condition you are in, so that you can recognize the small changes for the better, when they happen. Cancer can make a person feel old quickly. But have a sense of humor—older people do. They know it makes things easier. It's okay to laugh about your feeble state. Cancer or not, being younger and stronger is what we all dream of.

Between Us

January 20, 2004

When I feel the blankets being pulled over me, I open my eyes to see who is bestowing this kindness upon me. It's my mother. She has brought a glass of water and, bending the straw, she holds it to my lips. After I've had a long drink, she flips my pillow to the cool side before I lay my head back down, and this makes me cry again. This time it's because I know that at seventy-six, she should be the one resting. I should be taking care of her.

"I have most likely shaved five years off your life, Mom, with all of this." *One year for each of the past five weeks of worry and work.*

"Now, that's all right, don't you worry about me, just see if you can get better so you can take care of that baby," she says.

"I will...but how will I ever lift him out of his crib again? He's getting bigger faster than I'm getting stronger."

"Oh, you'll catch up to him. You'll see."

"Well, I've lost thirty-four pounds—how can I gain that back?" I ask, truly concerned. "I can barely eat, Mom. You know that."

"Well, I don't know. Now, I'm so fat that I need to go on a diet. It's too bad I can't just give it to you," she says. We both smile.

"I'd take it, believe me. I'd trade with you, and *be fat,* in a minute. I wouldn't say it's a party to be stick thin and have cancer," I tell her. "But *you* wouldn't want to trade with me."

"Oh, yes, I would. Take your cancer so that you could be well? I'd do it in a minute. What do I want with more time? Now I've already lived my life, but you're young yet and those kids need you."

Up to that point, she'd been walking around my room, picking things up and simultaneously folding a basket of laundry. But now, her feelings stopped her at the end of my bed. She paused there, holding the bedpost and looking at me deeply, binding my heart to the sadness in her eyes. "Oh, I'd trade with you, honey, that's for sure."

Is she really saying this? That were it an option, she'd be completely willing to forsake her own life to save mine? These are the dormant secrets within the heart of a mother. They are rarely spoken. They are not meant to be. That my mother is expressing this to me now must mean she senses the end to be very near for me.

This is one of those extraordinary moments I'll never forget. My mother's desire to save me is so honed and clear that I can feel her kneeling beside me, untying the knots that bind me to the rails of this track I'm tied to. It's true—because of her love for me, she is willing to free me from my burden and take it on herself.

Inside a mother's love resides a strength unlike any other. I know that I would feel the same way if one of my children were as sick as I am. But because I'm so worried about the outcome for my own kids, it has never occurred to me how deeply my own mother longs to see me well again. How uncanny that we are both afraid for our children at the same time.

I am overwhelmed with a surge of emotion that contains within it the history of every mother terrified that love would not be enough to save her child, not even her will to trade her own life. I can feel the preternatural anguish of every mother trying to will her very spirit into the body of her dying child...*anything, God...just take me and bring her back*. Through a knowledge that can only be gained in times of terrible sorrow, I feel a deepening and broadening of empathy for that grieving mother.

I know I will never again look at a painting of a mother watching over her mortally sick child without thinking of this astonishing moment.

"Now, you'd better try to sleep a little. I'm going to give the kids their dinner," she's saying as she closes my door.

I pray for my mother's broken heart to mend, while at the same time, I'm stuck with the realization that the only way to fix that broken heart will be to outlive her. I hope that I can do that. But from this bed, my pain meds magnifying my every emotion, it all looks grim. What distance remains between me and the river?

Seamlessly the early evening blue light of winter fills the sky. Its color intensifies and deepens as portly snowflakes lazily pirouette down, lifting and falling. My thoughts follow in big, slow circles, drifting down to sleep.

The Elephant

January 23, 2004

Cancer does a good job of directing a lot of people's conversations to the subject of religion. It might have to do with the point at which a person who hasn't seen me for a while comes onto my scene and notices that I look nearly dead. This has a way of making him worry about what will happen to my soul if I die. Or, more precisely, what will happen to *his soul* if I die and he didn't try to save me.

Cancer just might throw the idea of God directly into the center of things, making Him the elephant in the room. I'd say that, cancer or not, it hasn't turned out to be a good idea to hash out my views on religion with people I'm close to, unless I'm in a boisterous bar, where at least half of what I say can't be heard.

Various well-meaning people in my life have attempted to convert me to their religious beliefs in order to make sure that I don't end up a wandering spirit without direction when my number is finally up. They see my illness as an invitation to straighten me out. My having cancer is proof to them that I have "issues" which need fixing. Cancer has made me the target of an amazing array of unsolicited advice as to my spiritual well-being.

These conversations generally go in one direction, then end up sitting there like a giant boulder in my path, making me feel as if I'm not going to arrive anywhere anytime soon. This is not the first time that this has happened in my life; it's just the first time since I've been sick that I've had to look at how incredibly disturbed my having cancer has made the people around me feel.

Right now, I don't want to waste my energy trying to find common ground with anyone but myself. For healing to happen, the light of energy is what I have to protect.

These "religious episodes" involving family and friends are not completely without benefit. They let me in on the fact that cancer has a blackout effect. Now that I have been immersed in total darkness, I observe the light in a much different way. I know now that light is a gift, one that allows me a deeper spiritual understanding. I do not want to obscure any of it by choosing to become involved in unnecessary dialogues. I want to absorb all of the light possible right now, so that if cancer shoves me back into the churning river, I will have something to keep me afloat.

I've come a long, long way from the bend in the river where it was pitch-black and sucking me under. I was alone, and the road back has been ragged. I've seen that some rocks in the road just sit there like large elephants. Better simply to notice those, walk peacefully around them, and smile.

Feeling

January 31, 2004

I met Erlinda at St. John's Catholic School in the fourth grade, when we were just nine years old. Having been my friend for thirty-one years, she's seen me in nearly every stage of my life, physically and emotionally, but living in Sacramento spares her from seeing me like this.

Alone in the house, a rare thing these days, I call Erlinda to wish her a happy birthday. I'm instantly calmed to hear her voice and to picture her family, her three kids and her husband, Mike, who is also healing from cancer.

"I'm doing much better and it's really kind of a triumph that I've made it through the first month of this year. I'm just so happy to be home. I have to say, though, that it's a drag not being able to drive," I tell her.

"What? I'd go nuts!" she says.

"I haven't driven for three months now. I'm trapped. It reminds me of how we were at fourteen or fifteen when we had to get our parents to take us everywhere. I can definitely relate to feeling like a teenager, but at least *they* can walk. I can barely do that."

"Remember when we were like ten or eleven, taking the number-six bus down 8th Avenue from Capitol Hill all the way downtown to Woolworth's? Remember splitting the grilled cheese at the lunch counter? We'd buy our dolls clothes, or a goldfish or something else." We reminisce together about the innocent times we had known growing up.

"Even though it was Denver in the seventies, can you believe that our mothers let us do that?" she asks me.

"I know, can you imagine? We *could never* let our kids do that now."

I've mustered up a little pep from just connecting with the outside world and from chatting with my old friend for a few minutes. After we hang up, I light the stove and start to boil some water for tea. Five minutes later, when reaching toward the back burner of my stove to lift the steaming teakettle and fill my cup—a simple act that I have done without thinking a thousand times in the past—I discover the most unbelievable thing: I cannot lift it, this shiny kettle, half full of water. My body is that weak. *No.*

I am flooded with a surreal sense of disbelief. I sit down painfully on a wooden chair, whose woven-straw seat I had never noticed was hard before. I am skin and bones. I lay my head on my arm and shut my eyes. The inside bone of my right elbow presses uncomfortably under the weight of my head on the wooden table. It seems as though all of my efforts to pick myself up, to feel a moment's relief, to enjoy Erlinda's voice and her laughter, lead to tears. I'm tired of tears. I want them to stop, but they keep coming.

I find myself having to rely on others to help me with things that one never even considers: opening the inside lining of a box of cereal, pushing a grocery cart, lifting my baby from his crib, handing my teenager her backpack, lugging wet laundry out of the washing machine, even pulling on my lucky boots. Simple everyday actions have become mountains to climb.

I want to suffer privately, but I can't, because for the most part my house is constantly full of people, people I need. I can't walk far enough down my road to get the mail, much less to get away. I am grateful for all of the help, yet I want to take my house back. I not only want my privacy, my house and my children back, I want the little things back, too, such as my once-womanly figure which filled out a dress, dinner dates with my husband, where I look pretty and can actually eat, or even just sit, for longer than ten minutes. I want to drive, to blow my hair dry, to pull the freezer door open, to reach above my head for something in the cupboard, and at the risk of sounding insane, even to go to the grocery store, *alone*.

I sit here with my head down, tears streaming over the random wishes parading through it. Just as suddenly as a small fire is taunted by a fierce gust of wind and explodes tenfold, my tears ignite into an angry rage. I let out a primal scream. A scream I've never heard before. It doesn't scare me, though, it just fuels me on. Knowing that no one can hear me invites me to scream louder. I'm angry, angry that cancer has pretty much taken away all it can, including my being able to make a simple cup of tea without having to involve someone else.

With my right arm, I sweep an impressively folded stack of towels off the table, onto the floor. Their unsatisfying, silent collapse enrages me further. Pushing up from my chair, unable to tolerate its unbearable seat of woven straw one more second, I try to throw it down, but it just sits there. The chair wins without a fight. This makes me crazier. Looking across the kitchen at my stove, I decide on that teapot. I hobble toward the stove to grab it. I'm going to take it…and hurl it…as far as possible…into the field off the deck of my kitchen! Thrusting my arm toward it, I stop. My eyes squeeze shut, my mouth opens with a sharp inhale. Clenching my fists, I stop breathing. A single stab of pain sears my abdomen and slices straight down through my groin, simultaneously getting my full attention and reminding me that the condition I'm in is what sent me into this rage in the first place. *I'm pinned down to a body that I don't like. Weakness is overwhelming my sense of dignity.*

Gritting my teeth, and panting like a wild animal in pain, I sink down to my knees, which grind harshly against the rigid wood floor. Resting my forehead in my palms, the only soft surface I can find, I cry like a frustrated child. I stay there staring at toast crumbs around the legs of William's high chair. I don't want this, I don't want it! I want my old life back. I *want* my old life *back!* When will the healing happen? When?

The Winding Path

"A minute for every second. What does that mean?" I ask Dr. Gottlieb after I've explained my delayed arrival. *That's sixty to one—have I become sixty times slower than I was? It sure feels like it.* He is as quiet as usual, having no need for hasty conclusions the way I have.

His office, located on the side of a small hill, took me *ten minutes* to reach by walking up the winding path to the front door. I had to stop *five times* on my way up. About the fourth time I stopped, I was shaking my head, totally unwilling to accept that this was *me*, struggling along a small path that I normally waltz up in *ten seconds*.

"Your body, the well, has run dry." He pauses to stretch his answer. "You can fill it back up, but it will take time. You'll need to be patient."

Great. I kind of knew that he would say that. He's right. But we already know that patience is not my strong point.

No matter how badly I want to snap back to the old me, that's not the way it's going to happen. It's been a month since my last Mayo visit, and at ninety-seven pounds, it feels like there's so little of my body left to work with that I don't know exactly where to begin. But I figure that the new me, after treatment, with less cancer or no cancer, is really the only place to start.

Being an athletic outdoors girl, I have a sense of somewhere to begin with my body at least, but my emotions are fine and tangled, like fishing line in an ungainly mess. The only way to go forward is to cut the line and start with a fresh end, so I nip myself free of dealing with the emotional mess for the short term, knowing that eventually I will have to sit down and untangle my feelings as well. For now, though, I'm going to concentrate on my physical state.

Some doctors see beating cancer as strictly chemical warfare, to be gotten through and dealt with. And a number of them say that nutrition has very little if anything to do with beating the disease. But cancer or not, nutrition has everything to do with the body repairing itself. I do know that much. And I still feel the need to re-educate myself on nutrition, vitamins, minerals, teas and herbs.

Having completely fallen apart physically, I have to take miniature steps to begin with. Comparisons aren't really useful. They truly fail to serve in the healing process, so the first thing I stop doing is comparing myself to others, on any level.

I call the Boulder Book Store, and they put the seven books I've ordered on cancer, the immune system, nutrition and healing all under my name in the usual spot, at the desk in the children's section.

"Here you are, book delivery!" Amory announces happily that evening when he walks into the house.

I begin to look through the table of contents of each book, slowly, dreading all of this new information. How will I get through it? I'm intensely interested, but I feel overwhelmed. I am going to try and coax my immune system back into full form.

As it turns out, the right nutrition has everything to do with my gaining not only weight, but peace of mind. So I read on, making notes and laying out what will become my map back to essential health.

I decide to train my body back to life, one minute at a time, and I want to see each of those minutes as they pass.

"You know I don't like anything digital, but check it out, Amory, I bought my first digital watch today," I tell him, pleased with myself.

"Nice," he says with a wry smile, knowing that I'm aware of the way it looks clunky on my bony wrist.

I start by walking ten loops around the main floor of the house. I add the stairs to that. After several weeks, I feel ready to head outside—I need the fresh air, and I'm restless. The first day I start with three minutes. I walk down my road for exactly three minutes. Then I stop, turn around, and walk home.

Six minutes—aha, I can do this.

I notice that six minutes become ten, and then ten become twenty. When I hit twenty-five one way, I'm walking a mile from my mailbox to the corner. The days Sara joins me are soulful. Sometimes this means tears, other times frustration and fear, but she's right beside me for all of it with her gentle spirit. Her friendship feels like the cool shade of an old tree.

"Hey, I walked to the corner and back today. Two miles," I tell Amory in a satisfied voice when he comes home that evening.

"Good for you! Good job! See, you're going to get strong again. You keep walking and then you can start hiking again."

While I'm walking my way toward strength, I decide to enlist the talents of Dr. Gao, an expert in Chinese acupuncture. Thus begin my biweekly, two-hour-long treatments to stimulate my immune system and my chances of getting rid of the tumors on my lung and spleen. It might just work.

I don't enjoy all of this fussing over myself. It's a total bore. But I vow to stick to this "beating cancer with my nutrition-walking-acupuncture regime" for three months. Then in July, the masters at Mayo Clinic will unveil my condition once again with a CT scan and a series of lab results. I tell myself it's worth a try.

Healing my body is a long, arduous labor of love. Noticing my body, accounting for what it needs in order to right itself, while trying to remain patient, is a challenge. I want to give myself every chance of winning, so this is how I march the scrap of a body I have left, humbly and step by step, back into my life.

Thinking

Somehow, in spite of all of the support of the people who love me dearly and are there each day, I'm back to the beginning. I'm back to feeling alone. How can I keep my head up? How can I keep taking the extraordinary pile of vitamins that I've combed through seven different books to research so thoroughly? At this point, it seems highly unlikely that vitamins will prolong my life. How can I keep anything in perspective?

Right now, my well-thought-out and clean diet full of lean protein, organic fruits and vegetables is beginning to look like a fool's dream. As usual, a painting pops into my head. I picture my profile transforming itself into one of the four seasons, as Giuseppe Arcimboldo's 1573 allegorical portrait *Summer*. It's an amusing piece, in which the subject's face and head are a compilation of fruits, vegetables and grains: peach for a cheek, mushroom cap for a forehead, cherry for an eye, cucumber for a nose, ear of corn for an ear, peas in a pod for teeth, garlic for a jaw line, pear bottom for a chin and so on. Even his fetching jacket is made of golden wheat, with the artist's name and the date cleverly woven in. Yes, that's me all right, a perfect portrait of all of the delightful and abundant foods that the earthly gardens have to offer.

I picture my head made of vegetables and a noose around my neck. As I'm standing on the scaffold, waiting to be hanged, I find myself wondering if a different kind of rope might solve my problem. What kind of thinking is this? Desperate thinking, that's what kind. Will a new variety of rope keep me from hanging? No. And this is about how much credibility I'm giving my vitamins this morning. Also, I am so steeped in green tea that I think my skin is beginning to take on the lucky-leprechaun hue. But is my chakra-correct, chi-inspired, supercharged diet really the currency I need to buy myself more of the future? Am I selling myself my own absurd short stories again?

This kind of hideous thinking invites panic to my front door, and when it knocks, I want to run out the back, down to my local pub to eat a pile of hot, salty, French fries and down them with a pint of beer. While I'm at it, make it five pints—to help with that extra weight I'm trying to put back on—accompanied by several shots of anything that will knock the sense out of me. It's true, I am having destructive thoughts, but as cancer will dictate, now is not the time to drink. So I call my doctor.

"This whole deal is definitely too intense," I'm telling Dr Sitarik. "Can you refill my prescription?" I ask. I want the same anti-anxiety pills that he had prescribed before my surgery, an attempt to help me to dull the extreme nature of the emotional experience that I was having. The one where I couldn't sleep and couldn't feel my legs, the one that I'm having again, regardless of the fact that now I only have two known tumors. As all of us with cancer have figured out that where there is "known" there is also "unknown." Our doctors seem to understand the significant stress that this fact can cause us, and so they prescribe the right dose of the appropriate medication to calm what is left of our ravaged nerves. They know that we will require our nerves to be steely to get through this.

This is the pill that I will take when the mortality factor gets right up in my face and I can't see much else besides my funeral. This pill lets me ride in the backseat for a while, so that I can look out of the window at the landscape going by without having to see the road right in front of me, the one that leads straight to my own grave.

My family and friends don't want to know this, but this is the kind of stuff that crosses my mind because I'm the one with the cancer. I'm glad that they cannot look inside my head, and are thus spared the little vignettes that cancer plays on the big screen in my mind: *private showings, patients only.*

I have no doubt that my brother-in-law Jack has seen these films. Despite his tendency toward quiet, Jack remains, for me, the one member of my family who really gets it. After surviving cancer twice, I guess he must feel that he's at the end of his cancer road, because he bestows upon me a talisman, a weasel about two and a half inches tall, carved out of turquoise, standing on its hind legs. He explains that the weasel has seen him through both of his fights, so now the weasel's going to watch over me.

It's an odd gift to be sure, but Jack, being an artist, has the ability to observe things in a way that most people can't. He senses the layers, and so do I. At times, I'm aware that we see them together, but we never decide to talk. Talking isn't always as useful as people think.

While at times quiet makes me uncomfortable, I'm becoming more and more grateful for it. I'm beginning to feel that we might all benefit from using fewer words.

At least I've already come to realize that any variety of incessant talking—including the type in my own head in the form of non-stop thinking—seldom resolves any issue the way that listening to the sound of my own breath can. I hope to find someday that I have indeed grown wiser as well. Incidentally, if you actually listen to your breath, you can't "think" at the same time...isn't that delightful? This is perhaps one small piece of what the enlightened guru knows about the virtue of silence.

* * *

Cancer is like that. As we go along with this disease, we learn that a pill may ease things now and then. But we know it is only a temporary fix and that the truth is that we're all we've got. We can order the offending words, which make up those grainy little black and white movies, out of our heads. You alone can do this. Take a deep breath and invite your solitude in, as close as possible. Nestle into it, take yourself there, and breathe. Find the quiet and settle into it like a seed in the warm, dark earth. Honor it for the strength of its darkness, for the hidden space it provides. Have faith in yourself and take shelter there. Trust that spring will come. You can be in the dark for a while. You can look at this, at your possible death. You just about have to, in order to revisit your life. You have yourself, and you are everything you need.

Wishing

March 11, 2004

"D on't miss any," I'm saying to my kids in the kitchen, as I hand over two packs of the standard, multicolored variety of birthday candles.

"Mom. We won't. Just *let us* do it," Marco frets.

He's spreading icing on a double-layer chocolate cake that we've all come to treasure on our birthdays and any other time we can give him a reason to bake one. The secret is how he takes a Betty Crocker devil's food cake mix then adds a stick of butter to it. Butter improves everything. Then he whips up chocolate icing from the recipe on the back of the Hershey's cocoa can, more butter.

While he and Chanel are dripping wax all over the top while lighting the candles, my mind takes a long walk into the future. I go ahead and write myself another indulgent short story, with a happy ending.

I'm sitting at a table set with the finest linens, crystal and silver, and a china tea service, upon which hand-painted butterflies abound. In front of me are my favorite champagne and a fancy cake of three layers, with pale pink fondant, topped with roses, candy pearls, and seashells, and seventy candles all aglow! My personal triumph. I'm looking at my children and grandchildren. Then they're singing me "Happy Birthday." I smile quietly to myself, because I'm here, a long, long way from there. The End.

* * *

Then, back in my dining room, I look across the glow of the forty-one candles on Marco's sweet cake into Amory's eyes. We exchange a glance that says, "We've made it this far, let's keep going" and smile. Before I blow them out, I close my eyes and get my wish ready. I wish one day to be seventy.

"Did you make a wish, Mom?" Marco asks.

"I sure did!" I answer as I pull that wishing candle from my cake and tuck it away, picturing myself placing it at the top of my cake twenty-nine years from now.

Then I open a small gift, beautifully wrapped, from Amory's parents. I start to cry when I remove the lid. Inside the first box I see another: an enamel box, the kind that I collect. Cobalt blue with tiny gold stars all over it. In the center, the message reads: *Believe in Miracles.*

Immediately, this box becomes a treasure because of the love with which it was given, and as a reminder that anything is possible. Miracles are possible. Apparently, my mother and father-in-law think so, too. When I open the gold-hinged lid, a single gold star is painted inside. I pull my blue and white candle stub from the back pocket of my Levi's and place it in the box. Then, I actually believe, if only for that one precious instant, that I will get my wish.

In this small moment, I feel that my hopes might in fact come to pass, and in that feeling, happiness is mine. Who decides my future, I'm not sure, but I do know that I decide how I want to see it. It's okay to feel some happiness when it happens to spring up naturally. It's okay to dream a little, to let in a wish or two. I want to believe in miracles. Someone's got to.

Doldrums

April 20, 2004

Contrary to my own good advice about anything, I am now under a cloud that just won't lift. I'm a person who used to think that smelling a fresh lemon was enough to pull a person out of the dumps, but this is different. Having just returned from Mayo Clinic ten days ago where I've had my three-month postoperative CT scans and checkup, I'm not bouncing up and down.

I pretend that I'm nobody's mother and watch old movies all day. It's Hitchcock for me this week, so the queue is *Rear Window, Vertigo* and *Psycho.* Is Alfred trying to tell me something? Next, I watch *Rope.* I decide I'd like to strangle the person who said that life starts at forty. I don't agree.

My in-laws, a lovely and uplifting pair, have gone back home. They had come to visit and lend support. It seems that since their departure, I've hit the doldrums. I have not left my house for the past three days, my bedroom for the past two, and I'm not considering doing so any time soon.

I want to drop into the isolation that I feel. It's more than that. I want to disappear, to become the isolation. My tremulous sense of loneliness makes me think of Shelley's "man-monster" in *Frankenstein.* I think about the way that he can't find his way out of the woods and into society, the way he can't ever really be whole. The way his body has been brought from death to life. The terror he feels at being chased by the townsfolk, something evil and collectively more powerful than himself, makes me begin to weep. This is exactly how I'm feeling about having cancer. With its torches and pitchforks, it chases and terrifies me. Yet I'm unable to turn and talk to it. It only wants to kill me. That is all.

I close my eyes and begin to replay a conversation in my head, the one I had with Dr. Nagorney eleven days ago...Dr. Nagorney comes in to review my scans with me. He is followed by his quiet, attentive entourage of residents, who press themselves into a corner and try to be invisible while paying close attention to our interaction.

"I don't see anything new," he begins.

"Oh, wow. Great," I interrupt him, feeling my spine lengthen with my exhale.

"I still see the tumor in your spleen, that we didn't remove, and the small one on the lung...that, for now...we're leaving as a marker."

Thrilled that he sees nothing new on my scans, I feel a certain kind of bravery taking the place of the worry that I have felt up until now.

My brave self asks, "So will it just stay like this? Because I feel *really* good and it doesn't seem to be spreading, right?" I am chipper, and waiting for a green flag to celebrate the stabilization of this crazy disease. Instead, what I get is an answer I wasn't prepared for, an answer that sends me down through the rabbit hole, down a hundred floors with lightning speed to the dark basement where I will have to start to dig myself out once again.

"No, it won't stay like this," he says quietly, as though turning down the volume on what he is saying will make it impossible for me to hear and I will be able to go home as happy as I was thirty seconds ago.

"No?" I answer. "What do you mean?"

"Well, it comes back. It's the nature of this disease, of carcinoid." He pauses. "It comes back." Silence shoves itself into the tight space like a splinter.

"Well, that's not what I thought." I panic, hearing the child's voice cracking open the room, sealed shut by clearly well-informed adults, all of whom already know what I'm *just now* finding out.

I hear a child who feels betrayed. The child to whom someone, anyone, should have found a way to explain that she doesn't get to leave the maze she thought that she was finally nearing the end of. That child starts to cry tears for which no one has an answer, tears from which there are no safe havens. I can barely even see Dr. Nagorney through the thick wall of salt water that separates us.

"What should I do?" I hear the child asking him, shattered, as he kindly offers me the box of Kleenex.

"Just go on back home to those Rocky Mountains, and enjoy your beautiful family. Enjoy feeling good, and eat lots of ice cream. We want to see you gain some more weight, okay?" he says with a genuinely warm smile.

What else can the man say to someone who is on the slow boat toward her eventual death from a cancer with no cure? I try to think about what else he might have said if I had written this script. As I wait for the elevator, instead of following through with that thought, I switch to thinking about the meaning of the word "elevator." I decide that since I am not feeling "elevated," the elevator is not doing its stated job. I hate elevators.

Now in the lobby, I walk through the giant revolving door of the Gonda building. Still on my elevator roll, I notice for the first time the irony of the revolving door. With that thought I go straight over to my hotel, where I hope to smother these annoying observations by sticking my head under a pillow.

When I get to my room, I crawl into the bed fully dressed, right down to my lucky boots. Although I'm wearing a knee-length coat and have a hat on, it's no relief for the deep chill that I feel. I pull the thin and ugly floral polyester bedspread completely over my head and tuck it behind the low, wobbly headboard to make a tent. I'm going to stay in here until the maids come and kick me out, or until I can think of what to do next.

Three seconds later, Marisa's calling. It figures. She must hear the river, must sense that I'm back in the freezing-cold water again. But this time I can't pick it up. I don't want to hear myself say what I know.

Next, I see "Home" flashing across the screen of my cell phone. I don't pick that up, either. I tell myself that I'll call Amory when I know what has just happened, when I know what to say. Now that I am hiding under the blankets all alone, I know that I should have allowed Amory to come out here with me. I had insisted that he stay at home to greet his parents when they arrived last night for the Easter holiday weekend. I was so sure that this was going to be so quick and easy. "I will go and come right back," I told him. "No problem."

I can't tell all of them what they just told me. Or does my family already know this about carcinoid, that it comes back? Am I the only one who thought I was coming to the end of this thing? If I had known this before my surgery, would I have gone through with it, knowing that it would come back so that I could have more surgery? How many more surgeries will I need? *What?* I have to live like this for the rest of my life, with cancer, with carcinoid tumor as a permanent part of my list of things to get rid of? I won't ever get to be cancer free? Why didn't they tell me this?

Deep inside of my tent, I open my cell phone, illuminating my little cave. I hit D and begin scrolling the "doctors section" of my phonebook, Dr. Diagnosis...Dr. Second Opinion...Dr. Anxiety...Dr. Keeps Track of My Cancer in Boulder...Dr. Keeps Track of My Cancer at Mayo Clinic...Dr. Echocardiogram...Dr. Eyesight...Dr. Teeth...Dr. Braces for My Kids...Dr. Balances My Meridians...Dr. Mammograms and Pap

Smears and...Dr. Pull Me out Of the River, Dr. Nagorney. I click and press Send.

"Good afternoon, Dr. Nagorney's office," his secretary answers with pep.

"Is Dr. Nagorney in, please?" I ask in a barely audible voice.

"He is, but he's not taking calls right now," she says sweetly in a singsong Friday-afternoon voice.

"I'm...pretty sure he'll take mine," I whisper in a crackle, trying not to cry. "Would you mind telling him that it's Carrie Host?" I manage, my voice lackluster and without expression.

"Yes, just a minute."

The next voice I hear is his.

"Yes, Mrs. Host?"

I don't try and sound upbeat or even open with common novelty. I just ask the question that was last on my list.

"Why didn't you tell me that it would come back? Why didn't you tell me that?" the child asks, completely sincere in wanting to know the reason, isolated in her tent.

"I don't think you asked me about that aspect of it until today," he says slowly, pausing before continuing, "I truly don't believe that anything would have been gained by telling you when you were at your lowest point, right before your surgery. Knowing this would not have been helpful to you during your initial recovery."

I stay quiet, waiting for more.

"This isn't information that would have helped you three months ago," he finishes intelligently, unapologetically. What he's saying rings true, so I agree that does make sense; he's right.

"Okay, thanks for taking my call."

"We'll work with this," he adds in a fatherly fashion.

"Okay."

"I'll see you in July," he confirms.

"Okay."

"Hang in there," he ends off.

"Okay."

Once again, the river has no banks and time has no edges. You can't reach out to touch anything, as you float down, to give yourself a sense of its passing.

According to the clock on my phone, it's already been over an hour and it's now 3:11 p.m. The maids still haven't come. Maybe they don't know that I've already checked out.

Suddenly, I want to be home something fierce. I crawl out of my tent and make my way to the lobby, in a numb blur, where the shuttle will arrive in twelve minutes to take me to the airport. I don't want to be hanging around the lobby. I don't want people staring at me all blown apart. So as the elevator doors open, I cruise across the room at a clip and, refusing to go through yet one more revolving door, push through the door to its left. I step into the slap of icy air outside, yanking my suitcase out behind me.

Leaning against the stone wall of the hotel, I call Amory. Unable to say much, I get to the point, which is what he is waiting to hear anyway. "He said that it will come back." Both of us are silent about that one for several seconds. Then he says lovingly, in a scratchy whisper to keep back all those tears that he's saving for when we hang up, "Come home, honey. Come home."

At once, I'm overtaken with the emotion of hearing myself say that this cancer will come back and by his immediate response to come home to him. Tripping over tears and raw feelings, I've fallen back into the river.

"I feel like giving up. I'm tired, Amory. I can't keep surviving these surgeries forever—you know that, don't you? Look at me!" I cry as if he were standing in front of me. "There are only so many pieces that they can take out. This just doesn't work; it doesn't go away. Radiation doesn't even kill these stupid tumors; they just eat it for lunch, and keep on marching! Why you would want to do this with me makes no sense at all. You shouldn't live with this, too. Don't you understand that you'll have a wife who always has cancer? You don't need to do this, Amory. This is a long road and there's no cure. I feel that all I am any more is a burden to you and the kids. I'm a complete drain on this whole family, emotionally and financially. I don't want that. Frankly, I don't believe that you can want me like this, forever." I stop, sorry that I've been raving, but more so because he's had to hear the truth from so far away. Clearly, he's heard the desperation in my voice.

"I'll be standing right there with my arms wide open when you get off that plane. I need you, we need you. Carrie. You can do this," he's saying. "Come home, honey. I promise you, I'll never let you go there alone again. I'm sorry I let you go alone, but I'm right here. We're all right here for you...we need you to come home. Okay?" he says very quietly with pure love. Just as the old one expertly threads the needle, Amory threads the tiniest filament of courage through the eye of my heart.

"Okay...the shuttle's here," I answer from the corner of my fear. "I have to go. I'll see you at the airport. I love you, Amory."

"Okay. I'll see you in a few hours."

Quietly closing the phone and dropping it into the pocket of my coat, I hear it make that chiming sound that tells me the battery's dead. It shuts off. Thanks to my stupid cell phone I'm wondering *how many cells are left in my battery, before I shut down?*

Stepping up into the shuttle van, I take the third row and squeeze myself close to the window; it's a shoulder to lean on. I start to cry and can't stop. I think it's a good thing that it's only me and another girl in the van all the way to the airport. She keeps to her book two rows ahead of me, and I keep to my window with the trees and farmhouses streaking by. Farmhouses I now know by sight, as I've been on this same one-hour rural drive seven times before in the past twelve weeks.

The driver keeps his eyes on the road ahead, yet he's fully aware of the stream of tears behind him. He's delivered a lot of tears, both to and from this place. I suppose he's accustomed to the sight of a person who has come undone.

Cancer is like that. Sometimes we truly don't see how we will muster up the courage to keep going. When we can only see death staring us in the face, fear just knocks us flat out. This is where the people we love the most can help us to lean on their courage and stand up again.

Chanel's Poem

May 11, 2004

Now that I am finally starting to heal physically, I don't want to bother with my emotional rescue. I figure that because I was alone in my physical suffering, the same will be true of entering the door marked Feelings. I leave that door shut, partly because I don't really have the nerve to look into my feelings, and partly because I am just too tired. I want to wait until I have more energy, wondering if that day will ever really come.

Surviving thus far has been a dark experience. It is as though I have been sitting in a dimly lit space for a long time, and my eyes have adjusted. When people enter from outside, I see them but they are unable to readily see me, because it's too dark and they are moving too fast. They have just stepped in from the bright sunshine of life without a frightening disease attached to it. It feels as though people move through my space rather than into it. This makes me feel all the more separated from the "world out there." Alone as I am feeling, I am relieved to see people who are glowing with health, because it helps me envision reaching that point.

I notice that my family's humor and camaraderie have vanished, as I struggle to do a quarter of what I was doing just six months ago. I try to instill the same joy that was once there, but I am completely drained. No one's saying so, but I know that they all miss the marvelous aromas that once filled the house from my nightly cooking.

They miss Billie Holiday, and the Preservation Hall Jazz Band,

Benny Goodman, Stan Getz, Frank Sinatra, Diana Krall, Nat King Cole and Muddy Waters. These are the musicians who they claim to dislike, who their mother loves, and who have stopped filling the house with their music. It isn't only the mood it set but that it was once accompanied by my kids' rolling eyes. I'd grab one of them and start to dance around the kitchen, the way my mother used to do with me.

"Oh, no, Marco, here she goes...help meee!" Chanel would scream as I'd pull her, my first unwilling partner, into a dance with me, as she feigned the desire to be released. Then Marco, yelping for deliverance, but loving every minute of it. Until now, I had never noticed how entwined my health and my happiness were, how once they danced together without a care.

It's all of these gleeful moments that have fallen away to nothing but a memory. I can tell that the cancer has weakened the easy laughter and outward strength that my kids used to see in me. The fresh roses that used to embellish my favorite crystal vases weekly are gone, as is my repeatedly telling them: "Buy yourselves flowers, kids. Fill your lives with the things you love, don't wait for someone else to do it."

Having been a lifelong lover of fine art, I know very well the unseen importance of each tiny brush stroke. While they may disappear onto the canvas never to be seen again individually, each stroke constitutes the finished work of art. My "family painting" is suddenly on hold. I start trying to justify the loss of my capabilities by thinking that I'd previously done too much for all of them. I wonder if they ever really even noticed any of my effort. My defense for feeling so weak is to feature myself becoming remote to my family's needs. To think that when I am well I'll be less involved with everything and just let everything take care of itself. I'm thinking not only of becoming distant, but that if I could leave home and lift the burden that I have become, I should.

This makes no logical sense. It is crazy and unsound emotional navigation, but this is what has become of my mind as it struggles to deal with my body. I have no energy and I feel like giving up. I can't deal with me anymore. It is taking everything I have just to take care of myself and my myriad of physical ailments, much less the family.

On top of this, the symptoms caused by a body on the mend create the need for certain medications, and the side effects of those same drugs are making my personal list of miserable experiences longer. I am overwhelmed with both the physical and the emotional side of this illness. I want to sleep for a year and wake up when I'm strong and healthy. I just don't care about anything at this point, including my future.

Lying on the couch in my room, I'm sinking deeper into this depressing thought when my daughter taps shyly on the door and enters. She asks me if I want to read a poem that she wrote for an English assignment at school. I perk right up as she tells me that they had to write a love poem. Of course I am at once terribly excited to get a glimpse inside of my teenage daughter's heart and to maybe even discover that she has a secret love. Nothing prepared me for this:

The Size of Love

I hike a mountain to the very top—
I think of your determination.
We drive that drive that we've never driven before—
I think of your courage.
I see a tree big and tall with its arms reaching wide—
I think of your strong beliefs.
The sky gets gray and clouds of thunder fill the air—
I think of your optimism.

When I wake to the smell of bunny eggs—
I think of your motherly touch.
As I walk by the gallery where you used to work—
I think of your strength.
I see your brilliant smiling face—
I think of your true beauty.
When I hear the word *poet*—
I think of your creativeness.

I see yet another gift you're giving—
I think of your generosity.
I enter the house, the table is set waiting for the family to sit—
I think of your perfection.
I see you twirl and spin—
I think of your spirit.
I see your eyes bright and wide—
I think of your curiosity.

When you get dressed up in your heels and pearls—
I think of your class.
You always lend a hand to those who are down—
I think of your friendship.
The house is suddenly redesigned—
I think of your joy in art.
Every time I smell fresh roses—
I think of your passion.

I hear a story of the house on Williams Street—
I remember your past.

I hear a story of myself and our family—
I think of your present.
I hear a story of the most tremendous success—
I think of your future.

Because it's the little things when placed together,
That make you my most special love.
—*Marlena Chanel Host*

"The Size of Love"? My daughter wrote *this?* About me? Tears fall from my eyes onto the page in my hand.

"This is beautiful, honey..."

"I knew you would cry, Mom, that's why I never let you read anything," I hear Chanel teasing me from the doorway on her way out.

Sometimes our lifelines are thrown to us by angels—not the ones in paintings, but the ones right here in our lives.

This poem in my hand makes me decide that I will not give up. All I do for my children does not go unnoticed. How I decide to go forward definitely matters. How I feel about myself will determine how I live the rest of my life, however long or short that may be. More important, how my children see me live the rest of my life will ultimately influence how they will see and *live* their lives.

Reading what she's written, I begin to understand what I mean to Chanel. This is so healing that I feel my body shift onto a different plane. In this moment, it feels like every cell is sparkling and the glimmer is good.

I have an undeniable new urge to beat this cancer. I want to take up my brushes and finish this work of art, my family painting. While the reality of the moment is that I can't do that just yet, the thought that one day I will return to my canvas gives me hope.

Part III

Floating

Bermuda

Bermuda is a place I have dreamt of going. Like a lot of things that I had been saving for "later," I decide to go now. Sparking my plans is the fact that Amory will be sailing there from Norfolk, Virginia. His friend Mike has invited him to crew aboard his fifty-foot *Quester.* In roughly a week, he'll be sailing into port at St. George. The kids and I will meet him. We'll spend a week together on the island and then fly home.

Shortly after we arrive, night begins to fall over Hamilton, and I begin to notice a strange sound that I've never heard before. I ask the bellman outside the hotel what the enchanting noise is. He breaks into a huge grin, apparently happy to share the answer, as I'm sure he's done a thousand times before.

"Tree frogs. They're only about the size of my thumbnail, but they can really sing, and they sing every night," he's saying in his pleasing British accent. I'm thrilled to know that their songs will be my lullaby.

Something about this place resonates deeply with me. The rare cancer that lives inside makes me feel isolated like this island, alone in the middle of an immense ocean. I'm in a place that relatively few people will ever see, much less relate to.

Strange things begin to happen. The old me would never enter any cave, much less drop into its cold water and swim around. But here I am: floating on my back, not fearing the dark water but dissolving into it. Melding with the interior seclusion of this cave, I'm absorbing the hidden beauty into my body. Pulling myself up onto a rocky ledge, I sit still and look up at the stalactites dripping water slowly down into this pool. I take the damp smell of cool clay into my nostrils and the strange echo of every drip drop into my heart.

One afternoon I sit, digging my feet into the pink sands of Horseshoe Bay stretched before me. As waves roll in and crash down, sunlight glitters upon the wet sand from beneath my rented umbrella and beach chair. I'm watching the kids build a sand castle. I never want to leave this lazy afternoon. But I know it will end and be replaced, just as each receding wave brings another. This is the eternal cycle of life. Why should this disturb my peace?

I'm seeing more and more clearly that this moment right now is the only one that really exists. With that, I try to stop worrying about the next week, month or year, and how many or few I might still have to share with my children. Here on this island I'm solely focused on the time that is the present.

That evening, all five of us are standing on the dock of our modest cottage in Salt Kettle, showered and dressed for dinner and admiring the last fading colors of the sunset. A rogue wind begins to whip about, rocking the dock.

"The ferry leaves for Hamilton in fifteen minutes. Shall we head over for dinner?" Amory asks, offering to save us from the sudden change of weather.

With a quick glance over my shoulder, I can see that Chanel has spun a different plan altogether, one she knows is ridiculous and not about to happen, but one she throws out there anyway.

"I *dare* you, Mom," Chanel says to me, a crazed anticipation in her voice, a wild look in her eye, sizing up my silk dress blowing in the wind and then raising her eyebrows while tipping her head toward the white-caps on the water. She knows full well my utter fear of dark water, rough water, or of any body of water at night. This makes getting me to even think of jumping into this water a complete impossibility. She knows that I absolutely won't. But I can see that somewhere, way deep down, she's hoping that I might.

"You dare me?" I reiterate. Watching her eyes widen, I simply can't resist the challenge. Kicking off my heels, I head down the dock at a clipping pace, jumping without a moment's hesitation and shrieking with delight. I hear the kids screaming "No way!" as I hit the dark, choppy water. As my head pops up, I look up at them all standing on the edge of the dock, an absolute thrilled disbelief on all of their faces, especially Amory's.

"Come on! I dare you!" I shout. One by one, they jump in. We're all splashing around, high on the temporary insanity of what we've just done. We climb out to William's clapping and laughing; he's still dry, sitting in an Adirondack chair on the dock. We stand there together, dripping wet and pleased with ourselves. We see the angry innkeeper who is marching down the hill toward us, wagging her head and her finger in unison scolding us too late to ruin our fun.

"I can't believe you did that, Mom," Marco hisses, half blaming me for the trouble we're about to get into for taking a dip in a no-swimming area.

"I can," I say, matter-of-factly and at total peace with myself. I smile at myself, at my pounding heart. I'm in love with the whole moment and truly loving life. The scowling woman who's heading down here right now to put me in my place doesn't realize that I'm already exactly where I need to be.

Back inside our cozy cottage after four hot showers, I happily whip up the scrambled eggs and toast that we were going to have for break-fast tomorrow, smiling the whole time. Marco and Chanel are stretched across the bed looking over the souvenirs they bought earlier at the Gibbs Hill Lighthouse. We're all smiling together, genuinely, in an easy way that has been missing for some time.

For no reason loftier than "now," I had jumped off the dock. What Chanel had dared me to do was so much more than jump into the ocean. She had dared me to live. And I took her up on it.

I'm doing it. I'm jumping into my own life, now. The raw material of cancer has made a different person out of me.

Cancer is like that. It not only changes the way in which we see and hear things. It ultimately changes the way we respond to the world around us. Laughing is good for you. Children laugh an average of four hundred times a day, while adults pale in comparison at only twelve. With cancer, we have been ushered into the now, and we can take this as an opportunity to return to the mindset of children. We were once this way, not thinking as much of the future as we did of the moment at hand. Let's feel the wonder of our lives again, the thrill of taking chances, the joy of laughter. Let's take the one life we do have in front of us right now and jump in.

Party List

***

O n the flight home, William sleeping in my lap, with his head in the crook of my left arm, I decide to make a list. A pen in my right hand, I am poised and ready to go to work. I think of every doctor that I have seen over the two years leading up to my diagnosis until the present, whether for a consultation, a procedure or a surgery. I go back to April of 2002, when I became pregnant with William, and start with my obstetrician. I list them all, reflecting on which of those doctors, either by word or by action, has had a positive, life-changing effect on me.

Chanel glances over to see me wildly scratching down names, one after the other, on the back of an envelope that I had pulled out of my purse. She wants to know what party I'm planning and who is on my list. With that, I am forced to picture all twenty-eight of the doctors whose names I have just listed gathered together in one room! Eyes wide, my mind shapes itself into a version of Edvard Munch's painting *The Scream.*

Between *obstetrician* and *oncologist,* there exists a mental chasm the size of the Grand Canyon. In my opinion, those two words have no business appearing in the same sentence. The fact that they are in alphabetical sequence lends me some demented comfort.

But her question leads me to really consider those twenty-eight doctors. Which ones would I invite to my imagined party—not just invite, but truly welcome? Oh, now, that is an easy question to answer.

"Just seven," I say out loud to myself.

"Seven?" Chanel repeats, confused.

"But, if I had to choose just three...I could easily do that." I continue to think out loud. Looking up I can see, by her "you're *so weird,* Mom" face, that now I have really managed to boggle her.

Cancer has worn me down with lists and questions, then all at once, given me that twenty-twenty vision I've been wanting, without the LASIK. It just feels good finally to be able to see. I mean really see. I know instinctively what I need, and whom I need. I'm going to keep trusting myself.

Camp Marisa

August 5, 2004

Visiting Jack and Marisa in Aspen is like going to camp. I decide that since I'm hiking four to five days a week in the foothills of Boulder, I'll demonstrate for myself how well I *really* am, at least physically, by hiking up Ajax, Aspen's ski mountain. I'm somewhat unsure if I should attempt this, but my camp counselor, Marisa, lets no one hesitate, including her recovering sister. Marisa isn't letting this fish off the hook.

"I don't know. Do you think I can do it?" I'm saying, trying to swim away.

"Yes, you can. Totally! Here, let me give you my double water-bottle holster. No, forget it, let me get you my new Camelback. I have what you need."

Before I can back out, she's marching ahead of me, across the yard toward her garage, Gear Central, where she starts shaking sports drinks like they're martinis and grabbing various clothing items, to suit me up to *her* standards. She's getting me fired up to head out alone to climb the face of Ajax, Aspen's ski mountain, where you start in town at 8,000 feet and climb 3,300 more to reach the top at 11,300 feet in roughly three miles. It's what I'd call steep.

"Stop and see Knansee at Goldie's on your way," she calls after me, giving me an order that will land me close to the base of the mountain and conveniently into the hands of her friend. I'm sure at this moment she is calling her to instruct her on how I must be encouraged, and sent up the "hill." Marisa is that kind of person. She tells us all what to do and how best to do it, and we love her for it. Also, she leaves us no choice.

As I walk downtown toward the base, I think about how much I appreciate Marisa's spirit of action. She's great about sharing her gear and her friends and anything else she has in her midst to help a person get going.

I stop by and see her friend Knansee at work, just as I was told. She greets me with open arms, eyes bright with delight. She's a walking ray of light, beaming. She's one of those rare people who when you think of them, all you can picture is their smile. I pretend to be shopping, as I ask a bunch of other useless questions. Sensing my hesitation, and no doubt having received Marisa's call, she walks me out of the shop and to the corner.

"Stay on *this* side of the lift," she points out—the trick to finding my way up.

"Do you think I'll run into a bear? I wouldn't amount to much of a meal, I suppose," I say, laughing about my still somewhat meager body.

"Don't worry. Aspen's bears come to town at night for dinner," she laughs, adding, "Seriously! One just snatched a doggy bag from a guy on Hyman Street a couple of nights ago. It had steak in it." The details convince me it's true.

Right off, the first thirty steps of this hike are extremely steep. I push my way up. I'm imagining that with each step I take, I'm delivering a blow to the cancer. Blow after blow, two hours and forty-five minutes later, sweat streaming front and back, I have the summit in sight—and with it, the sense that I'm taking my body back.

Finally, I make it to the top. I reach the Sun Deck in just under three hours. I stand there out of breath, holding on to the railing for a long time, not thinking about anything. I go in and get a cold drink and take a seat out on the deck.

A purple finch lands on the railing, innocuously framing himself with the stunning backdrop of glorious peaks. I take a mental snapshot of this tiny creature, with his even tinier claws and beak, amid these massive mountains. He takes to the sky, inspiring me to do the same.

I take the gondola down to spare myself any further test of my physical strength. Back at the base, drained, I trudge home. Pushing through the gate that feels as if it took years to arrive at, I stumble into Marisa's backyard. She's up out of her chair and heading toward me with a ready high five.

"I knew you could do it. I knew you'd just smoke up that thing!" she says.

"I'm not sure you'd call it *that*," I counter, practically falling into a chaise where I plan to stay for eternity. "It took *three hours*."

"That's actually a decent time," she says. "You kick ass, sister."

I'm so glad to hear that she knows about my hidden ability, and about how *"kick-ass"* I am, because I've had to wonder. If there were ever a person who could sift through my invisible fears, it's Marisa. It's as if she hears the microscopic voice in my head saying, *so what? Anybody can do anything once.* So I try to change the subject before she homes in.

"I'm glad you think so. Does this mean I'll be skiing with you this year?" I propose to hassle her.

"No. You know I don't do mercy runs with the *lame*," she says without any sense of injustice toward me whatsoever.

"I can't believe you just said that to me," I say, trying to sound offended while suppressing my desire to laugh.

"Yes, you can," she says, giving me that six-year-old's in-your-face look, forcing me to smile. "And don't go trying to change the subject. Do you want to hike it again, day after tomorrow, or not?"

"Yeah, I'm ready," I answer, glad she dug up my self-doubt and dangled it out in front of me.

"Good. My friend Marcy's a great hiker. I bet she'll go with you. Here, let me call her," she says, finishing dialing the number before her sentence. Two seconds later, she's making sure that I won't be able to flake out, with every syllable of "So, day after tomorrow? Eight-thirty? *Definitely.* In front of Little Nell? She'll be there, for sure," she seals my fate, hanging up. Ever the camp counselor, she schedules my next activity for me, regardless of what I might think might be a better option, like hiding in my cabin. She's already figured in tomorrow, a day for me to recover.

This time, I hike Ajax with Marcy and Amory—who decides to pop William into the Kelty pack and take him along, too. I can't tell if I'm truly slower this time, or if having two people who are both healthier and stronger up there in front of me is making me feel the way I really am, recovering. Amory just marches up Ajax, William and all. I'll come to a small meadow and he'll be smiling at me, sitting there with William out of the pack playing while he "takes a break." Marcy turns around to check on me every so often, and I keep pushing up the mountain till we all reach the top. Now I've made it to the summit twice.

There are moments when cancer challenges me, and moments when I challenge it. How did I get stuck in this tug-of-war? It doesn't matter. I'm digging in my heels.

Heave-ho!

Adrift

August 8, 2004

I t's extraordinarily dark on Highway 82 over Independence Pass after the sun has set. Surviving cancer feels a lot like driving this road at night. I'm traversing the most challenging mountain pass by focusing on what's in front of me right now, this bit of poorly illuminated road. As with cancer, it is no use to try to drive five turns ahead of the one I'm driving now, nor to needlessly fill my head with what lies beyond my headlights. I can only see this bit of the journey, right now.

I'm regaining the appearance of total health, and compared to the condition I was in just nine months ago, I am healthy. But those who were not along for the ride have no possible way of imagining the path that led me here. This makes me feel a deep sense of separation; I feel that I'm alone. While I'm actively participating in my life again and it's full of those I love, I continuously feel sad when I should feel grateful. With all of these wonderful people in my life, I still feel lost and isolated.

I rarely tell anyone anything about my cancer, unless I feel the need to enlighten the person on the freak-show nature of the disease or unless I want to see the look of astonishment and utter disbelief on someone's face. Visualizing cancer while staring at a radiant mother of three in the checkout line at the grocery store, her one-and-a-half-year-old toddler strapped in the seat and smiling, is a challenge.

They can't get their minds around that. Can I blame them when I can barely get my own mind around the idea that I'm on the recovery side of it, or any side of it for that matter? Telling anyone that I have cancer involves too much energy and explanation. On the other hand, I wish I had someone new to talk to without bringing the burden of my unsettled questions to my friends. I'm virtually 98 percent cancer free and holding together pretty well. Actually, it feels better than pretty well.

I return home, back to the incessant piles of laundry, dishes and mail. Now what? I won't go to Mayo Clinic for another set of scans for seven weeks. So how do I live in the meantime? I have the sense that I'm in a constant yet varied state of waiting. These stupid questions follow me everywhere: What is this in-between place? Should I be hopeful? Hoping keeps me from experiencing where I am now, the present. In a strange way, hope keeps me tied to the future. Is this hope business a good idea? What do I do next? I picture myself pen in hand, writing a short story something like this:

Today, I will overcome the odds that are stacked against me. I will beat this cancer. When I've done that, my body will be reminded of the unmatched machine that it is. Then I'll have won the biggest battle of all, and the rest will be a piece of cake. The End.

I like that type of story. It doesn't leave a sliver of room for that little devil Doubt to slip in. So for a long time, I tell myself this story. This way, I have it as a flashlight to help me in these still-unfamiliar rooms, where I'm still tripping over things in the dark. The rooms I haven't memorized yet by day, so that I can navigate them at night.

Whatever my definition of *navigation* was, it has changed—as I have, into something stronger. For me, that means picking myself up from where I got dropped on my head by cancer, way back in my old life, the life I've been idealizing as irredeemable.

I want to picture a destination other than death, a death that all of the statistics and even some of the doctors have predicted. I'm realizing that grabbing hold of life—my life, right now, because I might not be here later to do the grabbing—is something I wish I had done before this cancer came along and gave me the lowdown on how it really is.

We already know that all any of us truly has is now. It's just that, for those of us with cancer, we seem to have an especially clear "insider version" of how this is true. We are blessed to have this insight. It is important to remember this as we go along.

If I can just hold my own hand and remind myself of this truth in the middle of the night when I'm too disturbed to sleep, pacing the house and watching hazy *Cheers* reruns to keep my brain from wandering off to places I don't want to go, I'll be all right. I'm finding out that, like me, a lot of people who have cancer or another illness that's nearly killed them, are now where I am: *here.* They are also asking, "What do I do now?" That seems to be the main question that we all ask from the middle of this river.

This in-between place I decide must be Purgatory. Purgatory is a perfect place to hang around and be assaulted by my past sins or current misgivings, a place where I'm decent enough to be put on a waiting list but not good enough to see the pearly gates. It's a place Sister Katherine Anne taught me about, where people wait for God to decide.

"But what do you do there, Sister?" I had asked.

"Why, practice patience, of course," she'd answer. Then sweeping her pointer and her gaze to include the entire class, she'd go on to say, "Patience is a virtue." She'd find it reasonable to say this several times a day, first tapping the pointy black rubber tip of her thin wooden stick on someone's desk, then aiming it toward the blackboard where it was written for all of us to see—in perfect cursive, of course.

Since I am not the patient type, I have never considered going there, even for a visit.

In the first grade, at St. John's Catholic School, Father Morfield had a one-sided discussion with a whole room full of six-year-olds. He told us our options for after we'd died. Apparently this was an age-appropriate subject in 1969. He did give us a choice, however, with pictures to match: Heaven or Hell.

And then there was Sister Katherine Anne's Purgatory, a cave that God had carved out somewhere in the Earth's crust for those he couldn't make up his mind about. I decided, right there, at six years old, that I didn't like the sound of the last two choices. So I figured that when I died, I'd be going straight to Heaven.

Thirty-five years later, I'm not even dead yet, but I find I've been thrown into Purgatory. The bizarre fifteenth-century paintings of Hieronymus Bosch come to mind. Reaching for some type of definition, I lean over and pick up my *Webster's New World Dictionary*. I want to see if Purgatory is still in there waiting. "Pur-ga-to-ry / n. 1: an intermediate state after death for expiatory purification." That explains it, then. The truth is that I've already died and I'm in denial about that, too. Okay, and all this time, I thought Purgatory was a place God set up just to torture aspiring writers and artists.

Carcinoid Island

September 2, 2004

It takes a year on Carcinoid Island before I decide to go and visit the club to which I already belong but have never seen. I sit in with a Thursday morning cancer support group at Rocky Mountain Cancer Center here in Boulder. I have never met another person with carcinoid tumor, and it feels as if I'm driving around on this small and threatened island and going nowhere fast. I don't have the type of cancer which the various support groups claim to support. A zebra among horses, will I find help? What can a group possibly do for me? Even so, I begin to wonder if other cancer patients might be having a similar experience to mine.

First off, I'm not your "group anything" type of person. I prefer to be left out in the rain, if possible, literally. I am at once a loner and a social creature. I think it's a Pisces thing, two fish swimming in opposite directions. Entering the room, though, I take a look at the others and I see one thing right away. There is uncertainty here. I see it in everyone's eyes. Sitting with my back to the window on one side of the oblong table, I watch and listen. I find that I feel a direct and oddly immediate connection with each person's story or issue.

Having all been dropped over the Great Falls of Cancer, dumped out of our boats, mangled and spit out into the river brings us together. Some of us have made it to the bank of that river. Some of us have even been out on dry land awhile and actually feel good. Others of us are still in there swimming, treading water or just holding on. Nonetheless, during our two hours together, the newer people to the group, like me, all seem to look to those who say things like, *"I've been in remission for six years now."* We want to know how to get *there*. To me, that seems like a dream. I want to be able to say that, but I'm not in remission.

Instead of ending that last sentence with a period, should I have chosen a comma, followed by the word *yet?*

This is the kind of thing, which while seeming trite, has begun to toy with my emotions. I've begun to whittle away at every individual thought I have, knowing that thought contains energy. Energy heals. Do I accept the current truth about this disease, or do I add *yet* and daydream?

"I wish that I could have chemo and just kill all this stuff off, but I have a cancer that even resists chemo. I guess it's the cockroach of cancers," I say, telling the group something none of them has ever heard before, something that makes them reconsider cursing their chemo-therapy. They all look astounded that anyone would wish to be sub-jected to round after round of the stuff, but they get the point.

"But at least it's slow-growing, I guess I have that going for me," I say. What I don't say just yet, though, is what I don't have going for me.

How will I travel this precarious road? It's different than I had imagined, because the farther down the river I've gone, the less and less I feel that my immediate family is able to relate to my situation. Who can really continue to understand a journey like this? How can I expect the people closest to me to relate to the personal storm that I continu-ously experience, while they can't even see the overcast sky? But in this room, at this meeting, everyone is in the storm.

One particular meeting, a newcomer timidly shares with us the physically graphic, terrible and intimate details of the effects of one particular treatment on her body, and its heinous outcome. When she's finished telling us of her personal anguish, those of us not already crying openly with her are on the verge of tears.

A painful quiet surrounds us at the table, sort of allowing a space for all of us to recover with her. Tearfully, genuinely, she slowly asks us, her newfound friends, "*How* will I make it through this?" Then Dora, one of the shining stars of our group, embraces her despair completely, saying in her warm Greek accent, "We will get you through this." We all swiftly second this, nodding and looking in her direction, all equally grateful for Dora's strong and kind words. This is when I realize the powerful healing place that our group is.

Joe, our leader, seems undeniably aware of the way that, when it's our turn, we tend to want to stray off and talk about things such as how this or that person in our life is doing, or how we think our mailman is doing. Anything works, as long as we can successfully avoid talking about how we ourselves are actually doing. Joe gently steers us back to our own stories.

This is where we look at what is so hard to face: our true feelings. Speaking the truth about the way we're really feeling is something that we aren't comfortable doing anywhere else. Here, we unpack the suitcase of stuff that we aren't able to share with those closest to us. Our support group successfully doubles as a container, other than our heads, where we can put the frightening thoughts that plague us. Here, I feel heard while never having the sense that my thoughts are a burden to the others; rather, they're more like a contribution to our collective well, which has run dry.

The best part about my support group is that, no matter how tired I might be, not having to explain anything is a welcome relief, completely opposite from other interactions I'm used to, which require too much of the little energy I have. There are many more of us out here than I had realized. Cancer's really a club, of which I am now a member, so I might as well take advantage of it, Purgatory and all.

The Dark

January 22, 2005

The pain started right below my sternum. After bearing with it for three hours, I decide that I should probably go to the hospital. Having made it fairly well through the last half of 2004, I should have figured that since it's a new year, it was time for something to happen.

"I just wonder if this shot of Sandostatin is doing enough for me," I'm groaning out loud, more or less to myself, as Amory and I travel the familiar drive down Broadway to the emergency room. The doctor's thinking that my pain indicates a bowel obstruction. But after reading the X-rays, I find out that my pain is most likely from scar tissue in the many places where my bowels have been cut and then stitched back together. That is a lot of places.

"This may be an ongoing issue," the helpful doctor informs me just before he sends me home. *Great, just like the cancer itself,* I'm thinking.

"Well, I'll look into some other doctors this week and see what we can set up," my ever-supportive husband offers. Truthfully, I think that he wants an answer, too. We don't like the reintroduction of the unknown.

I feel as if I'm only just up and running again when some mysterious new factor hits me, and of course, I'm afraid of its source. I'm in the dark. I'm tired of trying to see in the dark and tired of pain. Every day, I have to choose the way I see the glass. Each new piece of information—which in my case, often involves a physical sensation that I've never before experienced—comes in and stirs me up. I want answers, but I have to settle for none. I have to somehow deal with the unknown, so I do. Usually I write myself a comforting short story to believe in, until a whodunit comes along and erases it.

A Stranger

March 10, 2005

New York City is cold and gray in March, but weather is not a factor in my mission to be seen by Dr. Richard Warner, a well-known oncologist in the field of carcinoid. Suffice it to say that he knows a bit about the disease. We had considered meeting him when I was first diagnosed, but chose the Dr. Rubin and Dr. Nagorney team at Mayo, due to their combined expertise.

Since my January trip into the emergency room in Boulder, Amory's assembled and sent my case collection, including my CT scans, to Dr. Warner well in advance of our appointment. Even biopsy tissue slides from my surgery at Mayo Clinic have been forwarded. We want his opinion of my overall care and current diagnosis and his recommendation for how I should proceed for the best outcome. In plain English, we're still shopping for the most time.

On the day of my appointment I'm taking an early morning train from Baltimore, where I have been catching up with my friend Janet. She and I have just spent the previous evening trying to talk through my reasons for wanting yet another opinion.

"I just don't want to miss anything that I might be able to do to get ahead of this, you know?"

"Absolutely. I think it's a good idea, I really do," she agrees. I know she's scared for me and wants the best for me, too.

Being a Colorado girl, I see trains as a novelty of the Old West. Other than the ski train to Winter Park, I'm not used to trains as a means of transportation. I board, walking forward two cars and find what looks like a perfect seat.

"Can I sit here?" I ask the woman across the table between the two facing seats.

"Sure." The "whatever" in her expression says clearly that I didn't have to ask, that no one cares where I sit.

Now slightly self-conscious, I keep my gaze glued to my window. After ten minutes of feigned East Coast indifference, I glance across the table that separates us. I see a woman with auburn hair cropped chin length looking out of the window as though she's trying to remember what she left behind. I become increasingly uncomfortable facing a person whom I haven't really even said hello to. I reach for my phone, thinking of calling my mom since she'll do all the talking and I can just utter an occasional "Uh-huh...right"

"I'm sorry, I might have to make a call. Hope that's okay?" I apologize before dialing.

"That's fine," is all she says. She's not looking like she's interested in further conversation.

Partly to put myself at more ease and partly because I decide that indifference just isn't me, I ask her a question.

"How are you?" I ask sincerely, meeting her eyes with mine. And something just short of two hours later as the train pulls into Newark, New Jersey, where she works, I manage to receive a complete answer to my question. Without knowing that I have cancer, she shares her story of how she's recently lost her husband Jim, to cancer. In return, I tell her the painful reason that I'm on this train headed for New York City.

"I'm going to see Dr. Warner. He's an oncologist. I'm trying to beat cancer myself," I say, and I tell her my story. We have that instant connection that you make with someone who has suffered the loss that cancer can bring.

As we approach her stop, I search in my purse for something to write down my name and number on.

"I don't have a card...although I've been tempted to get one that has 'Laundress, Driver & Cook' printed on it," I say sarcastically.

She laughs and gives me her card, saying, "Let me know how it goes in New York...and how you're doing...will you?"

"I will, definitely," I answer, meaning what I say. I'm so grateful for her insights on navigating the things that she wished she had known more about when she was helping her husband get to all of his appointments.

Finally, as the train slows she says, "Thank you. I finally feel like I understand a little better what my husband probably couldn't say." She's thanking me for having shared with her some of my own deeply hidden emotions and fears. Oddly, these are the same fears which remain a challenge for me to express to the people closest to me. In an attempt to put into words what largely goes unsaid by me, I'm healing.

"Carrie, you should write about this, you know? Like an article or something. I think a lot of people dealing with cancer would appreciate your insights," she suggests.

"Who knows, maybe I will someday." I smile at the fact that, blind to the knowledge of my passion for writing, she's bringing it up. Our eyes fill with tears.

"I'm so glad that we met, Kathleen."

"I'll be praying for you. Goodbye," she's saying to me as she steps off of the train, sorry to leave and sensing as I am that there's a lot more we could discuss. At once, I know that we've been invisibly stitched together in a way that will last over time.

Having grown up in the Rocky Mountains where a street most definitely could never be *above* me, rising to reach the street is a strange phenomenon in itself. As I emerge from the subway, I am struck by the way New Yorkers manage to appear completely isolated while pressed together like kernels ready to pop. Shoulder to shoulder, we hit the street and scatter.

Walking toward Dr. Warner's office, I spot Amory on the opposite corner giving me a wave. Once I've checked in, it's not long before we're led to the doctor's office to finally meet the king of Carcinoid Island.

"Hi," he says, introducing himself. "Dr. Warner. And...you are...the Hosts from Colorado?" He walks in, clutching a stack of files and a rumpled brown bag which he sets down on his desk while shaking Amory's hand with his free one. Then reaching across, he says, "Mrs. Host?" and shakes my hand with a no-nonsense grip, brief and firm. "Glad to meet you."

"My lunch," he announces, in a heavy New York accent, sitting down, lacing his thick fingers together and pressing them out toward me as he straightens his arms. Then, having gotten a good stretch, he pushes an assortment of files and stacks of books towering on every available surface out of his way. Poking the bridge of his glasses with his index finger, he sets them straight and re-laces his fingers. Then, setting his wide wrists squarely on the edge of his wooden desk and clearing his throat, he prepares to ask me a question.

"So, Mrs. Host, why, when clearly you have some qualified doctors managing your case, have you come all the way here to New York to see me?" His question strikes me as absurdly funny. *I'm here to buy more time, are you selling?* I answer to myself. A second later, my equally ridiculous answer springs forth.

"Well, I'm not looking for Botox, I can tell you that much. The truth is, Doctor, I'm in the market for wrinkles. Do you think you can help me out?"

He breaks into a huge easy grin as he laughs with me. "Well, let me see what I can do for you here. Does that sound all right? Okay," he answers for me, as he thumbs through a stack of files to his right, pulling mine free. "Let's start from the beginning here...October 31...2003...is that right?"

Sometime after I return home, I send my lady from the train a letter, thanking her for her openhearted sharing. I send the kind of letter people sent thirty years ago to someone wonderful they'd met on a journey. A letter in my own handwriting, with ink on paper, with a return address that corresponds to a real place situated on this Earth, with a front door attached. A letter with a stamp on it.

I'm not really thinking, as I drop it into the mailbox, that this is how cancer has given me a new friend. I may never see her again, but she will begin to send cards to me at that return address, saying that she has been praying for me, praying for a miracle. I will find that her words strengthen me.

And now I know what I will do with that "ending" that I wrote a year ago. The one I wrote after I remembered what Allen Ginsberg had told me, and then tucked away for "someday."

Later that night, in bed, I roll onto my stomach and lean down to retrieve the shoebox I have stashed under the bed. This is the box where all of the cards and occasional letters that I receive retire after they've lived out their time on my nightstand. Having all of these words of love and encouragement from friends and family, all tucked safely away below my bed, gives me a type of security. It's a way of remembering that I am loved when I can't feel anything.

I take off the lid. The piece of my own writing that I'm looking for is easy to find; it's the one I had folded too many times. I close the box and settle back into bed before I begin to open the stout square wad. I begin to weep as I slowly flatten it out in my lap and read.

I take a ratty, spiral notebook from the second drawer of my night-stand and then take several deep, even breaths. I begin to write the beginning. As the words flow onto the page, page after sacred page, I'm thinking, thank you, Kathleen, you beautiful stranger, you dear angel, for helping me see that while cancer is busy taking everything else away, I should, at the very least, take back my pen.

Kingdom of Cells

―――――⌒⌒――

April 4, 2005

No sooner have I received the letter from Dr. Warner—stating that he feels, based on his pathology reports, that my condition is stable and that I do not need to begin a course of Interferon as he had previously thought necessary—than I am being admitted to the hospital by Dr. Dughi with a fever of 105 degrees. *These conflicting messages have been brought to you by the Roller Coaster of Cancer. Thank you for tuning in; see you at the same time next week,* I hear the voice inside my head saying.

As soon as I have changed into a nice dry set of clothing, cancer drops me back into the river. I feel constant uncertainty. Just when I've talked myself into feeling somewhat confident about some aspect of my health, my confidence is shot down cold.

This is the fever that beats all fevers. Yet during my three-day stay in the hospital, I don't test positive for anything whatsoever. With a fever this high, I have to stay and be monitored until my temperature is normal. Also, they need time to try to find something with a name, which can be added to my chart as the main reason for my fever. Only then can I go home. I know this routine. But they never succeed in finding the cause.

In my old life, this fact would make me crazy with worry. Not today. Today I'm deliriously happy, because they can't diagnose me with anything! It may be the delirium that goes along with a fever this high, or it's having written a new and better short story with a happy ending, which gives me a false sense of security about this whole fever episode. My new story goes:

> My immune system has recognized its rightful domain. It is kicking into high gear. It is taking back its kingdom of cells by raising my temperature. It is killing this evil demon cancer. The End.

This is the story that I buy, and read over and over in my head for the next two weeks. I also tell it to anyone who will listen. These are the kinds of stories that cancer patients, half mad with the desire to beat this disease, tell themselves, their favorite nurses and occasionally, even their oncologists.

My story doesn't dissolve in Colorado. When I next get to Mayo Clinic, I'm happy to recite a well-rehearsed version of my new mini-screenplay, adapted from "Fever of Fortune," my award-winning short story about a fever which foretells my impending recovery.

In this expanded and even juicier version, the fever has practically taken on the properties of the Holy Grail. I've become bored with the original story, so I embellish the central facts with how I believe that the Holy Fever has annihilated the demonic cancer in my body. I feature myself glowing in the center of a Peter Lik photograph, sitting meditation-style atop the billowing cowboy clouds over the New Mexico desert, the rays of a fuchsia-pink sunset shooting out below, coloring everything a warm coral, a pure spectacle of light and magic.

Dr. Rubin, my oncologist at Mayo Clinic, appears to be listening with animated interest and is glad that I'm such an entertaining storyteller, not only because I come across so strongly, but because he is about to test my strength.

"It's nice to hear that you're feeling so well, Mrs. Host. Unfortunately, I must report that on your scans taken yesterday. We see seven new spots on your liver."

My storytelling has failed me. I mentally dash over to the museum for a visual: "Seven New Spots?" This should be the title of a mobile by Alexander Calder, or the name of an unfinished study by Georges Seurat. Jackson Pollock, help me out here. Wait! I can rewrite Dr. Rubin's bad script. After all, he's just a doctor. I'm a wordsmith, and it's my job to put words in his mouth.

Using the words I can barely hear issuing forth with his voice attached, I begin to collaborate, incorporate and constructively try to rearrange them to mean something different.

It's no use. There's a shortage of words, a bad topic and a volume deficit caused by a sound which I've gotten used to drowning out all others: the river. And just like that, I'm bobbing away.

"What?" is the only word that I do hear; it's coming from my own mouth, opened like a fish.

Open Sea

June 14, 2005

A tumor is a tumor is a tumor, no matter the size. Family and friends will try to save you and themselves from that fact by leaning heavily on the adjectives "tiny" and "small." When you're the one with the tumors, however, their evasions ironically become a magnifying glass.

Forever the optimist, I've decided to have a great summer in spite of the seven "tiny" tumors in my liver, which Dr. Charbineau saw on his super high-tech ultrasound in April... "Too small to remove now, so we'll wait and see this fall. If they've grown, then we'll remove them at that time. If they stay the same, then we'll be thankful."

Oh, good, now I can wait for the thing that is trying to kill me to grow. That sounds productive. It isn't fun waiting for something as deadly as cancer to grow, not just waiting, but allowing. All this, so that I can line myself up for yet another surgery, which as far as I'm concerned, may lead to another staph infection, one that I may not survive.

This fall I'll head back to Mayo Clinic for another set of scans and most likely surgery on my liver. I decide not to tell my kids now, going against all of the advice recommending that I should. I'll tell them in October; why worry them now? I figure that Amory and me worrying for the next six months is adequate family stress.

I'm completely confused. I've got several informed oncologists: one saying that I'm stable, another pointing out new tumors, and the third here in Boulder, at center court, looking from one to the other, then over at me sitting here in the stands. The odd part is that they are all on the same team: mine. Where do I run from here?

Mexico comes to mind. Not for alternative treatment, but just to have a good time, away from home, with the kids. Amory is sailing aboard the *Quester* again for a transatlantic crossing, so I take our three and my nephew to Puerto Vallarta. It rains six days out of seven, but it's a warm rain, a luscious thing that we never feel in the Rocky Mountains. In spite of the gloomy weather, we proceed to have a ton of sidesplitting laughs thanks to Stover, the family comedian, exactly like his father, my big brother Steve. His stout shape, sharp wit and continuous-fireworks smile keep us all happy.

Walking down the beach one afternoon, I stop to consider the wide triangular delta of the Rio Piteal, running smoothly out to sea. My bare feet squish into the cool wet sands of its wobbly bank as it merges into the ocean. As the tide flows in, it overcomes the mouth of the river so that it's impossible to say where one ends and the other begins. This is the exact visual of the way that I'm feeling now.

I'm not sure how my long, sometimes frightening journey down cancer's river has led me to find that I've been washed out to sea—but it has. I guess I'm out here bobbing around with all of the other cancer patients and survivors, many of whom are not sure how they ended up here, either. And while my current circumstances are relatively calm, this ocean is vast, an even more difficult place in which to navigate.

My Danish father-in-law, Stig, a devoted sailor, has given his wife, Jeanne, numerous opportunities over their fifty-three-year marriage to become "one with the sea." When asked how she'd describe sailing, she once summed it up darkly: "Sailing involves long, watchful stretches, interrupted by moments of sheer terror." Oddly, her description comes to mind as I think about surviving cancer.

Under a palapa, a warm misty rain falling, I'm safely planted on this damp, deserted beach, with Marco, Chanel and Stover playing cards. They're kneeling around a low wooden table, its wobbly legs sturdily planted in the sand. They're playing gin with a well-worn deck of cards, borrowed from the hotel. Marco's dealing, while Chanel's pouring hot chocolate from a large carafe. Have I said that Mexican hot chocolate is the eighth wonder of the world? It's probably the cinnamon, but I can't say for sure.

William is napping peacefully, spooned up beside me, wrapped in a sarong, his skin supple and covered in a micro-mist, his breathing imperceptible but for the rise and fall of his chest. And like all babies, the smooth underside of his chin moving with the sucking reflex, at seven-second intervals. If there were a way to be more satisfied than being with Marco, Chanel and Stover on this beach, while holding my sleeping boy, I don't know how it would look.

I begin thinking of Amory, even though the ocean I'm staring at is not the same one that he's sailing. Though I'm trying to focus on the kids' card playing, to keep myself here on the beach, in my body, feeling my right foot in the sand, I'm already allowing my mind to slip into the comfort of one more metaphor, to drop the mooring and sail out to sea.

Unlike the *Quester* that Amory is sailing, manned with a captain and crew who intend to live, on my ship, cancer is at the helm and I am its unhappy first mate. I'm sailing with a captain who intends for me to die and so heads straight for the tallest waves, darkest clouds and whipping wind every chance he gets.

It seems uncanny that I'm living a certain type of unpredictable open-water experience every single day. It seems that the moment I gain sight of land, the captain veers out to sea, silently taunting me with a sneer. One by one the birds vanish, and with them, my hopes of ever seeing land, much less coming ashore again. Amory may not see my cancer the way that I see it, but by sailing the open sea, he is sampling a microcosm of my life with cancer.

I batten down the hatches and just try to hold on through one more storm. The nausea and panic that come with being tossed about in a tiny container over which I have no control, minus air, overwhelm me. I want off. I'm stuck here against my will. Because my life is at stake, I remain vigilant, peering over the cresting waves, looking for any sign that I might make land after all.

"Aunt Carrie! Holy schh-nikes! Save me!" Stover shouts over his shoulder, while throwing wet sand at Marco, who's chasing him in big circles.

"I'm *out* of pesos, dude, I swear! Help, Aunt Carrie, he's crazy!"

"Get back here, lackey! Pay up. Now!" Marco yells, trying to suppress his laughter, and chases him into the waves.

Stretching her arms high, fingers spread, Chanel does a long, graceful cartwheel for herself. Tucking the sarong more snugly around William, I pull him closer and hold him tight.

Cancer is like that. It sweeps you into its world, without hesitation. It's not unlike a series of deep sleeps, followed by awaking each time into yet another seemingly impossible reality, good or bad. Yet you know how to do this; you know how to survive, and so you undertake the long passage toward that end. With cancer, we're dealing with an unfair captain—one who often tests us first, then teaches us the ropes. We've got to hang in here.

Remembering

July 1, 2005

Chanel will turn sixteen in two days, and her birthday brings up many complicated emotions. I'm alive and thrilled to see her turn sixteen, but I'm sad that her life has cancer in it. She seems frozen inside. She doesn't show it, at least not to me, but I know that my having cancer has weakened the foundation of her happiness. Cancer is always there, waiting to take her mother away. Can she laugh as fully as I did at her age? Can she love and even argue with me, with abandon, the way any normal daughter might with her mother? Or has my cancer torn the canvas of our emotions?

My own life at sixteen felt secure and full of promise. Having such a big, loving family meant I never really had to try to fit in anywhere else because I knew I had a fan club at home. I learned to love Italian-style, unconditionally—knowing even during arguments with my siblings, that we were going to make up, move on and still love each other as before. I wonder how it would have all been different if, like Chanel, I had had a mother with cancer.

July 9, 2005

It seems that, while I'm becoming less certain of my own situation, I'm becoming more certain and increasingly grateful for one of my old friends, Randy. As both time and the burden of my circumstance become too much for just about anyone to bear, Randy remains unwavering. He's there for the 4:00 a.m. phone call or the tearful report after a visit to the doctor's office. If even for nothing more than a blood draw. He's there for anything that I want to talk about, without judgment and with a great sense of humor. There's also his ability to call a spade a spade, which makes him a cynical delight.

Today, as it turns out, I couldn't be happier to have the friend that I made twenty-six years ago, when I was just sixteen. It's only really been in the past two years that I've become privy to the other element of his having become a diehard realist.

We were all so young, in our early twenties, when Randy lost his best friend, his true love, Joanne, to cancer. His beautiful bride died of leukemia, and when she did, it all seemed surreal to me, someone we knew actually dying, and dying so young.

The fact of her death lifted off my mind like steam off coffee, without ceremony of any kind. I didn't want to know more about death than I got from watching the movie *Harold and Maude*. I especially recall how quickly everything returned to normal again, for me anyway. I didn't know it then, but this is when Randy and I quit understanding each other as well. He left me in my easy world where everything always worked out and he began the irreversible journey that cancer sends you on. In losing his young wife, he was forced to jump ahead of me, carefree in my idiocy, to look at life from the fear-provoking angle that death draws.

I know now that the loss is with him still, and only today am I truly able to offer him words of comfort, words that until now I'd never really attempted. Words that somehow I feel I've earned the right to use—since cancer has nearly demolished me. All of these years, my dear friend has held Joanne in his heart, and along with her, this secret store of understanding for something that I could have never imagined would become my world. His empathy has kept me afloat.

Cancer has let me in on characteristics of things that up until now,

I never gave a second thought to, including my past and even my friends' pasts. Old friends hold the key to the door labeled Your Authentic Self. While examining my past has not seemed significant for most of my adult life, now that cancer has come to call, I want to spend some time getting clear about who I am and how I got here. This is where those old friends can help to lead me back, one memory at a time. There isn't anything that allows me the same comfort as remembering my past with someone who has been a witness to my life, to all of the separate occasions that have formed the person that I've become.

I want to support my family and friends as soon as I am able. This is not easy for them. They don't want to lose me. The truth is that, when I try to think about how it will feel for one of them to lose me, it just makes me acutely aware that I'm losing everyone I love. This is the part of this whole deal that is so hard to come to terms with, so I don't. Just like it is easier to deal with other people's fear instead of my own, it's also easier to look at them losing one of me, rather than to look at me losing all of them.

It is valuable to know that cancer doesn't just hit the life it's busy trying to take, mine. It deeply affects the lives of those who love me dearly. It changes their lives, too. I haven't really wanted to face this, because I feel so responsible for the stress and fear that my cancer brings, but I've learned that by acknowledging the burden my cancer makes them bear, I can better be the sort of friend my friends need me to be.

Sorting Socks

August 11, 2005

I officially abandoned my daily vitamin habit back in May. My six-month stint of twice-weekly acupuncture treatments has temporarily been put on the shelf. It's been just me and my injection of Sandostatin, a 30-milligram shot with the large and unpleasant needle attached, which is supposed to "fence the cancer in." I've taken to calling it the "fence with holes" since April, when it managed to let seven new tumors slip through, shattering my illusions of a normal life.

For me, the countdown of eight weeks until I'll be heading to Mayo Clinic begins now. I'll be going for my usual round of CT scans and blood panels and a twenty-four-hour 5HIAA, a urinalysis to measure the excess level of serotonin being produced by the tumors. It is likely that I'll have to have surgery.

Chanel and Marco will start back to school in two weeks. I picture myself telling them, *"I have some 'new' tumors that will most likely need to be removed."* Any way I try to slice it, it's not easy, not at all. Telling the kids is something I resent having to do.

I want magically to grant their wishes for my recovery more than anything else, but as I analyze my situation, I'm not feeling particularly hopeful. This is where denial is more useful than thinking. Dr. Sitarik likes to say, "De-Nile is a very long river." I think, *He's got that right.*

Amory's search for a full-time nanny has nearly come to a close.

Without debate, he's retained High Country Nannies to help us find the perfect candidate, someone who will mix well with the Three-Ts: two teenagers and a toddler, now sixteen, thirteen and two. He does this the same way he would do anything else having to do with managing a business, without a trace of sentiment. I begin to feel a complex amalgamation of emotions take me over.

Most wives would be pleased that their husbands had independently launched a campaign for help, but not me. I'm sad and disappointed. I know that his decision to hire help before we leave for Mayo Clinic, while clearly in the best interest of the kids, underscores the uncertainty that my cancer brings. Amory doesn't care for uncertainty, which is why he's spent his life planning. Logically, what he's doing makes sense, but to me, it feels like he is simply looking for someone to depend on in the role of caring for our children. That is what I'm hearing as the unspoken part of this whole nanny deal. High anxiety sets in. His helping unintentionally pulls me farther out to the sidelines.

I feel guilty that while the majority of cancer patients are financially wiped out by the extreme medical bills that go along with it, I'm fortunate enough to have adequate health insurance. This cushion makes it possible to have a nanny, a facilitation that I'm terrified of. I'm afraid that having another woman in my home will transform me into a ghost of a mother.

I'm dragging my feet about setting up interviews, and when I meet each young, *healthy* and cheerful applicant, my opinion is already tainted. I imagine that she'll be spending all that time with *my* children. Overnight, I've begun to behave like a scorned adolescent, pouting with no reasonable cause, and feeling as though my family is looking for ways to ruin my life. At least this is how I feel for the short term, but it gets worse when Amory clarifies, captain-of-the-ship style, that he intends to hire this person for a minimum of one year and potentially two, until William is in preschool. Mentally, he's walking me off the plank.

I am lacking any logical plan or alternate solution whatsoever, but I challenge him anyway. "I don't *want* a nanny, not to mention, I don't *need* a nanny," I begin, proudly staking my claim to my children and my household domain.

"Well, even if we get a good report at the Mayo, honey, you will still need help. I'm going to have a full schedule this fall." Then, trying to trap me with something sweet, he adds, "We'll need help if you're going to keep working on your book."

"Oh, don't worry about that. I can write the rest of the book in the middle of the night, since I don't sleep anyway." I'm chirping to him from the closet, where I'm organizing a sock drawer. Then it occurs to me: *I'm organizing a sock drawer.* This is an activity reserved only for three occasions that I can think of: the nesting portion of pregnancy, a new method of procrastination for would-be writers, or a last-ditch effort to deny that I am really going to have another surgery soon, to remove cancer from my liver! My whole life may be dumped all over the place again, so I'd better straighten up the socks.

"The fact that you don't sleep well, honey, is another good reason to have some help. If nothing else, you're going to need some rest." He keeps selling me. "Let's just look at the numbers for a minute. William is awake, needing care, roughly fifteen hours a day. That means, in a seven-day week, that he needs around 105 hours of your attention. Marco and Chanel need you, too." I hate when he starts making so much sense, so of course, he continues.

"Honey, I'm only suggesting that we hand over forty of those hours. You can even be here, resting...sooo...by normal working standards, you'll still have a full-time job...and a half," he finishes in that "there you have it—your man has solved the problem" voice, making perfect sense, with an actual mathematical equation to back up his theory.

I'm silent, still not seduced by the numbers. I stay in the closet and as close to my sock drawer as possible without crawling into it, allowing him just the pause he needs to wrap up.

"Aaannnd..." he begins, jutting his chin forward while dragging the razor up over his neck "...since you don't sleep at night, I'm going to make sure that you can sleep when you're tired, even if that's in the morning. Just ask Dr. Sitarik, honey. He'll agree that you need your sleep," he continues to reason out loud.

I watch him shaving his thoughts along with his jawline. Then looking into the mirror past himself, he sees the tears streaming down my face. He pauses to rinse the razor and turns to face me. He looks astonished that his wise and wonderful words have not rescued his damsel in distress, but instead have stung her like a bee.

"I don't want to sleep!" I shout, "I can sleep when I'm dead! Which, by the way things are going, isn't going to be long!" Setting down the razor, he pulls me to him. I can tell that he's looking over me through our bedroom out into the hall, making sure that none of the kids are out there overhearing us. "Shhh...don't say that...*please.*"

Pushing back from his embrace so he can look into my eyes and see that I mean business, I continue, "I'm afraid of a staph infection! Did you ever think of that? What if that happens? And it could. Then what? I don't want help with William—he's *my* baby and I'll take care of him! I don't want everyone else giving him a bath! I want to give him his bath! I don't want surgery! I don't want this stupid cancer! And I don't want a nanny!" I shriek, this time enunciating each and every word with a solid second wedged between each one, sinking onto the floor, crying hysterically.

September 1, 2005

All the good things that have ever happened to me have announced themselves the way the sun moves a shadow to reveal the landscape, both subtle and clear at once. This is the case with the timely arrival of Emily at my front door and into my life.

At about ten-thirty last night, I'm going through the résumés of two highly recommended, qualified applicants, both of whom I'd already interviewed twice, one of whom I will hire tomorrow. I return to checking my e-mail, rather than actually making a decision. I open one from Laura at High Country Nannies.

Hi Carrie, I know that you were adamant about not having someone who's just moved here…but I've got a new arrival from New York. She's absolutely everything you've asked for—except for the out-of-town part.

I've attached her résumé just in case you want to consider her. I know you're trying to hire tomorrow, since one of the two you're considering will take the job with the other family if she doesn't have a concrete offer from you by Sunday.

A little last-minute, but let me know. Laura

I print and read the first page of the attached four-page résumé and find I'm relaxing back into my chair, wanting to read on. I have this all-over good feeling as my shoulders involuntarily drop, the same way you do when the wonderful scent of chocolate wafts through a room, secretly taking over your senses, making you happy before the cake is even out of the oven. I already like this girl and the solid sound of her name, Emily Rockcastle. I say it quietly aloud to myself.

It's late to call, but I take a chance, figuring an East Coast girl will roll with it. Luckily I'm right. She answers, and enthusiastically agrees to come over first thing in the morning to be interviewed and considered, before the final decision is made. The same way that only a woman will—when she's looking into the empty living room of new house in July—picture where the Christmas tree will go, I'm keen that something delightful is in the works.

September 2, 2005

The moment that William takes a look at her from a distance through the window, he leaps forward from my lap and runs full tilt, diaper clad and barefoot, toward the front door. Before I can get there, he opens it, loudly saying, "Hi! Wanna come in?" We all know at that moment that the nanny of choice has arrived; he'd been hiding behind me while I interviewed the others. Emily enters the front hall with an easy stride, glimmering with a cool energy. With a small but strong hand, she gives me a concise, no-nonsense shake.

"Hi. I'm Emily Rockcastle," she says. Her very appearance embodies the resilient fortress her name implies.

She drops to one knee to greet William. "Hi, little man!" she says with a genuine smile. Her hair is swept up in a high, slightly messy ponytail. As she stands up she tucks the loose pieces behind her ears, revealing a fair and spirited face.

Chanel peeks out from the dining room, giving Amory and me a shrewd smile. Big sister approves! Amory and I exchange a conscious smile across the kitchen before the interview even begins. Our decision's already made. She's bagged the job, hands down, as William's gleeful hopping from foot to foot and clapping demonstrates for us. She really is going to be everything we had hoped for and more.

Unreasonable Thoughts

October 3, 2005

It's a clear autumn day. I'm sipping iced tea that tastes like the smell of moist pipe tobacco. It's been brewed too long. I'm sitting on the front porch and looking across the road. The ponderosa pines are standing like stout men along the coyote fence. I'm bouncing William on my knee, playing "This Little Piggy" when the kids pull into the driveway from school.

"Hi, Mom, hi, Monkey," they both say at the same time as they walk into the house. I hear their backpacks thud, thud, onto the floor. Halfway through listening to their stories of the day, I hear my cell phone ringing. It's much later that night when I listen to the message and I hear the voice of an acquaintance I haven't talked to in fifteen-odd years.

"*What?*" I think out loud. After the message is through, I push Repeat and listen more carefully this time, then I listen a third time.

"Hi, Carrie, it's Bernie," she begins. "I apologize for intruding on your life from left field, but I've heard through the grapevine that you're suffering with cancer. There's something I think might help you. It's called marine phytoplankton."

Some things I'm simply drawn to do, beyond my own reasoning. I suppose that logging onto this Web site at eleven-thirty at night is just such an activity for me. *Denial, denial, De-Ni-al* lightly taunts the voice in my head. *You're off a deep end...you're up late at night, thinking about eating like a whale...* this same voice narrates, as I stare at NASA's pictures of the ocean's "spring bloom" while reading about phytoplankton, a 3.2-billon-year-old life source, the food source of whales.

I'm being prompted to watch *Another Day,* a video which, by virtue of its title alone, gets my click. It's a fifteen-minute story of a sea farmer explaining how he'd begun eating plankton directly from the tanks in which he grows it, in a last-ditch effort to "do" something about fighting his rare cancer, mesothelioma. He explains his belief that eating his plankton daily over a period of time before his scheduled surgery resulted in his doctors finding that his tumors were inexplicably covered in a strange "white substance." He says that his surgeons had never before seen anything like it and could not explain it. The biopsies of the eleven sites taken during his surgery were benign.

This man and his daughter, Tiffany, somewhere on the Northwest Coast, are telling their story, and I'm listening. Instantly, they have taken that suspicious, negative voice in my head and tossed it out to sea. Just like that, my sense of hope is immediately restored to me, and with it, a surge of warmth runs through me.

Since reading my daughter's poem a year and a half ago, nothing has had the physical effect that this man's story is having on me. This hope is a tiny seed, and as it quickly spreads its roots through my body, I begin to weep uncontrollably for the sheer joy of possibility.

I'm pacing around the main floor thinking unreasonable thoughts: Is four hours from now, at five o'clock, too early to call a person whom I haven't talked to in fifteen years? I want to get some of this plankton, even if I have to fly to this man's sea farm to get it. I'm on a mission, driven by sheer instinct.

This is just the kind of mission that I imagine several of my doctors will quickly rack up as tomfoolery and try to discourage me from. I'm not planning to disrupt their busy schedules in order to get their permission, nor to trouble them for their opinions. The teenager in me has been resurrected. I'm now too smart for *stupid* advice.

Finally, at 4:00 a.m., I run out of spinning, slicing, dicing, fat-burning, butt-sculpting infomercials to watch as I grind through the last of my bowl of Grape Nuts. No longer able to keep this to myself, I wake Amory, the giant sleeping bear, and lead him to my den, to watch the video. He shrugs a heavy terry-cloth bathrobe over his flannel pajamas, trying to stay in the cocoon of sleep. He shuffles down the hallway and ambles in, squinting at the blue screen, trying to keep dozing through my words, while appearing to pay attention.

I ask and answer my own questions: "Have I gone completely mad, or do you think this could help me?"

It's definitely worth a try, I offer myself, sincerely.

"Could it help my immune system, and do something for me?" I ask.

"It could," I answer, and add: "We're going to the Mayo Clinic in thirty days, so we'll definitely know if it's starting to do any good. Right?"

He's quiet.

"I'm scared, honey," I whisper.

He watches the video and I watch his expressions and the tears in the corners of his eyes. When it ends, we both stand up. With his hands still in the pockets, he opens up his robe and pulls me inside, folding the robe around us. He ties the belt snugly behind me.

"There. Now you're trapped with me forever—now *that* should scare you," he says, hugging me tightly, here in the darkest part of night.

It seems Amory's at peace, sensing that somewhere beyond my fear, I'm full of hope. My hope, he never dashes.

October 4, 2005

The next day at 5:00 p.m., I'm at Bernie's house, drinking my first ounce of marine phytoplankton. While I continue to try and be logical,

to follow the numbers, I've begun to see how bleak the numbers can
It feels like it's time to go fishing with my instinct as my net, for some
thing unseen, something different

November 1, 2005

Twenty-eight days and eight bottles of plankton later, I'm thinking
that in three days, I'm scheduled for surgery to remove the seven spots
on my liver that they saw on my last scan back in April, six months ago.

Hope Swims

November 4, 2005

I'm not easily bought or sold these days, so when Dr. Rubin first delivers the good news, I'm not buying, at least not yet.

"Well, from what I can see here, your liver looks good, it looks clear."

Leaning far forward so as to get a better look myself, I nearly fall off the couch, the one that I've become so accustomed to being nailed to with bad news.

"What?"

"This looks really good," Dr. Rubin says mainly to himself as he cranes his head toward the flat screen in front of him.

"Do you consider reading CT scans to be one of your key talents as an oncologist?" I ask, after several seconds of pure hesitation.

"Are you asking me if I could be making a mistake?" he blurts, breaking into the first easy smile I've ever seen on his face.

"Well, frankly, if I can get away without insulting you, yes, I am," I quip.

"Well, of course I *could* be, but I'm not," he answers as a matter of fact. "Even if I had, then Dr. Charbineau would have caught it. He's already looked at them, and he doesn't see anything on your liver. In fact, he's already crossed you off of his surgery schedule for tomorrow," he says, backing up his first answer.

This might be someone else's scan. How can I be sure?

"What about my lung?" I challenge, refusing to celebrate.

"What about your lung?" he responds.

"Well, there's a pea-size tumor on the left side. Or there was. Did you see it?"

"To be honest, no, I didn't. I was just so focused on your liver, given the surgery, I really didn't look," he says.

"Could you look now?" I ask.

"Well sure, I suppose I could. Wait here, and let's just take a look-see," he says, heading for the door. *Please let this be me, let this be my scan and not a mistake, please. I* pray, back to begging God for unfathomable favors.

He's back. He's sitting down. "Yep, it's still there, but it's just a tiny thing."

It's me! That's my scan! Oh, my God! My frog legs, instead of jumping, go numb.

"So, no surgery, we can head home?" Amory asks, to be sure on one last level.

"You sure can."

"When do you want to see me again?" I ask.

"Six months." *Yes! I've graduated to six months, instead of three! Seven tumors are gone!*

"Now y'all don't run to the airport just yet, you still have to see Dr. Nagorney at three, all right?"

Just for the record, extremely good news can make a bed look more like a launch pad than something to crawl into. Back at the hotel, I'm off and jumping, nearly hitting my head on this old decrepit ceiling, jumping around in little circles like a six-year-old. I do a final bounce before I spring to the floor to head for my suitcase. I stuff it with my belongings as if the building's on fire, before the phone can ring, before a voice on the other end can tell me that they've made a mistake. *"...wrong CT scan, those seven tumors that have vanished were someone else's."*

"Do you think it could be the plankton?" I ask Amory.

"I don't know, but it's the only thing that you're doing that's different."

"My blood tests from the lab work done two weeks ago at Dr. Sitarik's office would show a change in the tumor marker, if it was already starting to happen, right?" I continue to dig.

"They should. We'll check on it when we get home."

I'm mentally searching out loud as I follow Amory down the hall to the parking garage. We're stashing our packed bags in the trunk of the rental car, as cowboys stash sacks of gold into their saddlebags, so that we can make a clean getaway with the mother lode after the appointment with Dr. Nagorney.

Five hours takes a good long time to stretch itself. Then, at three o'clock, Dr. Nagorney walks in and reconfirms the inexplicable news that we'd first heard from Dr. Rubin.

"We don't seem to be able to find those tumors that Dr. Charbineau was planning to remove with RFA, radiofrequency ablation, tomorrow," he says. But quick to stick with reality, I remind him of a different tumor, a quarter-sized one in my spleen.

"Well, let's just pull that up and have a look," he says, pressing his keyboard. Instantly, pictures of my abdomen like the slices of a loaf of bread are spread out on the large screen in front of us, checkerboard style.

"There's...your spleen...back in April...see that frame, with the dark spot? That's the tumor there." He guides my attention to the spot in question with the eraser end of his pencil. Then, with one satisfying click of the mouse, we're here on yesterday's date, November 3.

"It's gone! How about that?" he happily confirms for me.

"What? Can that be? Are you kidding me?" I say.

"No. We don't like to kid about stuff like this," he says, squinting at the screen as he clicks back and forth between the frames, playing now you see it, now you don't, until we've all seen it go away enough times to be completely satisfied that it is, in actuality, gone.

"So it's true?" I ask, still shocked.

"Yes, it is," he commits.

Then I take a solid look at him to be sure he's really there, behind the vast canyon of his words. He's got the smile you get when you've finally reeled that elusive rainbow out of the river, that fish you saw flash and disappear through water the color of tea. This is the slippery suspect that's been getting away for years. This one you don't release until your buddy snaps a photo of you and your fish, while you record the feeling that goes with this exact split second so you will have it for all time.

"What do you make of this? How is this possible?" I ask.

"Well, partly...That's the beauty of medicine—we don't really know everything," he offers wisely, reclining back, lacing his fingers over his right knee.

"Well, you may not know, but I'll take it!" I say, exuberantly.

"You do that!" he agrees, giving me my catch.

It's as if I've opened all of the windows after a big downpour, just filling the room with all of the sweet, clean air it can hold, a scent so full of earth and sky, it's stirring. An intoxicating sensation rushes up through the soles of my feet, elevating itself straight to my earlobes, where it dissipates into the fine mist of elation. Instinctively inhaling, I try to fill my head with something divine. It dives down my spine, naturally extending it, making me stand up taller. I'm illuminated with a gift from nature, unadorned, yet regal.

I'm standing on drier ground. There isn't anything more to want. I'm so relieved to look at the river from a bridge and I don't wonder what that bridge is made of. I'm savoring my moment. Letting it fill my body with the promise that it holds. I record this moment on high, so that I can revisit it again and again.

Flying

W̲e are practically jogging to get to the car. Once at the airport, we're running through the terminal we've come to know so well. We barely catch the last flight out for Denver. Takeoff never felt so right. We're flying; just as we should be. This time, we've made a clean getaway. Cancer can't hold us back. We're feeling inseparable, we're loving life, and life seems to love us. Holding hands, we keep trading looks with each other and bursting out laughing. We feel young, suddenly beautiful and thoroughly in love with everything that this moment has to offer. We don't know what the future holds and we don't care.

As we drive into Boulder, a celebration awaits us at the Hotel Boulderado. Our camp has completed its tenth year. We join our close friends and family at the event during the height of the evening.

"No *way!*" Steve, our camp director, shouts to me across the crowded room, obviously totally surprised to see us walking in.

"Yes!" I say, beaming. "See? I'm just not that easy to get rid of."

A real hoopla ensues. My parents are there, as well as many friends. Even though my mom and dad heard the news from me over eight hours ago, they become tearful at the sight of me and my smile, so fat it's making my face hurt. It feels as though the celebration is for us. And once we've shared our incredibly joyful news all around, we take leave fairly quickly to get home to the kids. Marisa has driven down from Aspen and is standing there in my kitchen with a bottle of champagne. I never remember bubbly tasting better.

"See, I knew you'd smoke that sorry-ass cancer!" she says in her "conquered that" voice while plowing across the kitchen to demonstrate the exclamation point with the world's greatest hug.

Navigating

―――――⤳

November 6, 2005

U nless you've won a large sum of money in a lottery, you probably don't know that really good news eventually leads to a giant question mark preceded by two words: Now what?

This is how it works. You stay in your post-confetti, flying, smiling-so-much-your-face-begins-to-hurt moment until you wind up with what feels like too many compliments on a sunny day. Suddenly you are popular with everyone, making you instantly suspicious. People you barely know are happy for you. Even the parents of your kids' school-mates, who have never approached you before, appear from nowhere and say things like, "Wow. I had no idea that you had been struggling, but I'm just so happy to hear your incredible story. Why, it's unbeliev-able." Translation: "I've never known anyone as poor as you, so I didn't think a conversation was possible. But now that you've won the lottery and are rich, your poverty is no longer a burden for me. Now I'm inter-ested in getting to know you."

I turn off the ringer on my phone and take to my bed for a few hours to see if I can quiet all of the voices in my head: I have to retrace my steps. I really have to try to figure out how this all happened. This is how I learn that bad news is not the only kind which forces you into facing "the unknown." Good news does that, too.

My good news of seven spots on my liver gone missing along with the single, quarter-sized tumor smack in the middle of my spleen has got me wondering: Why? How? What combination turned the key? These are the questions that I barrage Amory with before he drifts off to sleep, while silently narrating to myself between each one; before I get up to write it all down, to try to create a map, one that I will be able to follow if those stupid tumors come back.

"Do you think that it was the plankton?" *Because it may be that something that is this old is nature's lock-and-key mechanism for the human immune system.* "Or do you think that it was it because of the twelve weeks of acupuncture with Dr. Gao that I had before the plankton that opened the channels for the plankton to work?" *Because acupuncture's old, too, but at 5,000, it's young compared to plankton at 3.2 billion, but hey.* "Or maybe marine phytoplankton in conjunction with my Sandostatin injection is the bomb?...You know what, honey?...It could be because everyone's praying for me. People have put me in their prayer circles." *God may have only just started to take stock of those prayers.* "Or do you think that just my own belief that it would work made it work?...Or can stuff just vanish?" *That's what Dr. Hameroff told me. He says the place where religion and science meet is quantum physics.* "What if my thoughts about the tumors changed their growth process?" *Because that Japanese scientist, Masaru Enoto, discovered that molecules of water are affected by our thoughts, words and feelings. Thought itself can change the physical state of water. Are we not made of seventy percent water?* "Maybe plankton is the reason that whales don't have cancer." *Or is it sharks?* "Could this be a whole new frontier in health, harnessed from the ocean?" *Imagine if this stuff magnifies the positive traits of a drug like Sandostatin, or who knows what else, and just supercharges it?* "How can we know, honey? What should I do?" I finally stop.

"Be happy, honey. It's okay. Ask Dr. Sitarik...see what he thinks." Amory senses that my mind is alert and still turning questions. "It's okay. You can go to sleep, honey," he says in a slur as he drifts into a calm, thick slumber, the kind of sleep that a sailor gets when a storm has been gotten through and it's no longer his watch. Deeply exhausted and not spying a single cloud in any direction, as the sun stretches up to the horizon, changing the solid black night to lush indigo velvet, he goes below decks and sleeps, trusting that the sun will rise even if he does not stay awake to see it happen.

Suddenly I'm crying, finally allowing myself to feel the relief that my good news has brought Amory as I watch him sleeping.

I have to come to peace with the unknown, again. I try to reason with this, but I'm still full of questions. I decide that, in the morning when Amory wakes, I'll keep all of my questions to myself, at least for a while. I'll just let him enjoy the calm after this harsh storm which has worn us both ragged. I can let him enjoy the prospect of fair winds. It is a little trickier to enjoy the same thing myself. I think that being the person with cancer, the only thing that will give me this same feeling that things will be okay is time.

I don't know if my cancer's coming or going, or why. This is the reason I should sit down next to this moment and try and let it sit next to me. I don't need to be afraid. The present moment is like an old friend who doesn't need to talk.

November 23, 2005

Several weeks later, after all of the details of that amazing day have been properly rehashed a hundred times, we've all settled down enough to start really feeling that I might make it for a lot longer than we had first thought, even a whole lifetime.

Tomorrow is Thanksgiving and I will most definitely be giving thanks. I am cooking dinner for my family, a small group of thirty-six. I have set three tables with china and linen, begun to chop, sliver, sauté and pour love into every dish. Technically, I should be exhausted, but I've still got energy to include thirty-six more. I just want to celebrate in my favorite way, around a formal dinner table dripping with the trimmings.

Tonight, I'm lying in bed, waiting. I'm waiting for an answer that makes sense. How did I make it? How am I still here? I wait for the little noises to stop. I hear Chanel pitter-patter barefooted on the main floor, then the dryer open and shut—she's getting something out, something she wants to wear tomorrow—then Marco's footsteps, into the kitchen, a late-night bowl of cereal.

I let the house settle. I let the beating of my heart slow until it feels empty and open. Then I fill it with the sounds of my teenagers, now fourteen and sixteen, doing simple things on a Wednesday night. I'm still here, listening.

Sinking

December 1, 2006

I'll tell you how fast a whole year zips by when hope is swimming with the current: too fast. Every December now arrives at my front door with a very self-assured "Aha! I'm here. And so are you, I see. So let me in. Let's decorate the house, shall we? Let's take stock and celebrate!"

I think of Dr. Sitarik as a sort of walking "December," always ready to bring me good cheer.

"Well, hello, my miracle patient, how are you?" I picture him saying.

But this is what drowns out his happy greeting: "We see tumors on your ovary from this last scan...." And the sound of the river is back, swelling up out of season, getting ready to sweep me away again.

December 3, 2006

William's singing to himself, tipping his head from side to side in sync with each syllable. "...Then one frog-gy Christ-mas Eve, San-ta came to say, Woo-doff with your nose so bright..." We're strolling through the Christmas tree lot, hot cider in hand. Together, we are sizing up the tall, handsome candidates while mentally I'm packing a very small bag for my trip to Mayo Clinic two days from now. I don't plan to stay long, just one night, to prepare for my morning CT scan and tests, followed by Dr. Rubin giving me the green light. Then, that same evening, I'll be flying back home to continue making the pizzelles that I'm placing in tins for gifts. This is what I tell myself over and over.

December 7, 2006

Eight separate appointments later, including a mammogram, I am now *NPO*, the Latin prescription for *nothing by mouth*. In plain English, I'm being prepped for a five- to six-hour surgery tomorrow morning at 7:00 a.m. with Dr. Dowdy, a gynecologic oncologic surgeon. What? *A full hysterectomy?* I never liked that word. Now I like it less. Can't you do this by laparoscopy? No? It's too major? And "Dr. Mammogram" will remove the tumor they found in my breast while I'm under? They are not lacking in efficiency here at Mayo.

Oh, my God, what does this mean? I will not have time enough to answer that question for myself satisfactorily.

December 8, 2006

"Amory...do you realize that my first surgery was on December eighth...three years ago?" I'm asking just to hear myself say it. "Weren't we just tearing out of here last year, celebrating? How did this happen? Where did these tumors come from--Hell?"

I just cry quietly as the nurse preps me to receive that first injection. I whisper to her to bring a priest because I'm scared. And when I'm scared, I want to pray. Whom am I praying to? Why should I believe in any God at all? If this is God's plan, then He's fired!

"Oh, my God! *I am not* missing William's fourth birthday!" I bark. This is the last thing I say before my voice gets up and leaves the room. I have lost both my power to speak and my faith, all at once.

Wow. There *is* actually a state called Speechless and I am the governor.

December 15, 2006

Back in my own cozy bed, at home, I'm watching *A White Christmas* with Bing Crosby crooning away. It's snowing in the movie and outside my window. I feel my life's been a lot like the word "flurry" these past three years.

I've doubted God this week, and I'm starting to doubt God's plankton, too. I don't know what to believe in anymore, but decide to at least continue taking stock in the idea of the Holy Trinity. Of course, this makes no logical sense.

I settle matters by telling myself that surviving another major surgery, *three* years from the last one, on the *same date* is a sign. It's a sign that some very powerful entity will keep rescuing me from this river, at least once every *three* years.

December 28, 2006

"Plankton schmankton," I'm saying to myself as I check my reflection in the rear-view mirror. "I'm going fishing at Nieman's."

I'm buying a ridiculously luscious silk-satin dress. I'm going to dinner with my husband, and by all means, I plan to look and feel exquisite doing it.

Can a fabulous dress heal me? Yes, it is completely irrational. But then again, it's wonderful to be so completely willing to try it. As I'm zipping it up I'm thinking, *C'mon, 2007...I'm willing to try you on, too!*

"Mom, that's gorgeous! Where are you going?" Chanel gasps as I come downstairs that evening.

"To dinner with Dad. How do I look?"

"Soooooooooooooo, so, so, *so* pretty!"

Perfect.

The Chapel

December 17, 2007

I t's a year and nine days later; December has come again. It's a Monday morning, but not just any Monday: William is five. He slept in our room last night, so that I would not miss a single second of his birthday morning face. I just dropped him off at preschool where he will be king for the day or at least until 12:30 p.m. when I will pick him up. He will run to me wearing his crown and shouting, "Mama! Mama!" I will just kneel down and wrap this miracle in my arms.

But before all of that happens, I need a way of celebrating this milestone, alone. Pushing the solid wooden door, I slip inside the chapel. I light three candles again, one for each of my children—this time out of joy. I sit in the pew, the very spot where I sat four years ago, begging God not to take me so soon.

I am here. Chanel is eighteen, Marco is sixteen, and William is five! Finally, I'm not crying, but I'm smiling from the inside out.

The Shoe Box

December 20, 2007

It's eleven minutes past four, when night has become so silent that it feels like soft cotton has filled the floors. I slip out of bed and sit down beside it. I want to feel the hard floor beneath me. My mind quiets to a silent hush.

I know the date. It was four years ago today that I walked back into my home and into the beginning of my new life with cancer.

Reaching under the bed, I feel for my shoe box. I pull it out and I rest there with it in the dark. In the dim light of the hallway, I remove the lid as I sit down on the floor, then rummage through my collection of cards. I'm searching for my ending—the one I wrote almost three years ago, on the back of a prescription sheet, in order to find the courage to begin to tell my story. I pull out the thick folded square. My thoughts tremble. I more or less remember what I wrote, but as I begin to unfold it, I stop. Isn't that what life has done—unfolded? How strange.

I'm not quite ready to read what I had written. I try to recall the way I had felt three years ago. What had I envisioned when I thought about "the end"? I settle in and picture myself back there in 2004 at the beginning of this journey: on my couch, angry, bewildered and afraid, and simply unable to care about anything. Hadn't facing my own mortality and then writing that ending required me to carve out a place somewhere in the future? But the future doesn't exist. Perhaps that is why it is so inviting: it is something you can invent, unlike the past.

But to invent the way that I might arrive at the end of my life? This was a large assignment. Hadn't "the end" snuck in and led me to see the harmony of life and death? Hadn't it helped me to sort out the way that there's really *nothing* between me and the river?

It had.

On that very afternoon three years ago, I had been able—with absolute lucidity—to see my life as a grant of time, a generous allowance from nature which contained tremendous possibilities. I remember vanishing into the ocean-like sound of each breath as I am doing again now. I had felt the boundaries which divided my life from my death redefined. How could I say where one ended and the other began? What kind of words would I have to write?

I continue to allow myself the luxury of sitting here in the quiet of night where nothing will threaten to interrupt this effortless feeling of wonder. This is the joy of life's continuous unfolding. This precious emptiness has a sound. It is the sound of the river. It is the sound I resonate with. This is the uncluttered sound of being here. This is the joy of life.

Here is the ending I wrote that day so that I could find a place to start -an ending I could live with and live for. It made itself visible; it appeared and took me to a place without any words at all. My ending and I, we belonged together. I could feel it and I wasn't afraid.

Radiating pure light, I've surreptitiously come to a place with winter clarity along the banks of a magnificent river, its roar a vague whisper, a place with all words sleeping.

Resources

Books on Nutrition, Healing and Coping

The Cancer Recovery Plan
D. Barry Boyd, M.D., and Marian Betancourt
Avery, 2005

Beating Cancer with Nutrition
Patrick Quillin, Ph.D.
Nutrition Times Press, 1994

Nature's Cancer-Fighting Foods
Verne Varona
Reward Books, 2001

Spontaneous Healing
Andrew Weil, M.D.
Ballantine Books, 1996

Love, Medicine & Miracles
Bernie S. Siegel, M.D.
HarperCollins, 1990

How to Help Children Through a Parent's Serious Illness
Kathleen McCue
St. Martin's, 1996

Becky and the Worry Cup:
A Children's Book About a Parent's Cancer

Wendy Schlessel Harpham
HarperCollins, 1997

Raising an Emotionally Healthy Child When a Parent Is Sick
Paula K. Rauch, M.D. & Anna C. Muriel, M.D., M.P.H.
McGraw-Hill, 2006

To Find a Support Group in Your Area

American Cancer Society
1-800-227-2345
www.canccr.org

Organizations for Carcinoid Patients

The Caring for Carcinoid Foundation
www.caringforcarcinoid.org

The Carcinoid Cancer Foundation
www.carcinoid.org

*Organizations and Web Sites That Provide Comprehensive
Information and Resources for All Cancer Patients*

The Livestrong Foundation
www.livestrong.org

The Mayo Clinic
www.mayoclinic.com

The American Cancer Society
www.canccr.org

Acknowledgments

My gratitude to:

Amory, for always being my champion. You are the rock in my river.

Chanel, for your poems, paintings, doodles and songs. I love you, my Bird.

Marco, for your sideways sense of humor and quiet morning waves. I love you, Puppy.

William, for loving me at my weakest and always telling me the way it is. I love you, Bunny.

Mom and Dad, for the happiest childhood ever and teaching me to always believe in myself. I love you both so dearly.

My brothers and sisters—Jack, Steve, June, Wendy and Marisa—for creating the warmest and craziest memories of our life on Williams Street.

In memory of my aunt Florence, for teaching me about blind faith, how to "show up" in life and how to make superior pie crust.

Aunt Mary E. VonFeldt, for those late-night calls where you sincerely convinced me that you had made a deal with God on my behalf. I'm thinking you might have done just that!

Lex, for that devilish smile and never once backing away from the way things are, but always marching straight in.

My wonderful father-in-law, Stig Host, and brother-in-law George Host, for their singular talents with the English language and for braving the first drafts.

All of my many family members, in-laws and friends for coming to help me in very special ways when I was sick, and for coming back for dinner once I was well—I love you all.

Mary McClanahan, for wielding your super-sharp red pencil, your wonderfully warm wit and your unwavering belief in my book from page one. You kept me afloat in the largely late-night and continuous process of writing, editing and formatting, draft after draft after draft. You are a true gem.

Susan Heath, my editor, for taking on my project, seeing it through, and for making a better writer of me than I knew was possible. You possess a talent truly sublime—dancing with words.

Jill Kneerim, my agent. I am honored to have my book be one of your choices. Thank you for pulling it out of the river and sending it to the Big Apple.

Deb Brody, my editor at Harlequin, for your unsurpassed energy and confidence, and for being the purveyor of superior decisions in all the important places.

Dr. Max Mitchell at Children's Hospital, Colorado, for believing in my book at the outset.

Dr. David Nathan at Harvard Medical School, for giving me your vote of confidence.

Nancy Lindholm, for your rare courage and foresight in creating the Caring for Carcinoid Foundation—a beacon of hope for me and all patients with neuroendocrine tumors.

Susan Haskins, for your true spirit, heart and loyalty to the eccentric family we are.

Cathy at "Eight Days a Week," for smiling every time I'd walk through the door with a new and better draft to print.

My earliest readers, for their time, edits, insights and encouragement: Rebecca Zweig, Kristen Boedecker, Dr. Max Mitchell, Marisa Silverman, Dora Breigleb, Currie Barron, Joan White, Mercy Morganfield, Barbara Farland, Nina Paul, and Sara Wolfe.

Finally, to Emily Rockcastle, for being brave enough to enter where sorrow might hang its hat. In memory of your beautiful mother, Susie Bosley. Also to Susie, for teaching your lovely girl Emily love, loyalty and tenderness, and thus giving these precious gifts to me and mine.